THE ENTERPRISE OF A FREE PEOPLE:

Aspects of Economic Development in New York State

during the Canal Period, 1792-1838

Published under the direction of the American Historical Association from the income of the Albert J. Beveridge Memorial Fund.

For their zeal and beneficence in creating this fund the Association is indebted to many citizens of Indiana who desired to honor in this way the memory of a statesman and historian.

THE ENTERPRISE OF
A FREE PEOPLE:

*Aspects of Economic Development
in New York State during the
Canal Period, 1792-1838*

By NATHAN MILLER

PUBLISHED FOR THE

American Historical Association

CORNELL UNIVERSITY PRESS

ITHACA, NEW YORK

CORNELL UNIVERSITY PRESS

First published 1962

Library of Congress Catalog Card Number: 62-8487

PRINTED IN THE UNITED STATES OF AMERICA
BY VAIL-BALLOU PRESS, INC.

To My Parents

"The great and magnificent waters were left in the midst of our Empire, to call into action the moral, political and physical power and enterprise of our infant Republic."
WILLIAM JAMES, Chairman of a Committee of Citizens of Albany, 2 November 1825

Acknowledgments

MANY librarians, archivists, and others assisted me in the course of my research, among whom Wilmer R. Leech and Wayne Andrews of the New-York Historical Society, Martin P. Lanahan and Samuel Kohn of the New York State Department of Audit and Control, Edna Jacobsen, Juliet Wolohan, and Hermann F. Robinton of the New York State Library, and Robert W. Hill of the New York Public Library were particularly helpful. I owe an especial debt of gratitude to the staffs of the Economics and American History divisions of the New York Public Library for their courtesy and patience with my endless demands and questions.

For advice, aid, and enlightenment, which without doubt contributed much toward improving this book, I am indebted to Bernard Bailyn, Ernest Bloch, Alfred D. Chandler, Carter Goodrich, Lillian B. Miller, Richard B. Morris, Sidney Ratner, and Harold C. Syrett.

I wish to thank Randall D. Sale and his assistants in the Department of Geography of the University of Wisconsin for drawing the map.

The Committee for Research in Economic History and the Social Science Research Council were jointly responsible for the financial support that this study received in its initial stages, and I am grateful for the confidence that their support implied.

The New-York Historical Society, the libraries of Columbia University, and the New York Public Library have authorized me to quote from the manuscripts listed in the Bibliography.

N. M.

Milwaukee, Wisconsin
June 1961

Contents

MAP

Introduction

THE successful completion of the Erie and Champlain canals filled Americans with wonder and amazement. There was more to the achievement, they felt, than the visible manifestations of intelligent management, of bold technical improvisation, or of shrewdly conducted financial arrangements. The Erie Canal, particularly, seemed like the result of an intense concentration of impressive energies that foreshadowed even more spectacular accomplishments in the future. Almost immediately, therefore, this canal was endowed with a host of symbolic qualities that variously represented it as a verification of American republican "genius," as an indisputable omen of a great national destiny about to unfold, and even as confirmation that Providence was especially concerned with the course of economic progress in America.

That ideas of this kind were widely entertained in 1825 is understandable. The builders of the canals had encountered great and numerous obstacles; their success in overcoming them was astonishing and helped swell the stream of optimism and national self-confidence that had first begun to rise and flow following the conclusion of the War of 1812. Had not this remarkable technological triumph been wrought by men with no formal training in engineering? Were not unprecedentedly large forces of men mobilized to dig, grub, and haul at a time when the country as a whole suffered from a shortage of labor? Did not the state borrow and expend extraordinarily large sums in a period when capital was short and credit was limited?

The symbolic importance of the achievement, however, was overshadowed by the fact that the canals were built, owned, and operated by the state and that they represented the state's most striking commitment to the proposition that it had an active and extensive part to play in advancing the course of economic development. Those who participated in the ceremonies that marked the official opening of the Erie Canal alluded repeatedly to the state's economic role; it was a theme that speakers constantly merged with predictions of the future greatness of New York—a greatness that all were confident would be achieved on the basis of the energy and enterprise of individual New Yorkers aided and supported in their endeavors by the state.

The purpose of this study is to investigate some of the ways by which the state of New York furthered economic development within its borders between 1792 and 1838. But why the preoccupation with the Erie and Champlain canals, as the foregoing paragraphs suggest and the table of contents confirms? To begin with, the canals, enormous projects both technically and financially for their time, evoked a kind of public reaction and comment that other forms of state intervention in the economy were incapable of doing, and thus they provide a useful and workable record for the historian. Secondly, the canals marked a turning point in the tradition of state intervention in the economy. Previously, the state had restricted its activities to small-scale aid in the form of loans to manufacturers and farmers and of investment in privately sponsored canal companies and banks. The large-scale expenditures for canals, however, altered the picture. To make such expenditures, the state had to establish its credit in the money market as a solid, reliable borrower and to protect this status once it had been established. By 1820–1821, there was no doubt that the credit of New York State rested on an unquestionably firm foundation, a matter of considerable significance for future state enterprise and for the direct and indirect support that the public would extend to private sectors of the economy.

Thirdly, a study of the management of the Canal Fund reveals the record and policies of the commissioners who administered it. Together, these constitute an extremely valuable source of information about economic development in New York in addition to the body of information that they contain about the canals themselves. The Commissioners of the Canal Fund were charged with the responsibiliy of handling all the financial problems that arose in connection with canal administration. They supervised expenditures for maintenance and repairs, made provisions for borrowing and lending, and attended to the various mechanical details of arranging for the regular payment of interest and amortization of the canal debt. Time proved, however, that the commissioners' functions in connection with borrowing, spending, and especially lending had unexpected consequences for New Yorkers engaged in trade, farming, manufacturing, and banking. The commissioners had to consider the probable effects of their decisions on the total economy of the state before they determined on a measure or on a change in policy. Their daily activities therefore, and their decisions and records as a consequence, provide an opportunity for observing the changing economic scene from the vantage point of men whose actions impinged on the major sectors of the economy.

Historians have overlooked the Canal Fund and the commissioners who administered it despite their usefulness in contributing to an understanding of the process of economic development and the part that the state played in New York in advancing it. The fund and the commissioners have been obscured by the more obvious and dramatic story of the construction of the Erie and Champlain canals, by the striking reduction in costs of transportation that the completed canals made possible, and by the vigorous leadership of DeWitt Clinton in the movement for internal improvements in the state. Yet if Clinton had survived only ten years beyond 1828, he, too, would have been astonished by some of the functions that the Commissioners of the Canal Fund assumed as well as by some of the uses that the commissioners made of the revenues of the Canal Fund.

The generation of New Yorkers that built the canals was determined to exploit as fully as possible the large economic resources of the state. The broadening areas of economic activity appealed to the imagination of farmers, upstart businessmen, realistic politicians, and sophisticated men of affairs. Consciousness of expanded opportunities moved men to action and to thought about the special characteristics of the nature and structure of the economy in which they functioned. Theirs was a young economy; they were keenly aware of its youth and intensely involved in nurturing its growth toward a higher level of maturity. Whatever were the private hopes of individual citizens of New York State, they saw sufficiently beyond these to discern the bond that linked them in the common objective of stimulating economic development in the state. This developing economy and the state's role in it are inseparably bound up with the history of an optimistic people who were stimulated by the abundant resources at their disposal, were endowed with a tradition of savings and investment, and were motivated by a desire for personal gain. They were people who were convinced that economic development for the community was a worth-while end in itself and that the state could properly assume functions of an economic kind in order to advance the general good.

It is almost unnecessary to point out the present-day pertinence of this study. New York State in the early nineteenth century was—as compared to England—an underdeveloped area, constantly confronted by the difficulties that a shortage of capital presented. Like so many countries today in Asia, Africa, and Latin America that face problems of economic development, the state and its citizens realized their dependence on foreign capital and strove to obtain it. Similarly, New York State then, like many underdeveloped countries now, undertook economic functions that exceeded the capacities of individuals or private corporations. State enterprise or assistance by the state to private enterprise was characteristic of the period. What individuals or corporations could do themselves, New Yorkers never advocated as functions to be assumed by the public. On the other hand, where individuals or corporations required assistance or where they proved totally ineffective, citizens of New York approved state participation to the extent that the particular case seemed to require. Preconceived notions of a doctrinaire cast never bound the "creative" powers of the state. Instead, the capacities of individuals, corporations, and the state were looked on from an entirely pragmatic point of view in relation to tasks that had to be accomplished. The only test was what worked best.

Part One

THE CANAL ERA AND THE MERCANTILISTIC TRADITION

I

The Tradition

CONSIDERED in the light of its own past, New York State at the end of the eighteenth century faced a promising future. The state was a "seat of empire," according to George Washington; an expanding empire, the general might have said had he fully appreciated the steady retreat of its frontiers in the direction of Lakes Erie and Ontario.[1] From Washington's inauguration in 1789 until 1817, the year in which the state began building the Erie and Champlain canals, the evidence of continued economic change and development was pronounced. This was a period of intensified activity, one of change in business procedure and agricultural practice; it was a period of economic growth that proceeded despite the restraints that a shortage of capital intermittently imposed. But although the period was striking for the changes that took place, there was much about it that rendered it a consistent part of an unyielding past. The abiding mercantilistic tradition that presumed state regulation and intervention in the economy, that sanctioned state aid for new and old enterprises, was a vigorous one and, as time proved, entirely appropriate to the more modern setting.

What were the outstanding characteristics of the economy of

[1] George Washington, *Writings*, ed. by J. C. Fitzpatrick (Washington, 1931–1944), XXVIII, 127.

New York State during this period? What were the evidences
of growth during the time that separated 1789 from 1817? What
were some of the specific functions that the state assumed for
the purpose of sparking enterprise and economic development?

Between 1790 and 1820 the population of both the state and
the city of New York tripled, to make these the most populous
state and city in the Union. At the same time, the areas within,
along, and beyond the Mohawk Valley were being settled at a
rapid rate. Interested parties may have overstated the rate, but
their estimates, though exaggerated, were not unrelated to the
facts. By 1810, Peter B. Porter informed his fellow Congressmen
that settlement within the state had advanced to its "western
extremity." [2] The observable changes in the countryside, which
had been wrought in a brief period of time, seemed particularly
striking to Joseph Ellicott, the agent of the Holland Land Company. In 1810 he described the route between Albany and Buffalo as "thickly settled and well peopled"; he noted the number
of villages that were growing up and remarked in wonder on
how quickly "a whole wilderness had been turned into cultivated fields, meadows, and orchards." [3] Three years later, Aaron
Hamton, traveling across the state for the purpose of inspecting
lands that he had purchased in the vicinity of Lake Erie, was
similarly impressed by the "rich country, fine flocks . . . beau-
tiful farms, fine orchards" that he observed during his trip. [4]

External conditions, especially during the period of the Napo-

[2] In only fourteen years, between 1800 and 1814, the number of inhabitants of Madison County more than tripled, and that of Onondaga
County increased more than four and a half times. Between 1790 and 1814,
the population of Oneida County increased from less than 2,000 to more
than 45,000, and in the brief period between 1810 and 1814, that of Genesee
County rose from 3,600 to 9,400 inhabitants (*Census of the State of New
York for 1855* [Albany, 1857], xxv, xxi, xxiii, xxiv, xxxiii; *The Debates
and Proceedings in the Congress of the United States, 1789–1824* (Washington, 1834–1856), 11 Cong., 2 Sess., 1397 (henceforth *Annals of Cong.*).

[3] Robert W. Bingham, ed., *Holland Land Company Papers: Reports of
Joseph Ellicott* (Buffalo Hist. Soc. Pubs., XXXIII; Buffalo, 1941), II, 49–50.

[4] Edna L. Jacobsen, ed., "Aaron Hamton's Diary (II)," *New York History*, XXI, 431, 435.

leonic wars, directly affected the internal development of the state. These were years marked by a high demand for the agricultural produce of New York. They were years of prosperity, a fact that was reflected in the annual trade statistics of the country.[5] It was during these boom times, just a few years before the turn of the century, that New York City emerged as the nation's chief port as measured by the quantity of exports and imports loaded and unloaded at its wharves.[6] Thus, at an early date, the predictions of commercial greatness for the city, based on the acknowledged natural advantages that its harbor enjoyed and on an appreciation of its highly populated hinterland, seemed well on the way to fulfillment.[7]

This rapid commercial expansion was not limited to the city. Farther north on the Hudson River and on its tributary, the Mohawk River, were towns such as Newburgh, Hudson, Catskill, Albany, Schenectady, and Troy with local hinterlands of their own which they served as markets or as transshipment points in the river trade.[8] These, too, felt the quickening pace of economic development.

---

[5] Jefferson's embargo of 1807–1808 and the second war with Great Britain brought to an end a long period of rapid gain in the amount of seaborne commerce in which citizens of the United States were involved (Timothy Pitkin, *A Statistical View of the Commerce of the United States of America* [New York, 1817], 36–37, 52–54).

[6] Margaret Myers, *The New York Money Market* (New York, 1931), I, 4; Robert G. Albion, *The Rise of New York Port (1815–1860)* (New York, 1939), 8.

[7] Jedidiah Morse, *The American Geography; or, A View of the Present Situation of the United States of America* (Elizabethtown, 1789), 256, 262. Morse estimated that the population of New York City's hinterland, in which he included half of New Jersey, most of Connecticut, and part of Massachusetts, along with the area drained by the Hudson, was half a million in 1789. Albion defines the city's hinterland as the valley of the Hudson "and other upstate regions," including adjacent parts of Long Island, New Jersey, and Connecticut, and estimates its population for 1810 as 1,170,000 and for 1820 as 1,600,000 (Albion, *The Rise of New York Port*, 77).

[8] David M. Ellis, *Landlords and Farmers in the Hudson-Mohawk Region, 1790–1850* (Ithaca, 1946), 78–79.

For merchants of these towns, for farmers of the surrounding areas, and for resident and nonresident speculators in real estate, the need for improved roads to maintain contact between the ever-advancing line of commercial agriculture and the river towns increased steadily as time passed. As a result, both public and private funds were invested in highway construction before the century ended; and such was the pressure exerted for improved transportation facilities that the new century opened with a truly impressive turnpike boom that was a source of pride to many citizens. For example, Benjamin DeWitt, the scientist, expressed the belief that progress in the rate of development of internal improvements was a true measure of the prevailing rate of general economic development. Writing in 1807, DeWitt declared that "the excellence of public highways marks the degree of general improvement in this country." And to confirm DeWitt's judgment that New York was rapidly outstripping her sister states in terms of economic growth, the Secretary of the Treasury in 1808 issued data which indicated that the Empire State was leading all others in the total amount of capital invested in turnpike stock. Shortly thereafter, the state took the lead in the rate of actual construction as well.[9]

The rapid rate of settlement and the production of a "cash crop" heightened the market consciousness of rural New York, raised more frequently the problems of credit and investment, and clearly signified that the state as a whole was moving toward a higher plane of economic complexity and integration. This market consciousness moved rapidly westward, appearing even before the first shipment of potash and pearlash was on its way out of a newly settled area. In this connection, Peter B. Porter of Black Rock, New York, spoke with authority when he told

[9] Ellis, *Landlords and Farmers*, 79–82, 85–88, 132–134; *American State Papers*, Class X, Miscellaneous (Washington, 1834), I, 737; Joseph A. Durrenberger, *Turnpikes: A Study of the Toll Road Movement in the Middle Atlantic States and Maryland* (Valdosta, 1931), 61; *Transactions of the Society for the Promotion of the Useful Arts in the State of New York* (Albany, 1807), 190.

his fellow members of the House of Representatives in 1810 of
the basic difficulties of the western settlers. "The great evil,
under which the inhabitants of the Western Country labor,"
Porter declared, " . . . arise from the want of a market. They
have no vent for their productions at home . . . being all agri-
culturists . . . and such is the present difficulty and expense of
transporting their productions to an Atlantic port, that little
benefits are realized from that quarter. The single circumstance
of the want of a market is already beginning to produce the
most disastrous effects." [10]

Porter's statement reflected the growing pains that a recently
settled rural area of the state was experiencing in making the
shift from subsistence farming to commercial agriculture. The
state as a whole, in fact, east and west, urban and rural, was
racked with growing pains of different sorts, which were affect-
ing the thinking of farmers, businessmen, and officials on varied
aspects of economic affairs. Over a period of years, New Yorkers boldly seized on opportunities to engage in new enterprises,
and although frequently their boldness far exceeded anything
that their capital, good judgment, or both might have justified,
such men demonstrated their initiative by petitioning the legislature repeatedly between 1800 and 1817 for charters of incorporation for a variety of enterprises.[11] During that time, charters

[10] *Annals of Cong.*, 11 Cong., 2 Sess., 1388.

[11] Any enterprise, private, mixed, or public, which added to, stimulated,
or facilitated the total productivity of a community, region, state, or the
nation, was considered both a desirable and patriotic undertaking, and
those connected with it were customarily said to be imbued with "public
spirit." For use of this phrase specifically in connection with internal improvements, see Carter Goodrich, "Public Spirit and Internal Improvements," *Proc. Amer. Phil. Soc.*, XCII, no. 4, 305–309.

DeWitt Clinton, for example, used the phrase "public spirit" frequently.
See Clinton to Gov. Worthington, 23 April 1817; Clinton to the Governor
of Pennsylvania, 20 Sept. 1817; Clinton to Richard Riker, 16 June 1826:
DeWitt Clinton Papers, Columbia University Library (henceforth DWC
Papers); C. Z. Lincoln, ed., *Messages from the Governors* (Albany, 1909)
II, 1096.

were granted to banks and insurance companies and to manufacturing enterprises for the production of woolens, cottons,
paints, glass, nails, iron, and much else. In addition, the legislature created a good number of ferry, bridge, aqueduct, lock
navigation, turnpike, and stagecoach companies. Some of these
corporations never got beyond the point of receiving their
charters; but many others did, and they began to function in a
period when economic activity was being intensified and when
private, public, and mixed enterprises alike were receiving encouragement on the basis of the visible and palpable sense of
economic growth that seemed to pervade the community.[12]

By 1817, the year construction began on the canals, the economy of New York State had reached a level of maturity that
made the claims of the canal enthusiasts seem considerably less
visionary than they had appeared to be before the war. In spite
of short-term fluctuations in business and trade, the rapid economic development of the state, dating from the last decade of
the previous century, seemed to justify the optimistic view
frequently expressed in print regarding the destiny of the "Empire State" as well as its "Great Emporium," New York City.
The increase in population, the rapid settlement, the extension
of commercial agriculture, the widening commercial ties within
and without the state, the increased total mileage of roads and
turnpikes, and the development of manufactures was evidence
of past growth and a forecast of things to come.

The tenets of laissez-faire economics were seldom invoked
in opposition to the large entrepreneurial role that the state assumed in 1817. Where opposition to the state's canal projects

[12] Aaron Clark, "List of All the Incorporations in the State of New
York Reported to the Assembly," bound with NYS, *Ass. Jour.*, 42 Sess.,
49–53. It would be incorrect to conclude that, because of the large number
of corporations chartered for the purpose of manufacturing, agriculture
had ceased to be "the great business of the state." The real expansion of
manufacturing took place after 1825 (Ellis, *Landlords and Farmers*, 127;
see also Alexander Flick, ed., *History of the State of New York* [New
York, 1934], V, 339–356).

did arise, it was based strictly on what appeared to be a realistic
appraisal of the economic conditions of the time, untouched by
considerations rooted in previously accepted economic theory.
For example, in 1816, when by means of a parliamentary maneuver, Martin Van Buren succeeded in postponing the commencement of the canals for a year, his explanation for his action was
the entirely realistic one that the commissioners lacked the necessary data to begin operations.[13] Opposition to the state projects
in New York City stemmed largely from the belief than an increase in taxation would be necessary in order to pay for them.
Farmers on Long Island and in the Hudson River counties
feared the competition of western agricultural produce in the
urban market that the future Erie Canal would make possible.[14]
Even the Reverend John McVickar and Samuel Young, vocal
advocates of the doctrine of laissez faire during this period, en-
thusiastically supported the movement for the Erie and Champlain canals, despite the philosophical contradiction involved.[15]

[13] By 1817, while most members of his own party continued to oppose
the Clintonian canal policy, Van Buren took what he declared was an independent course and voted in favor of the canals. He later called this
vote "one of the most important . . . he ever gave in his life." See NYS,
Sen. Jour., 39 Sess., 299; David Hosack, *Memoir of DeWitt Clinton* (New
York, 1829), 437, 453; Martin Van Buren, "The Autobiography of Martin
Van Buren," *Ann. Rep. Amer. Hist. Assn. for the Year 1918* (Washington, 1920), II, 84.

[14] Robert Troup to Clinton, 25 Feb. 1818, DWC Papers; Hosack,
Memoir, 432. Hosack quotes a speech delivered by Judge Pendleton of
Dutchess County in which the judge expressed his fears that the canals
would depress real-estate values in the Hudson River Valley (*ibid.*, 446;
see also *infra*, 69).

[15] When McVickar expressed his enthusiasm for the state enterprises,
he side-stepped the obvious fact that, from the point of view of theory,
his support of the projects was completely at variance with his own well-
known principles. Perhaps because Young served as a canal commissioner,
he felt the inconsistency of his position more keenly than did McVickar
and was driven, therefore, to explain his brief excursion into the normally
forbidden area of state enterprise in a lengthy address that he delivered at
Union College in 1826. See James R. McCulloch, ed., *Outlines of Political
Economy . . . by Rev. John McVickar* (New York, 1825), 38. By 1830,

Indeed, New York's heritage of a mercantilistic ideology, scarcely influenced by whatever laissez-faire opinion existed, provided a hospitable culture in which the state's entrepreneurial ambitions might flourish and develop. Severance of its political ties with Great Britain did not mean that the state rejected its provincial economic traditions; nor was there during the Revolution and the period of the Confederation any attempt to narrow the bounds of economic activity within which the state was expected to operate. The wartime emergency and the peacetime depression that followed gave rise often to situations in which the state was forced to act. Between the outbreak of fighting in 1775 and Washington's assumption of the presidency in 1789, the legislature frequently intervened between buyer and seller, debtor and creditor, or simply asserted itself as a force in the economy. It fixed prices and wages, issued bills of credit, authorized the confiscation and sale of loyalist property, seized supplies for military use, granted bounties to stimulate manufactures, regulated weights and measures, and levied discriminatory duties on imports entering the port of New York in British ships.[16]

Young considered "internal improvement . . . eternal taxation" and warned against government "entering into competition with individual labor and individual interest." He strenuously opposed further state-financed canal projects, although he justified his earlier support of the Champlain and Erie canals because of what seemed their unique potentiality "to amply indemnify the state for their cost" (NYS, *Ass. Docs.,* 53 Sess., II, Doc. no. 195, 2, 15, 19). For a discussion of McVickar and Young and the "Northern Tradition of Laissez-faire," see Joseph Dorfman, *The Economic Mind in American Civilization, 1606–1865* (New York, 1946), II, 512–526.

[16] Thomas C. Cochran, *New York and the Confederation* (Philadelphia, 1932), 31–32, 36–37, 51–52, 64, 165n, 167; Flick, ed., *History of . . . New York,* IV, 116, 125–126, 135, 139, 143–144; Richard B. Morris, *Government and Labor in Early America* (New York, 1946), 114–115, 126; Merrill Jensen, *The New Nation: A History of the United States during the Confederation, 1781–1789* (New York, 1950), 287, 299. Sales at auction and rates of wharfage and cranage in the port of New York were also regulated (NYS, *Laws,* chs. iv, xxv, xxxii, 7 Sess.).

"To preserve the reputation" of the state's exports, a series of legislative acts dating from the period of the Confederation and extending well into the next century was passed. These acts provided for the inspection, grading, and branding of specified products and, at times, established packing requirements as well, in order to assure minimum standards of quality for products of the state destined for overseas consumption.[17]

As in commercial matters, so, too, in matters of a financial nature, the legislature of the state conformed to its mercantilistic tradition of aid, regulation, and intervention in the economy. After the Revolution, the necessity to alleviate the "great difficulties" that arose because of "a want of sufficient circulating medium" as a result of the "late calamitous war" became a matter for the urgent consideration of the legislature. Hence, in April 1786, the legislature authorized the issue of £200,000 in bills of credit and empowered county loan officers (collectively) to disburse a maximum of three-quarters of this sum in loans to individuals mainly on the security of unencumbered real estate.[18] Six years later, when the new federal Constitution that prohibited the emission of bills of credit by states was already in effect, New York lent instead "money belonging to the people."[19]

[17] Before 1800, provision was made for the inspection of wheat, flour, meal, bread, dressed meats, staves, headings, timber, board, flaxseed, pot and pearl ashes, butter, and lard that were intended for export (Sidney I. Pomerantz, *New York, an American City, 1783–1803: A Study in Urban Life* [New York, 1938], 165–166, 166n).
Added to this list later were fish (1807), fish oil (1818), hops (1819), and leaf tobacco (1828). There was also provision made for inspection of produce destined for the domestic market, as in the case of distilled spirits (1814), hay (1828), and unslaked lime (1829). The inspection of sole leather was provided for in 1784 (NYS, *Laws*, ch. xlvi, 7 Sess.; ch. clxxx, 30 Sess.; ch. cxxxi, 37 Sess.; ch. lxx, 41 Sess.; ch. cxix, 42 Sess.; ch. clxi, 44 Sess.; chs. cclxxv, cclxvii, 51 Sess.; chs. liii, clii, 52 Sess.).

[18] The annual interest rate was 5 per cent. Plate was also accepted as security. The remaining £50,000 according to the law was to be used as part payment of interest owed to citizens of New York on the state and continental debt (NYS, *Laws*, ch. xl, 9 Sess.).

[19] These loans were made in sums not less than £30 or more than £300,

In much the same way, the state aided distressed individuals in 1808 when Jefferson's embargo, a disastrous experiment in economic warfare as far as the domestic economy was concerned, brought about an almost total cessation of foreign commerce and a severe depression.[20]

The state also made loans to individuals or corporations engaged, or proposing to engage, in manufacturing. These were usually direct loans authorized by special acts of the legislature. Initially, the source for such aid was the unappropriated funds of the treasury; beginning about 1807, loans to manufacturers more frequently were made from the resources of the Common School Fund.[21] Clearly patronage of manufactures by the state was accepted as a normal and desirable function of the government. As early as 1790, for example, when the legislature granted a manufacturer of earthenware a loan, it declared that it did so because "the establishment of useful manufactures is closely

at an annual rate of interest of 6 per cent, with mortgages on improved lands taken as security (NYS, *Laws*, ch. xxv, 15 Sess.).

[20] The state borrowed $441,441, which it lent to individuals through county loan officers in 1808. The amount that the state had borrowed could, according to the comptroller, be repaid if necessary out of a much larger debt of more than $1,262,000 owed to the state by the Bank of New York (NYS, *Ass. Jour.*, 32 Sess., 81). The interest rate on these loans was 7 per cent per annum, and they were limited to sums varying from $50 to $500 (NYS, *Laws*, ch. ccxvi, 31 Sess.).

In 1834, a joint committee of both houses of the legislature cited the pecuniary distress that had prevailed in 1786 and in 1808 and approved the extension of credit facilities that the state had granted at those times for the "welfare and prosperity" of its citizens (NYS, *Ass. Docs.*, 57 Sess., IV, Doc. no. 350, 7, 9; NYS, *Sen. Docs.*, 58 Sess., I, Doc. no. 25, 2).

[21] The Common School Fund, established by law in 1805 for the support of the common schools, originally consisted of 500,000 acres of land which the surveyor general was authorized to sell. Periodically additional sources of income were added to the fund. According to the annual reports of the comptroller, the fund in 1812 amounted to $558,000; in 1814, to $882,000; in 1817, to $982,000 (NYS, *Laws*, ch. lxvi, 38 Sess.; NYS, *Ass. Jour.*, 35 Sess., 86; 37 Sess., 273; 40 Sess., 213; Don C. Sowers, *The Financial History of New York State from 1789 to 1912* [Studies in Hist., Econ., and Pub. Law, Columbia Univ., vol. LVII, no. 2; New York, 1914], 263-264).

connected with the public weal" and that "it is desirous to encourage the same." This policy was reasserted in action during
the 1790's by several succeeding legislatures, which were ready
to grant the few requests that manufacturers made for loans out
of state funds.[22] Only the fact that the first flowering of manufactures, in New York as in New England, took place under
the hothouse conditions generated by the European wars toward
the end of the first decade of the new century delayed more
extensive state support for manufactures until that time. Then
there began not only a shift of capital from commerce to manufacturing as a result of the disruption of foreign trade and the
accompanying reduction of British imports but also the emergence of a class of would-be manufacturers who possessed a
highly developed entrepreneurial sense, if little capital. Such
men sought aid from a sympathetic legislature with success,
partly because of the timeliness of their requests and partly
because the encouragement of manufactures was accepted state
policy. Jonas Morgan and Ebenezer Walbridge, for example,
proposed to establish an iron manufactory but were embarrassed by the "great expense and risk attending the erection
of such works." Similarly, Benjamin Peck and Job Wilkinson
wished to engage in the manufacture of cotton cloth but found
that the "expenses" involved would "be greater than they
[could] meet"; Charles Joy, who already operated a plant for
spinning hemp, linen, and twine, could, he claimed, with increased capital add to its "public utility" by making it "more
extensive." To these petitioners, the legislature authorized loans

[22] An act to aid manufactures in 1793 began with the following preamble: "Whereas cotton, linen and glass manufactories have been established in this state; and, whereas, it is proper to encourage the same with
a loan of money." Five specific grants in aid of manufactures were authorized in the 1790's for a total maximum sum of £18,000. In addition, the
Albany Glass Works was exempt from taxation for a period of five years,
and its agents, superintendents, workmen, and artificers were released
from highway and jury duty and from service in the militia except in cases
of invasion (NYS, *Laws*, ch. lvi, 13 Sess.; ch. xlvii, 16 Sess.; ch. xlv, 18
Sess.; ch. liv, 19 Sess.).

in 1807 and 1808.[23] Eventually, as the European wars began to impinge more directly on American interests and as British "depredations," the Embargo, the Continental System, and, finally, the War of 1812 succeeded each other as effective factors in shaping the conditions of overseas trade, the encouragement of manufactures, which had long been considered to be in the "public interest," also became a matter of patriotism; the result was a considerable enlargement of state aid to manufactures, particularly during the war years.[24]

Between 1812 and 1816 the legislature authorized twenty-eight loans, amounting to a total of $143,500, whose primary objective was the encouragement of the manufacture of cotton and woolen cloth and iron and steel products within the state.[25] In other ways as well, the legislature extended a helping hand to manufacturers. In 1811 a general incorporation law was enacted, by virtue of which one hundred and twenty-nine charters were granted to manufacturing corporations between 1811 and 1818; cotton, woolen, and linen manufactories were exempt from taxation, and manufacturers of such products and their employees were exempt from jury duty and service in the militia. Occasionally machinery and materials for manufacturing were declared by law free from seizure for the payment of debts, and the legislature showed considerable leniency in extending the periods of time in which the principal of loans that it made to manufacturers had to be repaid.[26]

Agriculture, "the first and best pursuit of man," also received

[23] NYS, *Laws*, ch. clxxviii, 30 Sess.; ch. cxlviii, 31 Sess. Morgan and Walbridge received the total sum requested. The comptroller's report is unclear regarding the actual distribution of funds to Peck, Wilkinson, and Joy (NYS, *Ass. Jour.*, 33 Sess., 167; 37 Sess., 81).

[24] NYS, *Laws*, ch. clxxxvi, 31 Sess.; Flick, ed., *History . . . of New York*, V, 344-345.

[25] NYS, *Laws*, chs. xviii, lxvi, cli, clxxvi, ccxvii, 35 Sess.; ch. clxxxv, 36 Sess.; ch. cxxxii, 37 Sess.; chs. lxxiv, cxc, 38 Sess.; chs. cxlv, ccxxx, 39 Sess.

[26] NYS, *Laws*, ch. ccxiv, 31 Sess.; ch. lxvii, 34 Sess.; ch. ccii, 38 Sess.; chs. lxiv, cxciv, 40 Sess.; Clark, "List of All the Incorporations . . . of New York," bound with NYS, *Ass. Jour.*, 42 Sess., 49-53.

the benefits of state patronage during the second and third decades of the century in New York.[27] It was widely believed at the time that the productivity of agriculture could be greatly improved if the farmer were educated in the latest methods of scientific cultivation and if, at the same time, he could somehow be instilled with a "spirit of emulation." The knowledge of improved techniques of cultivation combined with a more acute desire to excel, it was believed, could not fail to raise the standards of "husbandry" throughout the state and the nation.[28] To help attain these ends, the state regularly contributed funds to such an organization as the Society for the Promotion of the Useful Arts, whose membership consisted largely of gentlemen-farmers of a scientific and intellectual cast of mind, among whom the average "dirt" farmer would have been conspicuously out of place. Its members—men like Robert R. Livingston, Stephen Van Rensselaer, David Hosack, and Samuel L. Mitchell—were greatly impressed by the revolutionary advances that had been achieved in English agriculture, and they sought to popularize in their *Transactions* the findings of Jethro Tull, Robert Bakewell, and Charles Townshend, English pioneers of scientific farming.[29]

The state also provided the funds for premiums which the

[27] The quotation is Clinton's (Lincoln, ed., *Messages*, II, 898).

[28] The prevailing mode of thought may be illustrated by the following excerpt from the Preface of the *Memoirs of the Board of Agriculture of the State of New York*, II (Albany, 1823): "Our farmers, in striving to excel each other, learn how to put their lands into the most productive way, with the most economical means."

[29] For lists of officers and members of the society, see the various volumes of its *Transactions of the Society for the Promotion of the Useful Arts in the State of New York* (Albany, 1792–1819), where names of New York's outstanding scientists, intellectuals, and public figures appear conspicuously. Members were often in correspondence with the English agricultural writers; for example, Robert R. Livingston corresponded with Arthur Young (*ibid.*, I, 163–168). Also see Ellis, *Landlords and Farmers*, 98–99. The state contributed funds, too, toward the publication of the society's *Transactions*. See NYS, *Laws*, ch. clxxxiii, 30 Sess.; ch. ccxlvii, 34 Sess.; ch. cclxvi, 38 Sess.

society offered for the home manufacturing of woolens, stipulating that the raw wool had to originate in the county where the final product was manufactured. This was part of the society's effort to improve the quality and quantity of farm production and to stimulate the spirit of competition among farmers in connection with sheep raising and the manufacture of woolens. Over an eleven-year period, between 1809 and 1819, the legislature appropriated $23,000 for this purpose.[30]

The form that state aid to agriculture finally took in 1819, however, was more influenced by the "Berkshire Plan" than by the relatively limited efforts of the Society for the Promotion of the Useful Arts. This plan, advanced by Elkanah Watson, also accepted as its central principle the belief that by stimulating the farmer's competitive instincts the products of agriculture would automatically improve both qualitatively and quantitatively. Watson urged that premiums be awarded in as many categories of agricultural production as possible: for the best crops, animals, and household manufactures. An important aspect of the plan was the annual county fair, organized under the auspices of the local county agricultural society, where the exhibition of the prize-winning animals and produce, along with suitable public presentation of awards, was expected to give the farmer increased incentive for even greater achievements. The first fair of this kind in the state of New York was held in Cooperstown in 1817, where an enthusiastic audience heard Watson predict that the Berkshire Plan would soon spread throughout the state and the nation "either through national or state patronage." [31]

[30] NYS, *Laws*, ch. clxxxvi, 31 Sess., 8 April 1808; ch. ccxxx, 35 Sess., 19 June 1812; ch. ccxl, 40 Sess., 15 April 1817. For the act of 5 April 1810, see the society's *Transactions*, III, 230–234. Between 1809 and 1815, of a total of $20,965 of state funds awarded for premiums, $19,645 went to products of home manufacture and the rest to those of manufactories (*ibid.*, III, 226–250; IV, appendix, 6). Approximately $3,300 in addition was granted in premiums for the same purpose during 1818 and 1819 (*ibid.*, IV, 235–240).

[31] Elkanah Watson, *History of the Rise, Progress, and Existing Condition of the Western Canals in the State of New York . . . Together with*

In numerous counties throughout the state, agricultural societies were formed, based on local ties of friendship and kinship, until it became clear that the movement to found such societies was state-wide. The societies won the approval of men in high places; Governor Clinton esteemed them highly and emphasized the close connection that he felt existed between the establishment of such societies and "the prosperity of the agricultural interest." [32] Therefore, it was not unexpected that, after warning against "proscribing" the farmer from sharing in the "bounty of the state," Clinton should have recommended a plan of agricultural aid in which the county societies would participate extensively and that the plan should have won the approval of the legislature.[33] By 1819, the state was committed to a policy of matching amounts of money raised by the societies by means of voluntary contributions up to a stipulated maximum, provided that the funds so raised would be used for the purpose of awarding premiums to farmers who participated in county-wide competitions.[34] Between 1819 and 1825 the state expended $42,000 for this kind of aid. It also allotted further sums to a Board of Agriculture, comprising the presidents of the county societies, which distributed "useful seeds" and published several volumes of articles on animal husbandry, plant pathology, entomology, irrigation, and other subjects of interest to the farming population.[35]

---

the Rise . . . of *Modern Agricultural Societies on the Berkshire System* (Albany, 1820), 107, 150; Clifford Lord, "Elkanah Watson and New York's First County Fair," *New York History*, XXIII, no. 4, 437–448; Percy W. Bidwell and John I. Falconer, *History of Agriculture in the Northern United States, 1620–1860* (Washington, 1925), 187–188.

[32] Ellis, *Landlords and Farmers*, 139; Clinton to James Cooper, 1 Oct. 1817; Clinton to James MacIntyre, 7 Sept. 1819; Clinton to LeRay de Chaumont, 12 June 1818: DWC Papers.

[33] Lincoln, ed., *Messages*, II, 969.

[34] A total of $10,000 per annum was the amount allotted to the county societies under the act of 1819 (NYS, *Laws*, ch. cvii, 42 Sess.).

[35] NYS, *Sen. Jour.*, 49 Sess., 176–183. The societies were actually entitled to $60,875 between 1819 and 1825 but apparently failed to raise suf-

Many "practical farmers" believed that the state's program was unsound. They suspected "book farming" and pointed out that gentlemen-farmers, who could easily afford to ignore the high costs that would normally ruin the average dirt farmer, came off with the prizes in the county competitions.[36] The state, however, was guided by prevailing practice; when it adopted its methods of extending aid to agriculture, it naturally chose those which were most familiar to its citizens.

Evidence indicating to what extent the tradition of state intervention in the economy persisted was clearly given in the comptroller's report of 1817, which listed specific investments and revenues showing numerous close economic ties of the state with its citizens. Private individuals and officers of corporations made interest payments on state loans totaling more than $1,500,000 in 1817. Similarly, a large number of individuals who had purchased public lands and whose mortgages, held by the state, collectively amounted to $950,000 were annually reminded of this intimate economic relationship when they made their interest payments to the treasury. As an investor, the state held $833,000 of 3 per cent United States stock, but it did not restrict its investments to public securities alone. The state also owned stock in fifteen banks, an investment totaling three-quarters of a million dollars. In 1817, this investment yielded handsome dividends, with some banks paying as high as 9, 10, and 11 per cent. In addition, public funds amounting to $107,625 were invested in two lock canal companies; $92,000 of this sum represented an investment in the Western Inland Lock Navigation Company, which paid a dividend of 3 per cent that year. For the same twelve-month period revenues yielded by the state-owned saltworks amounted to $11,500. The state leased the sites and the

---

ficient funds by voluntary subscriptions which would have made them eligible for the total amount of state aid available (NYS, *Laws*, ch. cvii, 42 Sess.). Three volumes of articles were published. See *Memoirs of the Board of Agriculture*, I–III (Albany, 1821, 1823, 1826).

[36] Bidwell and Falconer, *History of Agriculture*, 186, 192.

use of salt water to private operators, who were closely supervised by a state superintendent and a corps of inspectors. Clearly,
the promotional and enterpreneurial role of the state was well
established; canal construction and operation would entail only
a change in form and extent and would be entirely in harmony
with prevailing economic tradition.[37]

[37] NYS, *Ass. Jour.*, 41 Sess., 520; W. Freeman Galpin, "The Genesis of
Syracuse," *New York History*, XXX, no. 1, 19–32; Joseph Hawley
Murphy, "The Salt Industry of Syracuse—A Brief Review," *ibid.*, XXX,
no. 3, 304–315.

II

Private Enterprise

as a Premature Experiment

AMERICA'S manifest destiny was expected to unfold in the vast interior of the continent, and no generation believed this more than the one that had borne the burden of revolution and had founded a nation. "As yet . . . we crawl along the outer shell of the country," reflected Gouverneur Morris in 1801, as he stood on the shore of Lake Erie and pondered the future empire of America in the West.[1] Where and how Americans would penetrate from the "outer shell" into the interior of the country would be determined by the compelling facts of geography, and these facts favored New York State. For in New York, the Appalachian mountain range—"the great ridge which divides the waters of the Atlantic from those of the Mississippi"—seemed

[1] Jared Sparks, *The Life of Gouverneur Morris* (Boston, 1832), III, 143–144. Morris was an early advocate of the Erie Canal and served for a time as a canal commissioner (*ibid.*, I, 495–504; *Laws of the State of New York in Relation to the Erie and Champlain Canals, Together with the Annual Reports of the Canal Commissioners and Other Documents* [Albany, 1825], I, 39, 41, 42, 46, 69, 70 [henceforth *NY Canal Laws*]).

to melt away.[2] Here, as DeWitt Clinton put it, the Hudson River "breaks through the Blue Ridge [and] . . . ascends above the eastern termination of the Catskills . . . [where] there are no interposing mountains to prevent a communication with it and the great western lakes." [3]

In 1792 the New York State legislature chartered the Western Inland Lock Navigation Company for the purpose of establishing an uninterrupted route of transportation via water from the Hudson River to Lake Ontario by improving and linking the Mohawk River, Lake Oneida, and the Oneida River. At the same time, the legislature incorporated the Northern Inland Lock Navigation Company; this company was authorized to provide an uninterrupted connection by water between the Hudson River and Lake Champlain. Under the guidance of Philip John Schuyler, merchant, extensive landholder, and revolutionary-war general, both companies, with notable lack of success, set out to accomplish in a very modest way what the state succeeded in doing thirty years later on a far grander scale through the construction of the Erie and Champlain canals. The northern company collapsed after a brief existence; the western company, which made limited improvements in the Mohawk River and Wood Creek farther west, collected tolls for the use of its facilities for about twenty-five years, until it sold its rights and its property to the state.[4]

Although its achievements were limited, the western company was a factor of some importance in shaping public opinion on the question of internal improvements in New York for at least a quarter of a century. The company's history became a

[2] Thomas Jefferson, *Notes on the State of Virginia* (London, 1787), 25, 27, 29.

[3] David Hosack, *Memoir of DeWitt Clinton* (New York, 1829), 408.

[4] A detailed account of the history of the Western Inland Lock Navigation Company may be found in Nathan Miller, "Private Enterprise in Inland Navigation: The Mohawk Route Prior to the Erie Canal," *New York History*, XXXI, no. 4, *passim;* NYS, *Laws*, ch. xl, 15 Sess.

matter of considerable interest after the War of 1812, when the proposed Erie and Champlain canals, designed to link the Hudson River with Lake Erie and Lake Champlain respectively, emerged as an important public question. Both supporters and opponents of these projects turned to the record of the private company for the kind of evidence that would support their contentions. There was no dispute about the fact that the projectors of the private company had failed; what the lessons were that could be learned from the company's experience, however, was a source of disagreement. To those who opposed state construction of the Erie and Champlain canals, the company's history proved that the contemplated projects, if undertaken, would soon be brought to a halt by insurmountable technical obstacles similar to those that had dashed the hopes of General Schuyler and his associates. Supporters of the Erie and Champlain canal projects declared that all the company's history demonstrated was the folly of allowing a private corporation to assume a task which properly belonged to the state, the national government, or both.

What were the details of the history of this company, chartered in 1792, that still interested New Yorkers in 1817? Aside from a few short canals that were equipped with locks and the link that was established between the Mohawk River and Lake Oneida through Wood Creek, the company had accomplished little. It had never improved navigation on the Oswego River, and this meant that it failed to achieve its purpose of providing access to Lake Ontario. Similarly, the company had never commanded the resources and the technical skills sufficient to eliminate the portage between the Mohawk and Hudson rivers. Here the descent of the waters flowing into the larger stream was swift and precipitous, and navigation was impossible. Directors of the company explained that this portage was largely responsible for the high costs of transportation on the Mohawk River, but they acknowledged that they were helpless to do anything about it.[5]

[5] Miller, "Private Enterprise in Inland Navigation," *passim.*

Contemporary observers judged the company harshly. Timothy Dwight, president of Yale College, who traveled through central New York in 1804, and Samuel Mitchell, who toured the same part of the state six years later, agreed that between Utica and Schenectady navigation on the Mohawk River was "so imperfect that merchants often choose to transport their commodities along its banks in wagons." [6] Transportation in the upper reaches of the river, between Rome and Utica, was apparently no better. When the water level was low, the "serpentine route" of the river posed difficulties enough for boatmen; in especially dry seasons, the entire stretch "became a portage." [7] The public grumbled at the company's poor service, inadequate facilities, and high tolls. Merchants of Geneva and Canandaigua protested to the legislature that the company's tolls were "oppressive"; boatmen and travelers heaped the "grossest abuse" on the company's collectors for the same reasons. In defense of its tolls, the company pointed to the poor returns on its investment and to the years when it skipped or paid low dividends. [8]

A closer look at the company's operations explains, at least in part, why its improvements scarcely extended beyond the Mohawk Valley. Waste and fraud were not unknown and added to the continuing difficulties imposed by the high cost of labor and technical ignorance. Because the company was always short of funds, it was decided, as a matter of economy, to allow General Schuyler to serve as the company's engineer. This decision was a step in the direction of technical and financial disaster. Schuyler was a self-confessed amateur as an engineer, and some of the company's financial losses resulted from errors that he commit-

[6] Timothy Dwight, *Travels in New England and New York* (New Haven, 1822), IV, 124. Because Mitchell owned stock in the Western Inland Lock Navigation Company, his criticism was especially significant.

[7] "Report of the Canal Commissioners," 31 Jan. 1818, *NY Canal Laws*, I, 367; Myron Holley to Clinton, 11 May 1817, DWC Papers; Hosack, *Memoir*, 393.

[8] Peter Colt to Gerald Walton, 11 Nov. 1796; Peter Colt to Philip Schuyler, 2 March 1798: Schuyler Papers.

ted. Young DeWitt Clinton, a keen observer and articulate critic of these proceedings, in an unsigned newspaper article denounced the general as a "mechanic empiric" responsible for "wasting the property of the stockholders." [9] The general, chastened and contrite, eventually admitted that his assumption of the duties of an engineer had been an error, but he explained that he had accepted the assignment only because he had felt that any delay "would have dimmed the hopes of the stockholders." [10]

That the "hopes of the stockholders" were uppermost in the general's mind and that he was determined to make the stock of the company "more productive than that of any banking or insurance company" in the state can readily be understood. If labor came high in the last decade of the eighteenth century, so did working capital; and it required the promise of large earnings to attract and retain an adequate supply. From the day that the company first opened its subscription books, it encountered considerable resistance in the money market. Three months passed before it disposed of three-quarters of its shares at $25 a share, and within three years, one-third of the subscribers had forfeited their stock when they either would not or could not pay the frequent and high requisitions levied on their holdings. [11] Requisitions and forfeitures made the stock even more unsalable than ever.

Who invested in this company, what were their resources, and why did they become involved in an enterprise whose future seemed shrouded in uncertainty? A large proportion of the stockholders and the directors of the company were merchants,

[9] New York *Journal and Patriotic Register*, 24 July 1793. For MS copy, see DWC Papers.

[10] Copy of Schuyler's letter, probably to Thomas Eddy, Aug. 1803, Schuyler Papers.

[11] Nine calls were made between 1792 and 1801, only one of which amounted to less than $25 a share (Miller, "Private Enterprise in Inland Navigation," 402–403; Receipt for Payment on Shares, 20 May 1801; Plan for Prosecuting the Canals [undated]: Schuyler Papers).

businessmen, and bankers in New York City. John Murray, Nicholas Low, and Daniel Ludlow, all prominent businessmen in the city, were early stockholders. Especially notable among the directors were businessmen who speculated in lands in the Mohawk Valley and its vicinity; fifteen of thirty-six known directors held lands that were expected to rise in value in consequence of the company's improvements.[12] Access to market meant profits to the real-estate speculator, and for this reason the company's subscription books carried the names of such large-scale operators as the Holland Land Company, LeRoy, Bayard & Company, Samuel Ward, Robert Troup, Melancton Smith, Daniel McCormick, and many others. Merchants of New York City saw the connection between real-estate prices and internal improvements, so that some of them, who had accumulated sizable fortunes in trade and had diverted their surpluses to investments in land, took shares in the stock of the canal company also.[13]

Private subscriptions, however, were insufficient to fulfill the company's capital needs. The company, therefore, frequently called on the state to assist it, a provision for a "free gift" in its charter setting the precedent for such aid. Eventually, the state advanced two loans to the company and invested in two hundred shares of its stock, thereby becoming the largest single stockholder in the company.[14] As a result, the state became eligible to receive such dividends that the company would declare and "to which . . . the people became entitled" and to appoint an agent to attend stockholders' meetings.

[12] George Scriba, a director of the company, speculated in lands in central New York. Advertising his lands in the New York *Evening Post*, 16 Feb. 1809, Scriba pointed out how much more accessible the lands had become as a result of the company's improvements.

[13] Miller, "Private Enterprise in Inland Navigation," 402, 403. Ward, Scriba, and McCormick, along with Robert Bowne, who served for a time as president of the company, Peter Kemble, Peter Curtenius, and William Constable, had had long and profitable careers as merchants before they turned to real-estate activities.

[14] NYS, *Laws*, ch. xxxviii, 18 Sess.; ch. lxi, 19 Sess.

It was easy to justify mixing public with private funds in a venture that promised to be so beneficial to the community. The benefits to commerce and agriculture were apparent, and any improvement in transportation could only facilitate the enforcement of law throughout the state. Governor George Clinton recommended that the legislature grant the company "every fostering aid and patronage" because of the obviously "great public advantages" that would result on the basis of a "very moderate expense."[15]

The legislature was no less favorably disposed toward the company than was the governor, and it accepted and acted affirmatively on all his recommendations. Indeed, legislative generosity was so great for a while that, besides the direct assistance that it authorized the state to grant to the company, it enacted legislation designed to make it possible for the company to draw on the resources of a foreign land company operating within the state at the time.

The foreign company in question was organized by a group of eminent Dutch bankers who, as the Holland Land Company, were speculating in lands in western New York. As foreigners, the Dutch had been handicapped in their speculations in New York from the start because, under prevailing state law, aliens were permitted to hold lands in New York only under a special act of the legislature. The Dutch had preferred speed and certainty to delay and doubt, and instead of petitioning the legislature for a special act, they had bought their lands through the agency of native trustees. Having acquired an enormous acreage in this way, they then took the necessary steps to win legislative approval for their *fait accompli*. The legislature's response dismayed the directors of the land company; by law, the company's tenure was limited to a seven-year period, after which the property would be forfeited to the state.[16]

[15] C. Z. Lincoln, ed., *Messages*, II, 320–321, 335.
[16] Paul D. Evans, *The Holland Land Company* (Buffalo, 1924), 2–6; NYS, *Laws*, ch. lviii, 19 Sess.

The Dutch immediately petitioned the legislature for more liberal treatment, since the directors of the company judged that it would be impossible for it to dispose of its large holdings in the brief period of seven years. Philip Schuyler, president of the Western Inland Lock Navigation Company and a member of the state Senate at the time, saw in the plight of the Dutch an opportunity for the enterprise over whose fortunes he presided. The idea of a Dutch loan had a ring of familiarity for the ex-general of the Revolution. Dutch wealth had aided the rebellious colonists in their time of trouble; would it not do the same for an American company in its hour of difficulty? With Schuyler's enthusiastic co-operation, the legislature granted the Dutch their request; they could retain their lands for a considerably longer period than had been originally stipulated provided that they lent $250,000 to the canal company or took an equivalent amount of its stock.[17]

Changing circumstances in the real-estate market in New York destroyed the effectiveness of this attempt to exert pressure on the Dutch company for the benefit of the canal company. The year 1796 was a disastrous one for American land speculators, particularly in New York; prices fell sharply, and those who were caught in the downward spiral thrashed about in search of some way to salvage their sinking fortunes. The possibility that foreign capitalists—if they were assured of their rights to hold land in New York State indefinitely—might rescue the native speculator occurred to more than one land-poor, over-extended gambler in real estate.[18] As a result of the collapse of real-estate prices in 1796, the Holland Land Company soon learned that a movement in favor of liberalizing alien land laws had developed in New York, backed by native real-estate operators, and that it might now well achieve its objectives without

[17] NYS, *Laws*, ch. xxxvi, 20 Sess.; Gerald Walton to Paul Busti, 18 May 1797, Schuyler Papers.

[18] Evans, *The Holland Land Company*, 208–210; William Constable to John Inglis, 23 March 1798; William Constable to Patrick Colquehoun, 3 June 1798: Constable Papers.

becoming involved financially with the canal company. The
Dutch gave this movement their full support; they hired Aaron
Burr as their "legislative representative" and provided him with
the necessary funds to supplement his considerably large personal powers of persuasion.[19] Meanwhile it became clear that the
legislature regarded the collapse of the land market seriously. It
accepted the proposed remedy—liberalization of the alien landholding law—as a means of meeting the crisis and enacted a law
authorizing alien landholding in perpetuity under certain conditions.[20] Schuyler, realizing that the Dutch were about to elude
his company's grasp, made a last desperate attempt to wring the
needed funds from the land company, but his attempt to bring
pressure to bear on the legislature to exclude the Dutch from
the benefits of the new law had little effect.[21] In the crisis, real-
estate speculators, foreign and domestic, remained firmly united,
and this unity embraced even those speculators who had also
subscribed to the stock of the canal company. Originally, Robert
Troup, William Constable, Ezra L'Hommedieu, and others had
subscribed to the canal company's stock because they recognized
that improved transportation would increase the value of their
lands; when they were forced to choose between the security of
their real-estate investments and the possibility of supplementing
the income of the canal company, they did not hesitate to join
forces with the Dutch. Understandably, their landed investments
came first, and any effect that their decision might have on the
affairs of the canal company they regarded as of secondary importance.[22]

19 Evans, *The Holland Land Company*, 212–213.
20 NYS, *Laws*, ch. lxxii, 21 Sess.
21 Philip Schuyler to Gerald Walton, 21 or 22 March 1798, Schuyler
Papers.
22 William Constable to Barent Bleeker, 22 Feb. 1797, Constable Papers.
Robert Troup revealed the activities of the "real-estate lobby" in 1802 to
Rufus King when a further extension of the rights of alien landholders
was sought. Troup wrote: "When I was last in Albany, Mr. Ogden in
behalf of the Holland Land Company, and I, in behalf of Sir William
[Pulteney] and Mr. L'Hommedieu, in behalf of himself, set on foot an

The canal company's failure to extract financial support from the Dutch marked its last vigorous effort to make use of the state in order to further its objectives. The company continued to operate the facilities that it had already completed on the Mohawk River, to collect its tolls, to pay dividends when it could, and to incur the hostility of those who patronized it. By 1808, the directors of the company abandoned hope of ever extending their improvements west of Lake Oneida to Lake Ontario, and the company surrendered its legal right to do so.[23]

The company's renunciation of its rights, which it had held for sixteen years, passed unnoticed, however. For some time, the city of Washington rather than Albany had become the important source of news regarding the general question of internal improvements. In 1806, President Jefferson had declared himself in favor of using the accumulating surplus revenues of the national government to provide the country with an improved network of roads and canals if appropriate constitutional changes authorizing the government to undertake such duties were made.[24] During the following year, numerous petitions poured into Washington urging national aid for specific projects and indicating not only that the President had correctly assessed the country's need for improved transportation facilities but also that his proposal to use the surplus revenues for such a purpose had considerable popular approval.[25] The Senate of the United States responded to this manifestation of public opinion and after a brief debate on the general question of internal improvements in March 1807, resolved to assign to the Secretary of the Treasury the task of recommending how, where, and to what extent the national government might participate in a program of pro-

---

act which passed our legislature" (Troup to King, 9 April 1802, Rufus King Papers).

[23] NYS, *Laws*, ch. ccxxii, 31 Sess.

[24] James D. Richardson, ed., *A Compilation of the Messages and Papers of the Presidents* (Washington, 1896), I, 379, 409.

[25] Carter Goodrich, "National Planning of Internal Improvements," *Pol. Sci. Quar.*, LXIII, no. 1, 26–28.

viding the country with roads and canals. The resolution directed the Secretary to present "a plan for the application of such means as are within the powers of Congress to the purpose of opening roads and making canals together with a statement of the undertakings of that nature, which, as objects of public improvement, may require and deserve the aid of government." [26]

New Yorkers did not doubt that a canal between the Hudson and the Great Lakes which would provide transportation facilities penetrating deeply into the heart of the continent deserved the aid of the government. From the national point of view, the primacy of the claim of such a canal on the resources of the national government seemed incontestable. President Jefferson's elaboration of his declaration of 1806 re-enforced the growing belief in New York that the national government was on the verge of shaping a policy in connection with internal improvements based on the national treasury's mounting surplus revenue. Referring to this surplus, Jefferson asked in 1808: "Shall it lie unproductive in the public vaults. . . . Shall the revenue be reduced? Or shall it not be appropriated to the improvement of roads, canals, rivers, education and other foundations of prosperity and union . . . ?" [27]

The legislature of New York responded to the President's statements as to a call for action. In February 1808, it appointed a committee which was instructed to initiate a survey of the "most eligible route for a canal between the Hudson River and Lake Erie." Legislators declared that they had reached this decision in order to accommodate the national government, so that Congress could "appropriate such sums as may be necessary to the accomplishment of that great national object." Simeon De-Witt, the surveyor general of the state, who took charge of the survey, explained it in the same way. "The step which the state has taken," DeWitt declared, "was in consequence of sugges-

[26] *Annals of Cong.*, 9 Cong., 2 Sess., 90.
[27] Richardson, ed., *Messages*, I, 456.

tions that the General Government contemplated the execution of such a work." [28]

When the *Report of the Secretary of the Treasury on the Subject of Roads and Canals* appeared on 4 April 1808, a federal program of roads and canals seemed imminent. The *Report* was a comprehensive survey of transportation facilities that were needed in the country, of some that had been completed, and of some that had been begun but had ended in failure. In the *Report*, the Secretary appraised the capacity of private corporations to assume the burden of financing and constructing roads and canals. On the basis of the national survey that he had conducted, Secretary Gallatin concluded that the resources of private enterprise were inadequate to finance the transportation needs of the country. The country was far too large, its population much too small, and its capital entirely too limited for it to depend on the efforts of private corporations to provide it with the necessary arteries of transportation and communication that a growing nation required. Of interest to New Yorkers was the fact that Secretary Gallatin classified the future Erie and Champlain canals among those of "national and first-rate importance" and he strongly advised the government to help finance projects of this kind.[29]

Gallatin's *Report* crushed any further attempt to build canals between the Hudson River and the lakes by means of private enterprise. The *Report* appeared only a few days after the surveyor general was authorized to survey the canal route in anticipation of national aid, and, just a week later, the Western Inland Lock Navigation Company surrendered its right to extend its operations west of Lake Oneida.

In 1810, a new canal commission, appointed by the legislature of the state of New York, emphatically declared that by the

---

[28] Simeon DeWitt to Joseph Ellicott, 13 June 1808, in Frank H. Severance, ed., *The Holland Land Company and the Erie Canal: Journals and Documents* (Buffalo Hist. Soc. Pubs., XIV; Buffalo, 1910), 4.

[29] *Amer. State Papers*, Class X, Misc., I, 741.

tests of efficiency, economy, and financial capacity private enterprise was incapable of building the Erie and Champlain canals.[30] "Too great a national interest is at stake," maintained the commissioners; the canals "must not become the subject of a job or a fund for speculation." Moreover, they agreed that the United States was a capital-short country: "Few of our fellow citizens have more money than they want, and of the many who want, few find facility in obtaining it." Only the "public," the commissioners declared, that is, the state or the nation, could "readily, at a fair rate of interest, command any reasonable sum." Finally, for purposes of more efficient administration, the commissioners also indicated their preference for public, rather than private, management: "Large expenditures," they concluded, "can be made more economically under public authority than by the care and vigilance of any company." [31]

This vigorous rejection of private enterprise as a means of building canals in New York, following Gallatin's *Report*, was a measure of the unquestioning confidence of many officials in

[30] The commissioners who took this position were, for the most part, enterprising individuals. Four were Federalists, three were Clintonians; the only one with Tammany affiliations—Peter B. Porter—turned Whig later in life. Gouverneur Morris, Federalist of considerable wealth, headed the commission. The others were Stephen Van Rensselaer, the great landlord and eighth patroon; William North, heir to part of the Von Steuben estate; Thomas Eddy, successful businessman and insurance broker; Peter B. Porter, businessman and speculator from western New York; Simeon DeWitt, the surveyor general; and DeWitt Clinton. Both DeWitt and Clinton had speculated in lands, but Clinton undoubtedly derived his chief satisfactions from public affairs. See Sparks, *The Life of Gouverneur Morris*, I, 283; Daniel D. Barnard, *A Discourse on the Life and Character of Stephen Van Rensselaer* (Albany, 1839), 6–7, 17–18, 25–26; Charles M. Robinson, "The Life of Judge Augustus Porter," *Buffalo Hist. Soc. Pubs.*, VII, 244–246; Ellis, *Landlords and Farmers*, 50–51; Samuel L. Knapp, *The Life of Thomas Eddy* (New York, 1834), 48–49, 54–55; Hosack, *Memoir*, 49–50; *NY Canal Laws*, I, 46.

[31] "Report of the Commissioners Appointed by the Last Preceding Joint Resolution of the Senate and Assembly," 2 March 1811, *NY Canal Laws*, I, 68.

the state government that the national government was about to
assume responsibility for the construction of the projects. As
time went on and the bold phrases of Gallatin's *Report* were not
translated into action, public officials found time to consider the
implications of joint activity with the federal government in the
field of internal improvements. The delay on the part of the
national government clearly meant that the state had to assume
a greater share of the initiative in the matter; moreover, in any
joint enterprise involving the state and the nation, it was mandatory that the state retain the upper hand.[32] Congressman Peter
B. Porter of Buffalo expressed this belief in an address in 1810,
when he urged the great economic need felt in western New
York for improved arteries of transportation in order to furnish
farmers with an outlet for their surplus agricultural produce in
eastern markets. As a member of a forwarding firm that mo-
nopolized trading privileges across the Niagara portage, an investor in turnpikes, a businessman on the "western frontier,"
and a vigorous advocate of internal improvements, Porter rejected "individual enterprise" as ineffective and inadequate where
large-scale internal improvements were needed and urged that
the state and the nation merge their resources in a common
effort in which the state would assume the dominant role. "The
Government of New York," said Porter, "have long seen the
advantages of such a navigation, and they have been for several
years desirous of making this canal. . . . They only wait in the
expectation that the General Government will aid them in this
work." [33]

[32] The commissioners wanted support from the federal government and
distrusted it at the same time. They looked for "prudent munificence" in
Washington but were careful to specify that it "must be the result of a
treaty" between the state and the federal government ("Report of the
Commissioners under the Act of April 8, 1811," *ibid.*, I, 72).

[33] William A. Bird, "New York State: Early Transportation," *Buffalo
Hist. Soc. Pubs.*, II, 21–24; Porter to Clinton, 11 July 1802, 17 Dec. 1803,
DWC Papers; *Annals of Cong.*, 11 Cong., 2 Sess., 1398–1400. Clinton main-
tained that both Gallatin's *Report* and Porter's speech "had awakened

In April 1811, the legislature authorized the canal commissioners to apply to Congress for aid, and two of them, DeWitt Clinton and Gouverneur Morris, were selected to make the trip to Washington for the purpose.[34] Plans were carefully made in advance to avoid any last-minute difficulties that might jeopardize the success of the mission. Congressman Porter consulted with Secretary Gallatin and President Madison to determine the best time for placing the matter before Congress.[35] In order to avoid arousing any sectional hostility to the projects, the two commissioners, together with a newly appointed canal commissioner, Chancellor Robert R. Livingston, took considerable care, in drafting the petition for aid, to emphasize the distinctly national advantages expected to result from construction of the New York canals.[36] Many of the ideas that Gallatin's *Report* contained, justifying national aid to internal improvements, were included in the commissioners' petition, partly because of the similarity of purpose of both documents and partly, no doubt, because with Gallatin in the Treasury this seemed like the politic thing to do.[37]

. . . the public attention and excited public solicitude" regarding the question of the canal (William W. Campbell, ed., *The Life and Writings of DeWitt Clinton* [New York, 1849], 27).

[34] NYS, *Laws*, ch. clxxxviii, 34 Sess.; "Report of the Commissioners under the Act of April 8, 1811," *NY Canal Laws*, I, 71.

[35] Porter to Clinton, 14 Nov. 1811, DWC Papers; "Copy of a Letter to the President of the United States," *NY Canal Laws*, I, 90–91.

[36] Robert R. Livingston to Clinton, 4 Sept. 1811; Gouverneur Morris to Clinton, 2 July, 4 Sept., 2 Oct. 1811; document entitled "Gouverneur Morris, Canal," 4 Sept. 1811: DWC Papers. The combined talents of Clinton, Morris, and Livingston produced a watered-down and uninspired message; this becomes particularly evident when the last draft is compared with its predecessors.

[37] Both the *Report* and the petition maintained that internal improvements would strengthen the Union, and both emphasized how such improvements would raise the value and increase the rate of sale of public lands. The *Report* asserted that the "system" advocated in it would "facilitate commercial and personal intercourse . . . tend to strengthen and consolidate the Union, and unite by a still more intimate community of interests, the most remote quarters of the United States." The petition

Responding to the petition of the New Yorkers, President Madison affirmed his belief in the utility of canal navigation and commended the state of New York for "its honorable spirit of enterprise." The President had first-hand acquaintance with the local need for canal transportation in New York, derived from his personal experience as a land speculator in the Mohawk Valley at an earlier period.[38] His message to Congress on the subject revealed an appreciation of the similarity of ideas contained in the application of the New Yorkers and in Gallatin's *Report*, for he declared that the application would "recall" Congress' "attention . . . to the signal advantage to be derived from a general system of internal communication and conveyance." [39]

President Madison's recommendation to Congress that it consider "whatever steps may be proper" to implement a "general system of internal communication" re-enforced an opinion that had been impressed on Clinton and Morris from the day of their arrival in Washington—that their objectives could be achieved only within the framework of a national plan. Members of Congress had informed them that their application "would not be separately attended to" and that "unless something was done for many of the states, the consent of the majority of the House of Representatives could not be obtained." [40] Gallatin also warned

---

stated that the projects of the state would "facilitate a free and general intercourse between different parts of the United States . . . [and] tend to . . . consolidate and strengthen the Union." The Secretary foresaw that the "system" would "increase the national wealth in every way"; the commissioners maintained that their projects would "encourage agriculture, promote commerce and manufactures." The *Report* singled out the Hudson-Erie Canal as likely to increase the value of the public lands; the commissioners expected it "to promote the speedy sale . . . and the payment" for "many millions of acres" (*Amer. State Papers*, Class X, Misc., I, 725, 740–741; *Annals of Cong.*, 12 Cong., I Sess., II, 2166–2167).

[38] Irving Brant, *James Madison, the Nationalist, 1780–1787* (New York, 1948), 339–341.

[39] Richardson, ed., *Messages*, I, 497.

[40] "Report of the Commissioners Appointed to Attend at the Seat of the General Government," *NY Canal Laws*, I, 93.

the two emissaries from New York that the condition of the
public finances precluded a grant of "pecuniary aid" at the
time. In the light of this information, the two New Yorkers set
to work to frame a bill that would be national in scope and
would embrace "the principal objects contained in the Secretary's *Report* of 1808"—which, it will be remembered, included
aid for the Erie and Champlain canals. Since the Secretary had
eliminated all hope of aid based on resources of the Treasury,
Clinton and Morris advanced a plan based on public land instead. They suggested that the national government make grants
of land to states that completed specific projects of internal
improvements, and under the terms of the bill that they proposed, New York State would have been entitled to a grant of
4,500,000 acres of land in the Indiana territory when the Erie
and Champlain canals were completed.[41]

Progress on the bill, however, once introduced into Congress,
was halted in committee, blocked by arguments of Congressmen
that grants in "land or money" were impossible at this time because of the threatening war with Great Britain and because
of the unfavorable condition of the public finances.[42] Clinton
and Morris disputed the committee's conclusions; they indicated
that their bill contained no provisions for drawing on the resources of the Treasury and therefore could not affect the government's capacity to pay the costs of war or to borrow for
such purposes should war come. Nor could the New Yorkers
see how grants of land would affect the nation's ability to pay
and equip its armed forces or limit its credit. It seemed evident
to the commissioners that the explanation for the rejection

[41] *Ibid.*, I, 93; "Proposed Bill, to Be Passed by Congress," *ibid.*, 95–100.
[42] "Report of the Commissioners Appointed to Attend at the Seat of
the General Government," *ibid.*, I, 93–94. Gallatin indicated to the Congressional Committee his approval of national aid in the form of a land
grant. The bill offered by the New Yorkers was not specifically mentioned
in the committee's final resolution; actually the resolution was taken on
the "Memorial of the Commissioners of New York State and Others,"
Annals of Cong., 12 Cong., 1 Sess., I, 1078–1079.

of their bill was not to be found in the committee's report.[43]

The commissioners believed that the bill's defeat could, in part, be accounted for by the fact that it was introduced in the House of Representatives too soon after the struggle for renewing the charter of the first Bank of the United States had been lost. There were many factors of local economic importance that had shaped the arguments for and against renewing the charter of the bank, but no matter how basic these were, the impression was created that at the heart of the controversy lay the question of whether Congress had the constitutional power to charter a bank at all.[44] When the bank was denied a new charter by Congress, the task of obtaining aid for the canals was made immeasurably more difficult because, as in the case of the bank, there was no constitutional authorization for the federal government to undertake or finance the construction of roads and canals. The commissioners believed that Congressmen who had observed how effectively the issue of constitutionality had been used against the bank found it convenient to press the same argument in opposition to aid for canals. Some, no doubt, did so out of sincere conviction that such aid was unconstitutional, and, if necessary, they could have cited Jefferson's proviso that a constitutional amendment would be required to empower the national government to build, or aid in building, roads and canals. Others, unquestionably, sounded the alarm of unconstitutionality only because they were motivated by a highly developed sense of state rivalry and feared that progress in New York would be achieved at the expense of neighboring states.

The commissioners were especially bitter about opposition of

[43] "Report of the Commissioners . . . to . . . the General Government," *NY Canal Laws*, I, 93–94.

[44] Bray Hammond, *Banking and Politics in America* (Princeton, 1957), 209–236; John T. Holdsworth and Davis R. Dewey, *The First and Second National Banks of the United States* (Washington, 1910), 98. Peter B. Porter touched on the major constitutional issues involved in his address to the House (*Annals of Cong.*, 11 Cong., 3 Sess., 627–628).

the latter kind, which they believed resulted from envy of New York State's great resources and large population. "State jealousy," the commissioners maintained, operating "with baleful effect, though seldom and cautiously expressed," accounted partly for the failure to win the support of the national government. Clinton and Morris complained that representatives from other states did not accept as an unprejudiced prognostication their assertion that the projects "would promote the prosperity of the whole union"; instead, the opposition "sedulously inculcated" the notion that its greatest benefits would accrue to the state of New York.[45] The implication that the commissioners had misrepresented their real opinions regarding the ultimate chief beneficiary of the canals added insult to injury. Their mission had failed; clearly there was little that the state could expect from the national government.

The only course left for the state to take was that of independent action; this the entire Board of Commissioners recommended. They declared that the canals should be "made" by the state "and for her account as soon as the circumstances permit."[46] They switched their arguments and, in their restricted appeal to citizens of their own state, threw discretion to the winds by boldly asserting what some Congressmen had suspected—that they believed the state would reap the lion's share of the benefits that the canals would produce. The commissioners pointed out to the legislature the urgency and wisdom of immediate action. Likening the state to an individual who failed to make the fullest use of his resources, they asked the legislators to consider "what should we think of his understanding, did he hesitate to double the value of his property and increase his revenue five-fold without labor [and] without ex-

[45] "Report of the Commissioners Appointed to Attend at the Seat of the General Government," *NY Canal Laws*, I, 92; Clinton to [Joseph] Hemphill, 13 May 1822, DWC Papers.

[46] "Report of the Commissioners under the Act of April 8, 1811," *NY Canal Laws*, I, 72.

pense." [47] Suppose this individual "to be an infant," they continued; "would his guardians do their duty should they let slip the golden opportunity to promote the interest of their ward?" The legislature, the commissioners concluded, "is the guardian of the State." [48]

Three months after the commissioners' exhortation reached the legislature, the nation was plunged into the "second war for Independence." In this conflict, the state of New York, from the Niagara River to the border of Vermont, formed the front line of offense or defense, as the fortunes of war determined. This meant that, while the conflict lasted, plans for internal improvements in the state would remain in abeyance.

[47] *Ibid.*, 86. The quotation continues: "Yet, such is the present case, unless it can be called an expense to run in debt for an object which will pay both principal and interest before the debt falls due."

[48] *Ibid.*

III

The Self-reliant State

AGITATION for the canals resumed almost immediately after the close of the War of 1812. New arguments were added to old and won the overwhelming approval of thousands of people, who signed DeWitt Clinton's memorial to the legislature setting forth the urgent reasons for state construction of the Erie and Champlain canals. According to the memorial, the construction of the canals would reduce the costs of transportation, communication, and travel; they would provide newly settled areas in western New York with access to markets; they would stimulate commercial activity and increase the value of public lands as well as speed their settlement. Specifically, the construction of the western canal was expected to strengthen economic ties between the east and west, prevent national disintegration, and destroy forever the commercial ties that were growing up between farmers of central and western New York with merchants in Montreal on the basis of the Lake Ontario–St. Lawrence water route. Finally, the canals would make New York City "the great depot and warehouse of the western world," an objective only second in importance to the expectation that they would bring "unparalleled prosperity" to the state as a whole.[1]

[1] "Memorial of the Citizens of New York in Favor of a Canal Naviga-

Wartime experiences gave birth to a new set of arguments in favor of canals. The complicated and difficult problem of sending supplies to Perry's base on Lake Erie over poor roads during the War of 1812 convinced many people that transportation facilities were an important component of national security. Partly for this reason, Governor Tompkins of New York recommended to the legislature in 1816 that the roads between the Hudson River and Lake Erie be improved. In Congress, James Tallmadge of New York, in urging the importance of improved roads and canals, called attention to the fact that the cost of shipping a cannon from Washington to Lake Erie during the war had exceeded the manufacturing costs of the artillery piece by four or five times. Canal "enthusiasts" not only made the most of such arguments but also linked them with others, which, arising after the war, were based on the assumption that the prevailing transportation facilities were inadequate even for purposes of normal peacetime usage.[2]

The idea of a self-contained economy, based on the concept

---

tion between the Great Western Lakes and the Tidewater of the Hudson," *NY Canal Laws*, I, 123, 126–127, 138, 140; "Report of the Commissioners, March 8, 1816," *ibid.*, I, 116–117; "Report of the Joint Committee on Canals on the Report of the Commissioners, March 18, 1817," *ibid.*, I, 51, 54, 63–64; "Report of the Commissioners under the Act of 1812," *ibid.*, I, 8–9, 75–80; NYS, *Laws*, ch. clxxxviii, 34 Sess.

[2] Alexander S. Mackenzie, *The Life of Commodore Oliver Hazard Perry* (New York, 1843), I, 132–133; Lincoln, ed., *Messages*, 853–854; Henry Clay, *Works of Henry Clay, Comprising His Life, Correspondence, and Speeches*, ed. by Calvin Colton (New York, 1897), I, 464. Thomas Hart Benton estimated that $60,000,000 had been spent for transportation during the war "over roads so abominable as to make cannon balls cost a dollar a pound" (*Cong. Debates*, 18 Cong., 2 Sess., I, 676; 19 Cong., I Sess., II, pt. I, 1511; B. H. Meyer, ed., *History of Transportation in the United States before 1860, by Caroline Gill & a Staff of Collaborators* [New York, 1948], 90–93, 137n, 137–139). Charles G. Haines, a canal "enthusiast" and a loyal Clintonian in politics, included Tallmadge's remarks in a book that he published for the purpose of spreading the gospel of canal transportation in New York (*Considerations on the Western Canal from the Hudson to Lake Erie* [Brooklyn, 1818], 18–19).

of the "home market," won increasing approval onee the war was over. For some time after the war, the overseas market for agricultural produce was highly erratic and undependable, although immediately after 1815 it experienced a brief period of prosperity. For manufacturers, the war's end meant merciless exposure to British competition.[3] "The home market for the productions of the earth and manufactures," declared Mathew Carey, "is of more importance than all foreign ones." [4] Carey envisioned an integrated national economy—isolated from the rest of the world by a protecting tariff wall—within which the products of farm and factory would be exchanged. Here was an easy solution to the prevailing economic problems that the "common man" could quickly grasp; it presented the attractive prospect of progressive economic development divorced from the uncertainties of foreign markets and secure against formidable foreign competitors. It was doubly satisfying because of its characteristics of national exclusiveness and self-reliance, for pride in nation and consciousness of nationality had been intensified by the outcome of the War of 1812. To facilitate the exchange of produce, improved means of transportation would be required. DeWitt Clinton summed up the current concept of the self-sufficient home market and related it to the need for canals in New York State in a single paragraph of his memorial. He pointed out that

the improvement of the means of intercourse between the different parts of the country has always been considered the first duty and noblest employment of government. If it is important that the inhabitants of the same country shall be bound together by a community of interests and a reciprocation of benefits; that agriculture should find a sale for its productions; manufactures a vent for their fabrics; and commerce a market for its commodities, it is [the legis-

[3] Percy W. Bidwell and John I. Falconer, *History of Agriculture in the Northern United States, 1620–1860* (Washington, 1925), 196; Ellis, *Landlords and Farmers*, 122–123; Victor S. Clark, *History of Manufactures in the United States* (New York, 1929), I, 243–245.

[4] Mathew Carey, *Essays on Political Economy* (Philadelphia, 1822), 26.

lature's] incumbent duty to open facilities and improve internal navigation.[5]

Sentiment in favor of public over private works carried over to, and was even increased in, the postwar period. Early adherents of the Western Inland Lock Navigation Company, for example, had long since abandoned hope for the private corporation; Thomas Eddy, for many years the treasurer and a director of the company, was completely converted to the cause of public enterprise and eventually served the state's Canal Board as its secretary and treasurer.[6] By 1816, Robert Troup, also an early and substantial stockholder in the private company, declared his loss of faith not only in the venture but in the capacity of any private company to do the job at which the Lock Navigation Company had failed. "Dependence" on such companies, Troup warned, would result in "future loss" and would prove that "we have depended upon a broken reed." Troup declared that the directors and the stockholders of the company had become "ardently attached to the success of the Erie Canal" and pointed out that they looked forward to transfer their right of operation and their property to the state "for a reasonable price." [7]

Offhand, it would seem that the directors and the stockholders were primarily interested in "price"; possibly some really were. But it is more likely that in 1816, just as in 1796, such stockholders and directors were also landholders and chiefly interested in land values.[8] They may well have concluded that, where the

[5] "Memorial of the Citizens of New York," *NY Canal Laws*, I, 123.

[6] Knapp, *Life of Thomas Eddy*, 55; Campbell, ed., *Life and Writings of Clinton*, 29.

[7] Troup to Clinton, 26 Jan., 3 Dec. 1816, DWC Papers.

[8] *Supra*, 25, 27–28. A small group of stockholders maintained that the company's failure resulted partly from the indifference of its directors and partly because it was a mixed enterprise. This group believed that only under a new private management, which would purchase the state's shares of stock, or under complete state ownership and operation could the enterprise be successful ("Memorial to the Legislature of the State of New York," 23 Feb. 1814, Misc. Ass. Papers, 6:22, NYSL).

company had failed to provide the necessary facilities which
could increase the value of their landed investments, the state
might, indeed, succeed; and therefore it seems likely that Troup
was reporting accurately the sentiments of the stockholders of
the company when he declared that they were "ardently attached to the success of the Erie Canal." [9]

Whatever were the motives of the directors and stockholders
of the western company, the Joint Committee of the legislature,
in any case, reflected the continuing firm support of public
enterprise that prevailed in that body.[10] An article that appeared
in the Albany *Gazette and Daily Advertiser* in August 1817 was
probably quite representative of the thinking of a majority of
the legislators as well as of those citizens of the state who had
given the question of public versus private enterprise any serious
consideration. In this article, the author declared that it was a
mistake to consider the English experience in building and
operating canals a guide to be followed in the United States.
In England, the writer declared, "the plenitude of private capital enabled . . . individuals to succeed"; but in the United
States, by contrast, such individuals "generally fail for want of
funds." The writer cited the history of the Western Inland
Lock Navigation Company to illustrate his point. This company would have been successful as a business enterprise had it
been able to provide an uninterrupted waterway between the
Hudson River and the Great Lakes. The fact that it failed to

[9] As it happened, the company protested that the price the state finally
paid for its rights and property was too low, and it petitioned for an additional payment, which it never got (NYS, *Ass. Jour.*, 44 Sess., 263, 1091;
46 Sess., 266).

[10] The committee rejected J. Rutsen Van Rensselaer's offer to assume
the obligation of building both canals on the basis of a contractual arrangement with the state. Van Rensselaer planned to organize a private company to undertake the job. The committee rejected the proposal in part
because it believed that the state "should retain the perfect control of the
canal in every period of its construction and future regulation" ("Report
of the Joint Committee on Canals on the Report of the Commissioners,"
18 March 1817, *NY Canal Laws*, I, 285–287).

do so, and therefore had failed also as a business enterprise, resulted directly from an initial lack of funds. It was forced to curtail its operations "at one-tenth the expense necessary . . . because individual capital was not equal to the undertaking." [11]

In 1816, the state legislature was well on the way toward authorizing immediate construction of the canals when Martin Van Buren, state senator from Kinderhook and future governor, mobilized sufficient opposition to block the necessary legislation.[12] Van Buren's opposition was largely politically inspired, despite his plea that technical and financial problems justified still another survey of the terrain and further investigation of the financial problems involved before the state plunged ahead with its plans. Van Buren's Democratic party was in the uncomfortable position of having relinquished leadership in the canal movement to a Federalist-Clintonian coalition. That the movement in favor of the canals was on the high road to success was clear; Van Buren's problem was to get the Democratic party on the band wagon while disguising the fact that it had scrambled aboard when the vehicle was already in motion. What better way was there to do this than by pleading for delay in terms of the welfare of the state and proposing one more investigation? Once the investigation was completed, the Democrats would be able to applaud the results and join the Federalists and Clintonians in a demonstration of great enthusiasm for the projects. They could then say that they were as "canal-minded" as the other parties but far more cautious, more scrupulous, and operating on a higher standard of responsibility than their political rivals.[13]

[11] Albany *Gazette and Daily Advertiser*, 6 Aug. 1817.

[12] *NY Canal Laws*, I, 175; NYS, *Laws*, ch. ccxxxvii, 39 Sess. For economic reasons behind local opposition, see *infra*, 66–70.

[13] Van Buren justified his opposition to commencing construction of the canals in 1816 in his *Autobiography*. He declared that further surveys and estimates were necessary before work could be started and that Clinton was anxious to undertake immediate construction for reasons of political advantage (Van Buren, *Autobiography*, II, 84–85; Albany *Gazette and Daily Advertiser*, 16 April 1817).

Van Buren's maneuver was successful. The legislature ruled
out construction that year; instead, it limited itself to appointing
five commissioners whom it authorized to conduct another survey of the routes for the two canals and to investigate the problems of finance once again.[14]

DeWitt Clinton, Stephen Van Rensselaer, Samuel Young,
Joseph Ellicott, and Myron Holley were the commissioners appointed under the act of 1816. For many years these men had
been abused by opponents of the canal projects as "visionary enthusiasts," and their appointment now indicated that the legislature had accepted completely the inevitability of state construction of the canals.[15]

Foremost among the commissioners was DeWitt Clinton,
whose interest in a western canal reached back into the last
decade of the previous century, when he had questioned the
abilities and methods of General Schuyler and had cast doubts
on the possible success of the Western Inland Lock Navigation
Company. In 1815, Clinton wrote his memorial to the legislature, authorized by a meeting of enthusiasts who met at the
City Hotel in New York. The memorial proved to be the greatest single factor in mobilizing public opinion on the subject of
canals after the War of 1812, and thereafter the name of its
author was permanently associated with the canal movement in
the state.[16]

Stephen Van Rensselaer, the patroon, had seen previous serv-

[14] NYS, *Laws*, ch. ccxxxvii, 39 Sess.

[15] Hosack, *Memoir*, 350. The word "visionary" was a favorite one with
the "anticanalites," and phrases such as "visionary enthusiasts" or "visionary projectors" occur frequently throughout the anticanalite literature.
Jonas Platt said that the term "hallucination" was the "mildest epithet"
used by the opposition to describe the mental processes of those who
favored the canals (*ibid.*, 386; see also Severance, ed., *The Holland Land
Company*, 89, 91).

[16] New York *Herald*, 3 Jan. 1816. The memorial was not only printed
in the *NY Canal Laws* but was reprinted and distributed as a pamphlet
(Samuel Wood & Sons, New York, 1816) and was included by Hosack
in his *Memoir*, 406–420. See also *ibid.*, 386, 378.

ice as a canal commissioner along with DeWitt Clinton in 1810, when both were members of the board that denied that private companies could carry out extensive plans of internal improvements effectively.[17] Van Rensselaer's interest in science and technology—as the institute that bears his name suggests—and his familiarity with earlier attempts to build canals and with the terrain for which they were planned, as well as his past activity as a commissioner, marked him, too, as an outstanding "enthusiast." [18]

Joseph Ellicott was probably the least "visionary" of all the commissioners. Resident agent of the Holland Land Company, Ellicott reflected the very practical interest of his employers in roads, canals, or any improvements that would increase the value of their property, and he became a tireless lobbyist for the canals and a staunch supporter of Clinton.[19] He urged legislators in Albany and Washington to exert themselves in behalf of the projects; he prodded his friends to lobby for the same ends too, and, in the west, where he was most influential, he encouraged the organization of public meetings in order to stimulate popular support for the canals.[20]

Commissioner Samuel Young's enthusiasm for public works is surprising in the light of his later career as one of the most articulate advocates of laissez-faire economics in the state. His

[17] *Supra,* 31–32.

[18] Daniel D. Barnard, *A Discourse on the Life, Services, and Character of Stephen Van Rensselaer* (Albany, 1839), *passim.*

[19] In June 1817, Ellicott wrote to his superior, Paul Busti, saying: "Should this Herculean work ever be effected, and the canal take the direction as explored under my instructions, it would in its passage through the Holland purchase intersect unsold lands belonging for the great part to our principals, and enhance the value of it" (Severance, ed., *The Holland Land Company,* 127; Ellicott to Clinton, 16 April 1817, DWC Papers; Evans, *The Holland Land Company,* 1–35, 218–220).

[20] Ellicott to William Peacock, 5 Feb. 1816; Ellicott to Jonas Harrison, 12 Feb. 1816; Ellicott to Chauncey Loomis, 14 Feb., 21 Feb. 1816; Ellicott to Micah Brooks, 30 Dec. 1816; Micah Brooks to Ellicott, 16 Jan. 1817; A. S. Clarke to Ellicott, 24 Jan. 1817: in Severance, ed., *The Holland Land Company,* 42–43, 46–48, 50, 55–56, 83–84, 95–96, 99.

wholehearted advocacy of the state-constructed and -operated
Erie and Champlain canals caused him a considerable amount
of discomfort, and, as early as 1826, he felt compelled to explain
his deviation from principle.[21] Young compiled his *A Treatise
on Internal Navigation* at the request of the other commissioners
in order to familiarize New Yorkers with the standard engineering techniques employed in England, the Low Countries, and
elsewhere. The book was published early in 1817, when the
legislature had the canal bill before it for consideration, and
its purpose clearly involved an effort by the commissioners to
allay the fears of many citizens who wondered if the proposed
projects exceeded the capacity of contemporary knowledge of
engineering. When Young's *Treatise* appeared, it was bound
with a reprint of Albert Gallatin's *Report on Roads and Canals*,
originally published nine years earlier as a public document and
reprinted for wider circulation in newspapers.[22] Young must
have winced at the intellectual company that he was keeping;
his own ideas and those contained in the *Report* were basically
in conflict. Nevertheless, he apparently was willing to compromise for the sake of assuring immediate action on the canals.

[21] Young explained his position regarding the Erie and Champlain canals
in an address delivered a year after they were completed: "The science of
constructing canals was not understood when the present works of the
state were commenced. These works were also too large and expensive to
be undertaken by individual enterprise; they were, besides, works which
without the grossest mismanagement and folly could not fail of indemnify-
ing the state for the pecuniary expenditure. These were the reasons and
the only reasons which could have justified the state in undertaking them"
(Young, *A Discourse Delivered at Schenectady, July 25, A.D. 1826, before
the New York Alpha of the Phi Beta Kappa* [Ballston Spa, 1826], Appendix VII). Clinton maintained that Young had initially opposed the
canals and reversed himself on the question only when he found it profitable to do so (Clinton to Young, 25 Feb. 1820, DWC Papers; cf. Jabez D.
Hammond, *History of Political Parties in the State of New York* [Buffalo,
1850], I, 426).

[22] Samuel Young, comp., *A Treatise on Internal Navigation . . . to
Which Is Annexed the Report of Albert Gallatin on Roads and Canals*
(Ballston Spa, 1817); Young to Clinton, 14 Dec. 1816, DWC Papers.

Certainly, republication of Gallatin's *Report* served a useful purpose: it rekindled the hopes of New Yorkers for aid to their canals at a time when the state seemed about to go ahead on its own, and it stimulated interest in the current activity of Congress, which had a plan of national aid for internal improvements under consideration.[23]

Myron Holley, the fifth commissioner, was an unswerving advocate of public enterprise. According to Clinton, Holley, as a member of the legislature, supported the cause of canals "with the whole force of his talents." [24] While serving as a canal commissioner, he helped to organize a large public meeting at Canandaigua, called "for the purpose of exciting general attention to the contemplated improvements, of giving a right direction to public opinion, and of pressing the construction of the canals as the work of the State." Holley drafted the resolutions approved by the meeting, which described the proposed canals as a potentially powerful factor in furthering the economic development of the state and the nation.[25] Actually, he did not believe that he had exerted himself excessively in the cause of the canals. He held that all the commissioners shared his anxiety for the "success of the enterprise . . . [which]," he noted, "we have all so much at heart." [26]

The commissioners at once directed their attention to the financial duties that the legislature had assigned to them. Of these, the most important was to persuade the national government, neighboring states and territories, "bodies politic and

[23] *Infra*, 51–52, 54–55.

[24] Tacitus, pseud. [DeWitt Clinton], *The Canal Policy of the State of New York, Delineated in a Letter to Robert Troup* (Albany, 1821), 45n. Holley warmly approved of an article published in the Albany *Gazette and Daily Advertiser*, 6 Aug. 1817, which explained the particular appropriateness of government participation in projects of internal improvements in the United States (Holley to Clinton, 9 Aug. 1817, DWC Papers).

[25] Hosack, *Memoir*, 424–428.

[26] Holley to Joseph Ellicott, 11 Jan. 1817, in Severance, ed., *The Holland Land Company*, 94.

corporate, public and private" to aid them in their enterprise
with "cessions, grants and donations." [27] The possible achievements of the complex form of mixed enterprise that would have
resulted had the commissioners successfully accomplished their
mission would be a matter of interest, particularly if all the
participants sought a voice in the management and construction
of the projects.[28] But the state was spared this experience, because external aid, both public and private, was generally restricted to verbal encouragement. Thus, when Clinton, in his
official role as president of the Canal Board, suggested that because the states of Ohio, Kentucky, and Vermont would "enjoy the benefits" of New York's projected improvements they
"should also participate in the expenses," he discovered that
these states could give more readily of their enthusiasm than of
their funds.[29] As W. W. Morris described the situation, these
other states were "full of ardor" for the projects "but destitute
of pecuniary resources." [30]

Prospects for aid from the federal government seemed to
have improved considerably since the time when Clinton and
Morris had made their fruitless excursion to Washington in 1811.
By the end of the war members of Congress were keenly aware
of the shortcomings of the nation's transportation facilities.[31]
Early in 1816, the Senate of the United States authorized the
reprinting of eight hundred copies of Gallatin's *Report*, thereby
anticipating by several months its appearance as part of Young's

[27] NYS, *Laws*, ch. ccxxxvii, 39 Sess.

[28] Such an arrangement was not completely beyond the realm of possibility. Ellicott held that in cases of improvements, where the United States
participated equally with the state, "they would necessarily appoint their
own agents to superintend and reserve to themselves a jurisdiction over
such improvements in proportion to the sum of money which was respectively expended in their completion" (Ellicott to A. S. Clarke, 3 Jan.
1817, in Severance, ed., *The Holland Land Company*, 88).

[29] *NY Canal Laws*, I, 297–301.

[30] W. W. Morris to Clinton, 26 Aug. 1817, DWC Papers.

[31] *Supra*, 41; *Annals of Cong.*, 14 Cong., 2 Sess., 852–853.

Treatise under the sponsorship of the New York canal commissioners.[32] In addition, New Yorkers now learned that they had powerful allies in other states who favored a national program of internal improvements. Henry Clay of Kentucky and John C. Calhoun of South Carolina had thrown their influence behind a bill for federal aid to internal improvements which Calhoun had introduced in the House of Representatives. The bill provided that the bonus and the annual proceeds that the federal government would receive from the proposed Second Bank of the United States be used "as a permanent fund for internal improvements." Moreover, Calhoun specifically declared that the costs of construction of a canal between the Hudson River and the Great Lakes could be defrayed in part by use of the revenues that the national government would receive if the bonus bill were passed.[33]

New Yorkers appreciated the importance of the bonus bill as far as their own plans for canals were concerned. Referring to the bill, Clinton commented to Ellicott that "if it becomes a law . . . it will give us $90,000 a year," the total annual sum that the commissioners estimated at the time would be needed

[32] Twelve hundred copies of Gallatin's *Report* were printed in 1808 (*Report of the Secretary of the Treasury on the Subject of Roads and Canals* [Washington, 1808]). The eight hundred additional copies that the Senate authorized to be printed in 1816 appeared under the same title (*Annals of Cong.*, 10 Cong., 1 Sess., 332; 14 Cong., 1 Sess., 43, 107–111; Richardson, ed., *Messages of the Presidents*, I, 567–568).

[33] "Let it not be said that internal improvements may be wholly left to the enterprise of the states and of individuals," declared Calhoun. "Many of the improvements contemplated are on too large a scale for the resources of the states or of individuals. . . . They require the resources and general superintendence of this government to effect and complete them." Clay believed that certain projects "if not taken up by the General Government" in co-operation with the states would be neglected, "either for want of resources" or from the difficulty that the states interested in the same project would experience in "regulating their respective contributions." Among such projects, Clay included the Erie Canal (*Annals of Cong.*, 14 Cong., 2 Sess., 851–858, 866–868; Micah Brooks to Ellicott, 16 Jan. 1817, in Severance, ed., *The Holland Land Company*, 95).

during the first two or three years of construction.[34] Ellicott considered this form of national aid important only because it would serve as "an entering wedge for larger grants." [35] Generally, however, the bill stirred the hopes of the commissioners, and they urged all the members of New York's congressional delegation to rally to its support. The commissioners informed the Congressmen that if the bill became law the resulting revenues, combined with those that the state could provide, would permit the construction of the canals without the necessity of raising additional taxes for the purpose. They also suggested an arrangement for the distribution of this proposed federal aid. "A fair and unexceptional standard" of distribution, they maintained, would be one that was made on the basis of population. Such an arrangement would be particularly advantageous for New York State, since it was about this time that the "Empire State" surpassed the "Old Dominion" in population to become the most populous state in the Union.[36]

The prevailing congressional attitudes toward internal improvements undoubtedly re-enforced the tendency of New Yorkers to look to Washington for aid. One newspaper declared that such aid constituted a promise of long standing and cited appropriate messages of President Jefferson to prove the point.[37] Reflecting the hopes that events in Washington had aroused, the legislature instructed the commissioners to investigate the matter, and Clinton, for the second time in a period of five years, found himself in the nation's capital as a petitioner for federal aid.[38]

[34] Clinton to Ellicott, 14 Feb. 1817, in Severance, ed., *The Holland Land Company*, 116–117; *NY Canal Laws*, I, 326.

[35] Ellicott to Clinton, 21 Feb. 1817, in Severance, ed., *The Holland Land Company*, 119.

[36] *NY Canal Laws*, I, 311–312. See U.S. Census Office, 3d Census, *Aggregate Amount of Each Description of Persons within the United States of America . . . in the Year 1810* (Washington, 1811), 28a, 51a, 56; 4th Census, *Census for 1820* (Washington, 1821), Chart 2.

[37] Albany *Daily Advertiser*, 12 Aug. 1816.

[38] NYS, *Laws*, ch. ccxxxvii, 39 Sess.; *supra*, 34–38.

As before, Clinton emphasized the national "pecuniary" and "political interests" that the canals would advance and carefully subordinated the local advantages that the state would derive from their construction. The president of the Canal Board repeated many of the arguments that had been heard before both in New York and in the halls of Congress. The canals would be useful in peace and war; they would enhance the value of the public lands lying north and west of the Ohio River and accelerate the rate of settlement in those regions; they would reduce the costs of transportation and would divert the trade of the lakes from Canadian to American routes. To a people already appalled by the vast extent of territory that it had to govern and fearful of the centrifugal force of disunion, which large distances from the seat of government seemed to make increasingly possible, Clinton offered the alternative of a nation tightly integrated by the kind of improvements for which he sought support.[39] He noted, in addition, that a western canal by providing superior means of transportation for Americans would, in some measure, undermine the influence of the British in the fur trade and thus weaken their hold over the Indians. This suggestion, coming so soon after the close of the War of 1812, throbbed with emotional overtones, since it had been widely believed that the British had incited the Indians against the Americans; and, although the evidence for this belief at present is debatable, Tecumseh's alliance with the British, once the war had begun, was sufficient to convince a great many Americans of the truth of this charge.[40] In New York's canals,

[39] Ironically, it was John C. Calhoun who warned against the dangers of disunion that could result from the difficulties involved in governing a nation the size of the United States. "We are great, and rapidly—he was about to say, fearfully—growing. . . . Let us then bind the Republic together with a perfect system of roads and canals . . . so situated . . . we may reasonably raise our eyes to a most splendid future . . . neglecting them, we permit a low, sordid, selfish and sectional spirit to take possession. . . . We will divide, and in its consequences, will follow misery and despotism" (*Annals of Cong.*, 14 Cong., 2 Sess., 854).

[40] *Newburgh Political Index*, 10 Sept., 31 Dec. 1811; Julius W. Pratt,

Clinton saw a logical coincidence of state and national interests. He relied on "the enlightened public spirit in Congress" to manifest itself in a "measure of patronage as cannot fail to produce signal benefits to the nation." New York State, he assured members of Congress, was "not unaware of her interests nor disinclined to prosecute them, but where those of the general government are united with hers, and seem to be paramount, she deems it her duty to ask for assistance." [41]

The passage of the bonus bill on March 1 must have convinced those who shared Clinton's views that an "enlightened public spirit" truly pervaded Congress. Apparently, the same spirit did not pervade the executive branch. Two days after Congress had completed action on the bill, President Madison vetoed it as one of the last acts of his administration. The President held that the absence of constitutional authorization permitting Congress to build roads and canals and to improve "watercourses" meant that any attempt by the national legislature to do so violated the limits of its constitutional powers. He did not deny that the national government could perform a useful function in executing a program of internal improvements, which would contribute to the "general prosperity," but he insisted that any future role of this kind which it would undertake must necessarily be preceded by a suitable amendment to the Constitution.[42]

This strict construction of the Constitution angered the

Expansionists of 1812 (New York, 1925), 35–39; A. L. Burt, *The United States, Great Britain, and British North America from the Revolution to the Establishment of Peace after the War of 1812* (New Haven, 1940), 302–304. See also Reginald Horsman, "British Indian Policy in the Northwest, 1807–1812," *Mississippi Valley Hist. Rev.,* XLV, no. 1, 51–66.

[41] *Annals of Cong.,* 14 Cong., 2 Sess., 260–265.

[42] Richardson, ed., *Messages of the Presidents,* I, 584–585. It was true that only five years before Gouverneur Morris, who like Madison had played a significant part in the Constitutional Convention, had taken the opposite point of view. Clearly, despite the optimistic assertions of Clinton and Morris in 1811, they had failed to banish the "scruples" of the President on this question. See *supra,* 34.

friends of national aid for internal improvements, who felt that there were many like Madison who were strict constructionists only when the question of internal improvements came up for discussion. "If you can constitutionally create banks for the accommodation of the merchant," Congressman Peter B. Porter of Buffalo had told the House of Representatives as far back as 1810, "but cannot construct canals for the benefit of the farmer —if this be the crooked, partial, sideway policy which is to be pursued, there is a great reason to fear that our western brethren may soon accost us in a tone higher than the Constitution." [43]

Porter's resentment was characteristic of those who viewed the establishment of a national bank by Congress—an exercise of power not specifically delegated to the national legislature under the Constitution—as a precedent for an interpretation of that document sufficiently broad to allow for national aid to roads and canals. When President Madison, an opponent of the bank in 1791, gave the establishment of a similar institution in 1816 the full support of his administration, advocates of federal aid to internal improvements had reason to believe that the question of constitutionality no longer figured as a factor in Madison's thinking.[44] Moreover, by 1816, they could point to the impressive progress being made in the construction of the Cumberland Road, a national project authorized ten years earlier during Jefferson's administration, which had established a useful precedent worthy, in their opinion, of continuation.[45] Clinton

[43] *Annals of Cong.*, 11 Cong., 2 Sess., 1400.

[44] Madison's veto of a previous bank bill in 1815 was not based on constitutional objections but on the belief that the proposed bank would not serve the purpose for which it was intended (Richardson, ed., *Messages*, I, 555–556). The President suggested in his message to Congress in 1815 that it consider the establishment of a national bank as one means of restoring "a uniform currency" and stabilizing the finances of the nation (*ibid.*, 565–566; Adrienne Koch, *Jefferson and Madison: The Great Collaboration* [New York, 1950], 109).

[45] Meyer, ed., *History of Transportation*, 14–17; *U.S. Statutes at Large*, 9 Cong., 1 Sess., ch. 19. By 1818 there was mail service over the Cumberland Road between Washington, D.C., and Wheeling, Va. (Archer B. Hulburt, *The Cumberland Road* [Cleveland, 1904], 54).

maintained that Madison's veto would prevent any future federal participation in the development of new transportation facilities, especially because he saw little prospect that the states would approve an amendment to "resolve the difficulty." "After swallowing the National Bank and the Cumberland Road," he observed in a letter to Rufus King, "it was not supposed that Mr. Madison would strain at canals." [46]

The President's veto eliminated the national government as a possible source of aid for the Erie and Champlain canals. In Albany the reaction to the news from Washington was described by a reporter as one of "indignation," matching the extent of the "disappointment" that was felt. But the same reporter noted that a quick recovery in legislative and public morale took place: "The feelings of the people and of the Legislature were aroused . . . [and] a very general determination [prevailed] . . . that the State of New York should put forth her own energies and commence the proposed works." [47]

Private sources of aid yielded as little help in defraying the costs of the canals as did neighboring states or the national government. Owners of large tracts of land in western and northern New York had little in common with the speculators in land of the early 1790's, whose uncritical judgment and extraordinary optimism had characterized that period of "raging speculation." Those who had survived the collapse of the real-estate market in 1796, along with others who had acquired land later, realized that they would have to wait patiently and for a considerable length of time before they would enjoy an appreciable return on their investment. Their dealings with impecunious settlers who required long credits and generous treatment and whose lack of cash frequently made it necessary that rents or interest on mortgages be paid in kind made this apparent. Short

[46] Clinton to King, 13 Dec. 1817, DWC Papers; Tacitus, *The Canal Policy of New York State*, 44.

[47] Hosack, *Memoir*, 440; Tacitus, *The Canal Policy of New York State*, 45.

of capital and frequently in debt, too, the large landholder
necessarily developed an acuteness in business matters; he calculated his costs closely and, unlike his more speculative proto-
type of the nineties, maintained a conservative outlook where
ventures involving the risk of precious capital were to be considered.[48] Robert Troup, for example, agent of the Pulteney
Estate and a substantial owner of land on his own account, made
no gift to the Canal Fund, despite the fact that he was an outstanding "enthusiast" and actively engaged in mobilizing public
opinion in favor of the canals.[49] Yet, in the 1790's, Troup was
relatively a large owner of stock in the Western Inland Lock
Navigation Company.[50] Such landowners, and the small farmers
and leaseholders who were indebted to them, could make no
gifts to the Canal Fund through the agents who were appointed
in various localities to receive them.[51]

Excluding large portions of land constituting the right of
way, the contributions of private donors were small and their

[48] Aaron M. Sakolski, *The Great American Land Bubble* (New York,
1932), ch. ii, 57–58, 74, 81–82; Evans, *The Holland Land Company*, 218–
220, 434–435; Neil A. McNall, *An Agricultural History of the Genesee
Valley, 1790–1860* (Philadelphia, 1952), 25, 36–37, 41–42, 63–65. Ellicott
wrote in 1806: "That spirit of speculation which formerly prevailed and
which induced men of large capital to embark in extensive purchases . . .
has at present subsided . . . hence we may presume that the plan by retail
will . . . ensure the company the greatest possible success. We have
pretty uniformly found that men disposed to purchase by wholesale are
needy adventurers, who have nothing to lose, are willing to engage in any
speculation" (Bingham, ed., *Holland Land Company Papers*, I, 297; see
also *ibid.*, I, 202–203; II, 144–145).

[49] Hosack, *Memoir*, 423–428; John G. Van Deusen, "Robert Troup,
Agent of the Pulteney Estate," *New York History*, XXIII, 168–169, 180;
Troup to Clinton, 26 Jan. 1816, DWC Papers.

[50] "A Full and Perfect List of All the Subscribers to the Stock of the
Company to Be Known by the Name of the President, Directors and
Company of the Western Inland Lock Navigation in the State of New
York," Schuyler Papers.

[51] Form letter of Samuel Young, 18 July 1816, DWC Papers; "Copy of
Resolutions Passed 18 April 1817, by the Canal Commissioners," *ibid.*, VII,
12; NYS, *Ass. Jour.*, 40 Sess., 617–618.

value almost negligible.[52] Such contributions took the form of land cessions and totaled 106,036 acres. Of this amount, the portion ceded by the Holland Land Company consisted of 100,000 acres, which in Ellicott's private opinion represented "100,000 acres of mountains" but which, he slyly noted, "*seems to evince great liberality*" on the part of the company. Ultimately, the tract sold for $28,000.[53]

Failure to win financial support for the canals from neighboring states and from the national government was disappointing; to Samuel Young, the unsuccessful attempts to obtain assistance from private donors seemed both unbusinesslike and humiliating. Young regarded the role of a "mendicant" as unworthy of the Empire State, and he did not consider it fitting or wise to tie the fate of the canals to the unpredictable generosity of private individuals or corporations. Such a course, he declared, served only to "belittle the great objects in which we are engaged"; and he might have added that they yielded little by way of results.[54]

[52] *NY Canal Laws*, I, 332, 380.

[53] NYS, *Ass. Docs.*, 55 Sess., I, Doc. no. 5, 1; 56 Sess., I, Doc. no. 4, 15–16; Joseph Ellicott to Paul Busti, 21 June 1817, in Severance, ed., *The Holland Land Company*, 127–128; Evans, *The Holland Land Company*, 289.

[54] Young to Clinton, 24 April 1817, DWC Papers.

IV

Reconciliation of

Sectional Differences

UNSUCCESSFUL in fulfilling the financial functions that a "mendicant" state had imposed on them, the commissioners compensated for their deficiency in the skillful way that they prepared the citizens of New York for the great tasks that the state would have to assume alone. After all, as they themselves acknowledged,

in a free government where the people compose the sovereign authority, it is chimerical to contemplate the execution of a stupendous task of internal improvements without the adoption of a wise and economical system which shall conciliate the affections and secure the favorable opinion of those who are the ultimate sources of power.[1]

To allay the opposition of citizens whose hostility may have been based on the technical difficulties and the high costs that the projects were expected to involve, as well as to avoid waste and losses, the commissioners investigated such canal construction as had already been undertaken in New York State and

[1] NYS, *Ass. Jour.*, 40 Sess., 614.

elsewhere. They applied to persons who had dug short canals in order to supply mills with hydraulic power; they questioned officials of the Seneca Lock Navigation Company about the difficult problems that the company had encountered when it undertook to improve navigation between Cayuga Lake and Seneca Lake by the slow and costly construction of twelve locks.[2] John L. Sullivan, the superintendent of the Middlesex Canal, also furnished the commissioners with useful information that he had gathered in the course of his observations of the construction and operation of the canal that connected the Merrimac River with Boston Harbor. In addition, he permitted two of the commissioners to make a careful and detailed study of this enterprise.[3]

The commissioners did not restrict their explorations of canal construction to the American experience; one of the engineers employed on the Erie Canal, Canvass White, went to England to investigate what had been accomplished in that country in expanding the means of artificial navigation. Where direct observation of the English and continental experience proved impossible for the rest of the commissioners, they did the next best thing: they combed the technical literature of other countries, and their reports, as well as Samuel Young's *A Treatise on Internal Navigation*, indicate that their research was exhaustive.[4]

Limiting the projects in extent and cost would, of course, go

[2] This enterprise, like the earlier Western Inland Lock Navigation Company, received state subsidy and was later (26 June 1825) acquired by the state (W. L. Marcy to Reuben Smith, 12 Aug. 1826, Letterbooks of the Comptroller Relating to Canals, I, 6, New York State Department of Audit and Control, Albany [henceforth LRC]).

[3] *NY Canal Laws*, I, 607–614; Clinton to Sullivan, 3 March 1817, DWC Papers.

[4] Philetus Swift, the president of the Senate, Matthew and Francis Brown, Augustus Porter, and Judge Joshua Forman, all New Yorkers, furnished pertinent information regarding the cost of construction of short canals (*NY Canal Laws*, I, 320; NYS, *Laws*, ch. cxliv, 36 Sess.; NYS, *Ass. Jour.*, 40 Sess., 177).

a long way toward conciliating public opinion and toward mut-
ing the shrill cry of bankruptcy that was repeatedly raised by
people who had no faith in the projects. It was necessary to banish from the popular mind the formidable image of the major
canal: three hundred and sixty-three miles long, crossing rivers,
streams, and marshes on aqueducts, penetrating the lofty granite
escarpment at Lockport, and surmounting the sharp rise in the
terrain between the Hudson River and the Mohawk Valley.
Hence the commissioners proposed that a beginning be made
by constructing two small canals—the first to stretch between
the Mohawk and Seneca rivers and the second to unite the
Hudson River with Lake Champlain. The shorter the stretch
of canal to be built initially, the fewer, it was thought, would
be the engineering difficulties that were likely to arise; and the
fact that the estimated outlay for these abbreviated projects was
$1,500,000 as compared to $6,000,000 could only mean that
economy-minded legislators would look with more favor upon
the projects. For these reasons, the commissioners were willing
to pare down the projects, despite their "perfect conviction
. . . that these canals [could] be made without any serious inconvenience to the financial operations of the State." [5]

Obvious commercial considerations argued in favor of quick
construction of the middle section as a means of linking the
Mohawk and Seneca rivers and thereby providing a continuous
artery of navigation stretching halfway across the state. Lake
Ontario and the St. Lawrence River provided farmers of western New York with a Canadian outlet for their surplus produce;
the back door of New York was threatening to become its
front door, and increasingly New York City began to appear
less attractive to the inhabitants of the west than Montreal. Construction of the middle section promised to change this kind
of thinking and to alter the routes of trade in northern and
western New York at the expense of the Canadians and for the
benefit of the merchants of the "great emporium" at the mouth

[5] NYS, *Ass. Jour.*, 40 Sess., 614–615.

of the Hudson River. Here was a consideration that would apply with equal force to farmers of western New York and businessmen in New York City, since, despite the use that was made
of the St. Lawrence route, it was a hazardous one and many a
farmer's produce never reached Montreal because of the rocks,
rifts, shoals, and unpredictable currents in the river. To such
farmers, therefore, this proposal offered a far safer route to
market. The business community of New York City constituted
another powerful regional economic interest that had to be won
over to the project, and the commissioners obviously hoped that
the lure of a quick diversion of western trade down the Hudson River would be attractive bait.[6]

The commissioners' decision to confine initial construction to
a fraction of the total project for purposes of "conciliating"
public opinion was shrewd; it was wise, too, when considered
in terms of the lack of technical experience of the men who
would bear the burden of supervising the initial operations on
the canals. For all the confidence that the commissioners exuded
in public, in private they revealed, on occasion, their doubts
and fears in connection with the enormous task that they proposed the state should undertake.[7] For this reason, they maintained that "counsels of prudence," along with a solicitude for
public opinion, urged that the limited project be undertaken
first. The limited project, the commissioners declared, would
enable them "to bring the solidity of their opinions to the touch-
stone of experiment before the whole system is undertaken."[8]
Moreover, this middle section offered favorable conditions for
such experimentation. The nature of the terrain presented only

[6] Undoubtedly the commissioners emphasized this expectation in order
to conciliate businessmen of New York City who feared that the canal
project would mean higher taxes. The businessmen might have felt that
such fears were justified not only because of the expected high costs of
the canals but also as a result of the commissioners' recommendation that
a portion of the auction duties collected in the city and used for payment
of poor relief be used instead to pay the interest on the canal debt (NYS,
Ass. Jour., 40 Sess., 614).

[7] *Infra*, 64.   [8] NYS, *Ass. Jour.*, 40 Sess., 614.

the simplest problems in excavation and drainage; the required amount of lockage was small and therefore precluded the possibility that even novices could commit large errors.[9]

A whole decade later, DeWitt Clinton justified the experimental nature of the middle section and the wisdom of building it first. Looking backward, Clinton then declared that in the early period of construction "the services of civil engineers was [*sic*] little known" so that the middle section became the training ground for ex-lawyers and others who soon gained the reputation of being the foremost practitioners of canal engineering in the United States.[10] Both James Geddes, the chief engineer on the Erie Canal, and Benjamin Wright, frequently referred to as "the father of American engineering," had been lawyers and judges and, because of their frequent involvement in cases relating to contested land claims, had been forced to

---

[9] *NY Canal Laws*, I, 268. The commissioners' recommendation that the Champlain Canal, between the Hudson River and Lake Champlain, be started simultaneously with the middle section was a decision based on technical as well as political reasons. The technical problems that would be encountered on the Champlain Canal in terms of lockage alone were somewhat greater than those presented by the middle section. On the other hand, the Champlain Canal presented fewer technical problems than any single "section" that was undertaken as a unit on the Erie Canal, if the middle section is excluded. For political reasons, it was impossible to start on the western canal without starting at the same time on the northern canal. For twenty-five years, from the time that the Northern and Western Inland Lock Navigation companies were incorporated, western and northern schemes of internal improvement were thought of as a single project, and both these early lock navigation companies were incorporated under the same act. In 1816 DeWitt Clinton learned that inhabitants of the Champlain Valley thought of both canals as a single project when he toured that part of the north country. Logrolling, therefore, was the order of the day. "The people of the north country are very desirous to see this work [the Champlain Canal] executed," Clinton informed Commissioner Ellicott. They were "willing that the western canal shall proceed *pari passu*," and no doubt this is what the legislators of the north country held out for in the legislature (Clinton to Ellicott, 20 Sept. 1816, in Severance, ed., *The Holland Land Company*, 71).

[10] Clinton to F. M. Woolsey, 1 Oct. 1827, DWC Papers.

acquire a knowledge of surveying.[11] Near novices all, the "engineers" filled Canal Commissioner Samuel Young with fear when, with Young accompanying them, they set out to survey the summit level of the middle section near Rome. This was a "delicate, important, and difficult" task, Young confided to Clinton. "The whole project hangs upon an attentuated thread," which could "break and cause our destruction if we do not exercise the utmost care, caution and vigilance. A Mistake in the summit level," declared Young, would be "irrevocable damnation in this world." [12]

Young soon recovered his confidence as a result of the spectacular performances of the amateur engineers. Judge Geddes, for example, ran a series of test levels for a distance of more than a hundred miles in the general vicinity of Oneida Lake; when he closed the traverse, he discovered that the difference in levels at the junction point was less than one and one-half inches. With pride, the commissioners noted the "degree of care, skill and precision in the delicate art of leveling," which they believed "had perhaps never been exceeded." [13] The "versatile ingenuity" of the engineers was soon widely hailed, and the Erie Canal was esteemed as "one of the most excellent schools that could be devised for the study of engineering." [14]

No one could have foreseen the surprisingly high technical competence of the men who assumed the duties of engineers on the middle section. Here was a "native treasure unknown until called for by the occasion," Joshua Forman declared; and the combination of the occasion and the men produced a high yield of technical innovation that simplified the more difficult tasks

[11] Noble E. Whitford, *History of the Canal System of the State of New York* (Albany, 1906), I, 788–789.

[12] Young to Clinton, 11 Aug. 1817, DWC Papers.

[13] "Report of the Canal Commissioners," 31 Jan. 1818, quoted in Whitford, *History of the Canal System*, I, 789.

[14] New York Corresponding Association for the Promotion of Internal Improvements, *Pub. Docs. Relating to the New York Canals* (New York, 1821), xlii; Whitford, *History of the Canal System*, I, 786–807.

that lay ahead.[15] New mechanical techniques were devised to solve the special problems of canal building. New tools and machinery were perfected that accelerated and facilitated the difficult processes of grubbing, clearing, and excavating, and Canvass White perfected his hydraulic cement that would later reduce the cost of constructing locks throughout the entire canal system.[16] Technical innovation advanced so steadily that soon the commissioners declared that such innovation had to be anticipated as an expected by-product of their future operations. One of the significant achievements in the construction of the middle section, Clinton later declared, was the "augmentation of skill and acquisition of experience that resulted" and that "ultimately contributed to economy and improved workmanship." [17]

In view of the pains that the commissioners took to reassure the public, it is perhaps surprising they made no secret of the fact that they considered the work on the middle section experimental. Whether one favored or opposed the canals, the middle section was termed an experiment. After it was completed, easterners who opposed further construction westward took the position that the "experiment" in the "art" of canal construction was inconclusive. On the other hand, an enthusiast such as Robert Troup as early as 1818 hailed the success of the "experiment" and predicted that it would "strengthen and extend public confidence as to insure the undertaking of other sections," and supporters of Clinton looked upon the completed middle section and the portion of the Champlain Canal under way by 1819 "as a demonstration of the practicability of the Scheme." [18]

[15] Hosack, *Memoir*, 354n.

[16] Whitford, *History of the Canal System*, I, 791; "A Communication from the Canal Commissioners," 25 Jan. 1819, *NY Canal Laws*, I, 404–406; "Report of the Canal Commissioners," 31 Jan. 1818, *ibid.*, 374, 377.

[17] Clinton to E. J. Williams, 8 Nov. 1823, DWC Papers.

[18] Troup to Clinton, 25 Feb. 1818, DWC Papers; J. D. Hammond, *The History of Political Parties*, I, 492–495.

The commissioners were highly sensitive to the interplay of regional economic interests and their possible effect on legislative authorization for the construction of the canals. They understood the objections of the farmer in the Hudson River Valley, in Delaware, Montgomery, Schoharie, Rensselaer, and Washington counties, who would oppose internal improvements that would open lands in the west far more fertile than their own and would provide the farmers who cultivated them with access to the very markets in which they disposed of their products. Similarly, the farmers on Long Island could be expected to oppose a state project that would intensify competition in the produce market of New York City, to which they, too, customarily sent their products. Moreover, was there any reason to believe that businessmen of New York City were especially imaginative in outlook and that they were not frequently overwhelmed by a combination of timidity, myopia, and parochialism when faced with large plans that seemed to embody the necessity for increased taxation? Could they have believed that the proposed public works would not mean higher taxes? Businessmen of a cynical cast of mind may well have suspected that they were about to be asked to shoulder a higher tax burden less for reasons of improving transportation facilities within the state than to benefit scheming politicians who were hunting votes in western and northern New York. And, finally, had not an earlier generation of New York merchants invested in the Western Inland Lock Navigation Company only to discover the folly of undertaking projects that were well beyond the technical and financial capacity of Americans at the time?

Members of the legislature from New York City—Peter Sharpe in the Assembly and Peter R. Livingston in the Senate —protested accordingly against the commissioners' proposal that part of the auction duties collected in the city and earmarked for purposes of poor relief be diverted to the proposed Canal Fund.[19] Sharpe maintained that the city was already

[19] NYS, *Ass. Jour.*, 40 Sess., 614.

"drained" to the limit of its resources by taxation, that the "most respectable and opulent of her merchants are daily becoming bankrupts," and that under such unfavorable conditions he regarded the anticipated costs of the canals "too great for the state" at the time. "She will sink under it," he declared in reference to the anticipated canal debt and, alluding to the immensity of the task, maintained that "the magnitude is beyond what has ever been accomplished by any nation." [20]

Livingston, somewhat less temperate than his colleague, declared that only "a madman, fool or knave" would favor undertaking the construction of the canals in the light of prevailing high costs of labor, the uncertain foreign market for agricultural products, and the existing "oppressive" level of taxation. He doubted that "money lenders" would consider the revenues from duties that the commissioners proposed to allot to the Canal Fund as adequate security for loans. The day of the speculator would dawn, warned Livingston, if the state sought to execute the internal improvements program that its officials were contemplating. "From diggers on up," all would be involved in selfish speculation, and the outcome of the enterprise would prove what Livingston already knew—that there were "no worse managers of funds than the public." [21]

Largely responsible for weakening eastern opposition to the canals was the fact that some easterners were investing in real estate in central and western New York, especially in areas through which the Erie Canal would pass. Such investors, many of whom were Federalists in politics, counted on officeholders of their own party to support the proposed program of public works.[22] Federalist members of the legislature from anticanal counties in the east found themselves in the embarrassing position of having to choose between party policy and the hostile

[20] Albany *Gazette and Daily Advertiser*, 16 April 1817.
[21] *Ibid.*
[22] Dixon R. Fox, *Decline of Aristocracy in the Politics of New York* (New York, 1919), 147–157.

sentiment that their constituents felt for the internal improvements projects and especially for the western canal.

The commissioners were especially resourceful in the way that they rescued the embarrassed Federalists from their painful political position. Among their financial recommendations to the legislature, the commissioners proposed a real-estate tax on the property of those who would benefit most from the construction of the new canal. The tax would be levied in the areas where the improved transportation would have a direct affect on land values, which would undoubtedly rise as a result of the anticipated fall in transportation costs. Although there seemed to be an element of simple justice in this proposal, it attested as well to the commissioners' political astuteness. Federalists such as William A. Duer and Nathaniel Pendleton of Dutchess County seized on the commissioners' proposal immediately in order to extract from it as much in the way of political advantage as they could. The proposal enabled them to support the public works program in the legislature at the same time that it diminished the possibility of an unfavorable reaction among their constituents along the Hudson River. No doubt with his constituents in mind, Pendleton lectured western representatives on the essential injustices that the canal policy embodied. "Am I to be taxed and my money expended in an enterprise which will be of no value to me, to raise the value of your lands?" he demanded. "Can this be just? Will any man desire it?" Having struck a vigorous blow for his constituents, which would yield them considerable satisfaction when they read his speech back home, Pendleton could now turn his attention to the useful compromise that the commissioners had provided for legislators who happened to share his awkward position. The suggested real-estate tax would, to some extent, redress the balance of benefits that the proposed canal policy would bring to central and western New York. Pendleton was a reasonable man. "With such a tax," he declared, he was "willing to begin the work; but if the whole funds were to be raised by the State," he would be found in the opposition.[23]

Duer's position was much the same as his colleague's. Like Pendleton, Duer favored a land tax, levied on real estate in sections that would benefit directly from the public works. He called the attention of the Assembly to the fact that the future "canal counties" would experience special advantages as a result of the projects from the moment that work on the canals began. These sections, he noted, would be "greatly benefitted by the expenditure of money among [their] citizens for the purchase of lands, the hiring of workmen, etc.," justifying, as far as this legislator was concerned, "a tax upon those sections where the canal is first to be made and the money for making expended."[24] Elisha Williams, Duer's neighbor in the Hudson River Valley and member of the Assembly from Columbia County, was another enthusiastic advocate of the land tax, although seemingly with less reason than either Duer or Pendleton. For although Williams turned out to be a vocal backer of the tax, he was, by his own admission, a considerable investor in western lands, which he expected would be "enhanced in value four hundred fold" if the legislature approved the construction of the Erie Canal. Apparently, his unnatural desire to be visited by the tax collector on the basis of his western holdings disgusted one opponent of this type of taxation, who realized that Williams was as eager to remain in the legislature as he was to enhance the value of his lands. This gentleman declared that he, too, "should have been as willing to have his land taxed as the gentleman from Columbia, had fortune favored him with any on the route of the canals."[25]

It was Duer, however, who introduced and led the fight for a section in the canal law that provided for a tax on land and

[23] Pendleton's address is reprinted in Hosack, *Memoir*, 445–446.
[24] Albany *Gazette and Daily Advertiser*, 11 April, 12 April 1817.
[25] *Ibid.*, 12 April 1817.

property within twenty-five miles of the middle section of the Erie and for the entire length of the Champlain Canal. The section became a part of the law, and although, as it worked out, the tax was never collected, it proved to be the most useful device that the commissioners could supply to legislators from eastern New York who, otherwise, might have been unable to support the Canal Act in the legislature for local political reasons.[26]

The law authorizing the construction of the canals represented numerous compromises of a complicated nature, determined by considerations that were sectional, political, and technical. The general scheme of allocating some of the revenues of old or new duties to the Canal Fund, which had been incorporated in the commissioners' financial plan, was itself a matter of sectional compromise according to George Tibbetts, who played a large part in formulating the system of finance that was finally adopted, and may be taken as representative of the way in which the entire law was shaped. According to Tibbetts,

it was presumed that the City of New York (notwithstanding her representation opposed the canals) must be more than compensated by them for the loss of the share of the auction duties which she had so long enjoyed; . . . that the West, who were the exclusive consumers of the salt made there, would consent to a heavy tax upon it rather than not have the canals; that some of the towns and counties who were conceded to be benefitted would consent to a small addition to their ordinary taxes; that the state could . . . devote a section of its wild lands for this purpose; that a steamboat tax might right or wrong be imposed.[27]

[26] NYS, *Ass. Jour.*, 40 Sess., 790.

[27] Hosack, *Memoir*, 489. Not all of these provisions were included in the final act. Cf. NYS, *Laws*, ch. cclxii, 40 Sess. The canal bill was considered in a legislature that was sharply divided not only on sectional and economic and technical questions but politically, too, as a result of the current gubernatorial campaign. Clinton, a candidate for governor, was considered, with some reason, an unstable politician, a conclusion that his shifting political allegiances and alliances helped to confirm. He had an un-

In making their financial recommendations to the Joint Committee on Canals, the commissioners proposed that they be divested of all the duties and responsibilities for raising, borrowing, or soliciting funds, thereby reserving for themselves only the technical and managerial functions involved in the construction of the canals. They proposed that a new board be constituted to assume the duties that they had abandoned and recommended that the comptroller, the secretary of state, the attorney general, and the treasurer be made members of it. With the addition of the lieutenant governor to the membership of the board, their suggestion was incorporated in the Canal Act. Eventually designated as "The Commissioners of the Canal Fund," the board as a unit became responsible for administering the financial business of the Canal Fund.

The most significant provision of the Canal Act authorized the Commissioners of the Canal Fund to borrow on the credit of the state. In this way, the projects were established on a firmer foundation than uncertain gifts, donations, and grants could provide. In spite of this provision, the legislature found it difficult to abandon the long-standing expectation of outside aid that had been repeatedly considered as a possibility during the previous decade. By making it legally possible for the Canal Fund to receive "grants and donations . . . by the Congress of the United States, by individual states, corporations, companies and individuals," members of the legislature indicated their continuing hope that some unexpected windfall might eventually lighten the financial load that the state would have to carry.

---

usual ability to incur intense hostility among those who opposed him while, at the same time, succeeding in retaining devoted loyalty among his friends. The fact that Clinton was intimately associated with the canal projects, therefore, drew them rapidly into the orbit of political controversy. Under such circumstances, the passage of the Canal Act surprised some of its devoted advocates; and the vote in its favor in the legislature showed, in general, a division along party lines (Ellicott to Clinton, 16 April 1817, in Severance, ed., *The Holland Land Company*, 123–124; *The Coalition* (NYPL), 1–8; J. D. Hammond, *History of Political Parties*, I, 441).

The act authorized the commissioners to begin building the middle section of the Erie Canal and the Champlain Canal simultaneously. With respect to the middle section, the legislature accepted the recommendation of the commissioners calling for quick action in purchasing the rights and property of the Western Inland Lock Navigation Company. The timing of the purchase was left to the commissioners, who had declared in their financial report that "if the middle section . . . is made, before the rights of the Western Inland Lock Navigation Company are purchased, it may induce the latter in consequence of the increased value of their property, to rise in their demands." [28]

Specific revenues were set aside for amortizing the canal debt, and the law required as well that tolls collected on the partially or wholly completed canals and on the facilities of the private company be used for the same purpose when these should become the property of the state. Revenues from duties, both old and new, were allotted to the Canal Fund in the expectation that the combined receipts would be sufficient to pay the interest on the funds borrowed for the construction of the canals prior to the time when an income from tolls or from the sale of hydraulic power could be realized. The duty on sales of salt manufactured in the western districts, part of the duty on sales at auction, a duty on steamboat passengers, a portion of the proceeds of certain lotteries, and the tax on lands within twenty-five miles of the canals were expected to reach a total equal to the amount needed for interest payments on loans during the early years. [29]

[28] NYS, *Ass. Jour.*, 40 Sess., 615. For the Canal Act, see NYS, *Laws*, ch. cclxii, 40 Sess. The company's rights and property were acquired by the state in 1820 with the state receiving two-fifths of the purchase price as the largest stockholder, while the remainder was distributed among the individual investors. The company eventually fulfilled the expectations of the commissioners by petitioning the Committee of Claims of the Assembly for additional compensation but without success (*NY Canal Laws*, I, 503, 505–506; NYS, *Ass. Jour.*, 44 Sess., 263, 871, 1091; 46 Sess., 266).

[29] NYS, *Laws*, ch. cclxvii, 40 Sess. Cf. NYS, *Ass. Jour.*, 40 Sess., 616. Revenues from taxes on lands along the route of the canals and from lot-

teries were never realized. The provision to tax lands was suspended by law until the time when the legislature would direct an assessment to be made, and this it never did (NYS, *Laws*, ch. cv, 42 Sess.). Lotteries were banned in the state under Art. VII, Sec. 11, of the Constitution of 1821. In 1820, the tax on steamboat passengers was suspended, and in its place the North River Steamboat Company was required to pay $5,000 annually into the treasury of the state. Collection of this sum ceased in 1825, when the company lost its monopoly rights as a direct consequence of the decision of the U.S. Supreme Court in the case of *Gibbons* v. *Ogden* (NYS, *Laws*, ch. cxvii, 43 Sess.; NYS, *Sen. Jour.*, 49 Sess., 523).

Part Two

SOURCES OF CAPITAL FOR
THE ERIE AND CHAMPLAIN CANALS

V

The Fuse of Domestic Investment

INVESTMENT in a variety of undertakings was a common-place of American economic life in the first and second decades of the nineteenth century. If its intricacies as far as overseas trade was concerned were understood and practiced by only a select set of merchants in the eastern cities, almost everyone else was able to cope with the kind of investment that land speculation entailed. Undoubtedly, it was this form of invest-ment that had educated the average American as to the means by which he could use his own savings, or those of others, ad-vantageously. For anyone who may have had moral scruples about engaging in this form of gambling, which frequently took on the proportions of a national disease, he had but to note the speculations of such founding fathers as Washington, Robert and Gouverneur Morris, Philip Schuyler, Benjamin Franklin, Patrick Henry, James Wilson, and others in order to set his mind at rest.[1] These men, of course, had only maintained a long-

[1] For Washington's interest in land speculation and his concomitant advocacy of internal improvements, which usually accompanied such an interest, see Herbert B. Adams, *Maryland's Influence upon Land Cessions in the United States* (Johns Hopkins University Studies in History and Political Science, III, no. 1; Baltimore, 1885), 55-91, and Wayland F. Dunaway, *History of the James River and Kanawha Company* (New

standing tradition that reached far back into colonial history.[2]

Under the tutelage of Alexander Hamilton, the education of Americans in the ways of finance and investment was greatly advanced. Hamilton's financial program for placing the credit of the nation on a sound footing gave many Americans their first experience with government securities and bank stock, the impact of which was far-reaching and profound. By the end of 1790, the appearance of government securities unleashed a "rage of speculation," which disrupted the orderly processes of business. Newspapers were filled with articles on "scriptomania," "scripponomy," "scriptophobia," and "stockjobbing." Wide public interest in the new government issues hastened the emergence of the new profession of the stockbroker and quickly created a new place of business called the stock exchange. Sober citizens like Jefferson, who observed the bewildering scene, expressed their apprehension that capital was being withdrawn from productive enterprises "to be employed in gambling." Even before the debt was funded, Andrew Craigie expressed the opinion that "the public debt affords the best field in the world for speculation"; and many years later, Thomas Eddy noted that this was a memorable period in his life, when he "made a great deal of money." [3]

The tremendous popular interest in the fluctuations of the

York, 1922), 10–27. The first President also realized the potentialities of the Great Lakes–Mohawk–Hudson River system as a basis for internal improvements, as indicated in his letter to the Marquis de Chastellux in George Washington, *The Writings of George Washington*, ed. by W. C. Ford (New York, 1891), X, 324–325. See also Sparks, *Life of Morris*, I, 351–352; Ann Cary Morris, *The Diary and Letters of Gouverneur Morris* (New York, 1888), II, 378; Josephine Mayer and Robert A. East, "The Settlement of Alexander Hamilton's Debts," *New York History*, XVIII, no. 4, 379–383; Sakolski, *Great American Land Bubble*, 1–53; Joseph S. Davis, *Essays in the Earlier History of American Corporations* (Cambridge, Mass., 1917), I, 176; Ellis, *Landlords and Farmers*, 411–412.

[2] Sakolski, *Great American Land Bubble*, ch. i.

[3] Davis, *Essays*, I, 188–189, 195, 197, 199, 207–208; Knapp, *Life of Thomas Eddy*, 54.

new government securities and the strong competition for stock of the first national bank and of the Bank of New York at the beginning of the last decade of the eighteenth century signified a vigorous growth of investment-mindedness, firmly established on an unexpectedly broad foundation of available surplus capital.[4] But land, banks, government securities, and, of course, commerce did not exhaust the opportunities that were open to American investors. By the turn of the century, they had the choice of investing in more than three hundred chartered corporations that engaged in such varied activities as banking, insurance, water supply, manufacturing, and the construction of canals, bridges, and turnpikes.[5]

When the canal commissioners of New York opened their books for subscriptions to the first canal loan in 1817, therefore, investment in federal loans and private corporations was a well-established feature of American business. The same thing cannot be said, however, of state loans as far as New York was concerned. The loan that the state floated in 1815 on the basis of popular subscription, although not unprecedented, was not the most familiar device that the state resorted to in order to raise funds. Wartime expenditures were responsible for the loan of 1815 and accounted, too, for the fact that the legislature also levied taxes on real and personal property, which it heretofore had made every effort to avoid. During the first four decades of the state's history, the costs of government had been met largely with whatever revenues were yielded by the sales of public lands, investments of the state's funds, fees, special duties, and lotteries.[6] When the income from these sources failed to keep pace with the steadily mounting costs of government, the state resorted to loans from banks, so that by 1814 it owed a total of $1,503,000 to seven banks, on which sum it paid an interest of 6 per cent per annum.[7] The prevailing ap-

---

[4] Myers, *The New York Money Market*, I, 11–13.
[5] Davis, *Essays*, II, 8, 291.   [6] Sowers, *Financial History*, 114.
[7] NYS, *Ass. Jour.*, 32 Sess., 84; 33 Sess., 44; 34 Sess., 87; 35 Sess., 76;

proach to the question of appropriations in order to pay the expenses of government may be illustrated by an act of the legislature of 1808, which empowered the comptroller "to satisfy the appropriations made by law during the same session by borrowing the necessary funds from the banks." [8]

The War of 1812 burdened the treasury suddenly and heavily with a variety of new expenses that made it impossible for the state to continue to resort to its customary financial procedures. The state had to improve its defenses on the northern and western frontiers and to fortify the port of New York against attack from the sea. It had to raise the sum of $860,000 as its share of a direct tax levied by Congress to meet the costs of the war. It found it necessary to lend $350,000 to the national government to provide for the payment of its own militia, which had been ordered into federal service. [9] Facing up to these new demands on the treasury, the legislature tentatively suggested that the state dispose of some of its investments, a proposal which the comptroller dismissed as impractical and unwise. Apparently, there was no way of avoiding the comptroller's recommendation, and the legislature finally consented

---

36 Sess., 161; 37 Sess., 264; 38 Sess., 32, 153, 155; 39 Sess., 185; 40 Sess., 204. The loan obtained from the Bank of America is incorrectly stated on p. 155 of the *Ass. Jour.*, 38 Sess., as $550,000. It should be $557,000 as indicated on p. 165. By contrast to the total debt accumulated by 1814, the income of the state that year, exclusive of bank loans, amounted to less than $540,000.

[8] NYS, *Laws*, ch. ccxl, 31 Sess.

[9] NYS, *Laws*, ch. vii, 31 Sess.; ch. cxxxix, 35 Sess.; ch.cc, 37 Sess., par. xxxix; chs. viii, xxvii, lxxxiv, 38 Sess. Under these laws, $280,400 was expended by the state during 1814 (NYS, Ass. Jour., 38 Sess., 158). See also NYS, *Ass. Jour.*, 38 Sess., 164; *U.S. Statutes at Large*, 13 Cong., 3 Sess., ch. 21. By Sec. 40 of this act, any state that indicated its willingness to pay its allotted proportion of the tax into the national treasury before 1 May 1815, and did so, was permitted by law to reduce its payment by 15 per cent. New York took advantage of this opportunity and paid $731,240.76 to the Treasury under this act (NYS, *Laws*, ch. cxi, 38 Sess.; NYS, *Ass. Jour.*, 39 Sess., 191).

to a tax on real and personal property.[10] A series of swiftly accumulating incidents, however, made it clear that the revenues
from the new tax would neither be available soon enough nor
be adequate to meet the expenses of a costly war, which unfortunately for the nation had been characterized by expensive
defeats. Under these circumstances, the legislature authorized
the comptroller to issue "a public and transferable stock,"
amounting to $1,300,000 and bearing an annual interest rate of
7 per cent.[11]

The success of this loan was regarded pessimistically even
before the comptroller offered it to the public in April 1815.
The legislature, in fact, clearly indicated its doubts that the loan
would receive much public support when it enacted supple-
mentary legislation empowering the state to borrow from the
Bank of America and from the City Bank the difference between the amount that would be raised by popular subscription and the required total.[12] The comptroller, too, was not

[10] NYS, *Ass. Jour.*, 38 Sess., 12, 32–33; NYS, *Laws*, ch. xxix, 38 Sess.

[11] NYS, *Laws*, ch. clxi, 38 Sess. For evidence that this loan was intended
for the payment of the direct tax, see ch. cclxvi, 38 Sess., pars. xxv, xxxvi.
The time sequence here is of some importance. The Treaty of Ghent was
signed 24 Dec. 1814; Jackson's victory at New Orleans occurred on 18 Jan.
1815. The following day, the law which provided for a direct tax of
$6,000,000 was passed by Congress. On 7 April, more than three months
after the treaty of peace had been signed, the legislature approved the
bill providing for the loan of $1,300,000.

[12] The fact that the Bank of America "took" $557,000 of this 7 per cent
loan may easily create a mistaken impression of large resources in the possession of banks that were available to public and private borrowers. It is
hard to determine what the resources of any bank were and to what extent
a bank's notes were backed by specie reserves. Banking operations at this
time frequently began, and continued to be carried on, on the basis of a
small amount of paid-in capital in a capital-short economy. The amazing
thing is that there were not more bank failures than actually occurred
(*infra*, 85 note, App. III; B. Hammond, *Banking and Politics*, 275–276,
282; Fritz Redlich, *The Molding of American Banking: Men and Ideas*
(New York, 1947, 1951), pt. I, 44. Under the terms of its charter and sub-
sequent revisions, the Bank of America was required to lend to the state.

especially hopeful about the possible success of the loan. He predicted that only a "very small proportion" would be taken on the basis of popular subscription and expected that if both banks together furnished $823,000, the maximum that could be required of them under the law, there would still "in all probability be a considerable deficiency." Popular subscription, the comptroller believed, would account at most for $200,000, and the banks would have to be relied upon for the rest. The comptroller saw additional difficulty for the state issue because it would be competing with issues of the national government in the money market. The offering of the United States government, he noted, afforded the prospective investor "a fairer prospect of successful speculation," in spite of his belief that the state loan offered "very considerable . . . inducements to capitalists to become subscribers to it." [13]

This bank was incorporated in 1812 in order to fill the gap in banking facilities that remained as a result of the demise of the First National Bank. The legislature, obviously, planned to use this bank, as well as the City Bank, as a source of credit in lieu of taxation. The practice of requiring banks to lend to the state under provisions in their charters was not restricted to New York (NYS, *Laws*, chs. lxxviii, clxxv, 35 Sess.; chs. lxvi, lxxv, 36 Sess.; ch. xiv, 38 Sess.; Redlich, *Molding of American Banking*, pt. I, 12).

[13] NYS, *Ass. Jour.*, 38 Sess., 618. The benefit of hindsight indicates that fair prospects for speculation did exist in federal loans. On 14 April 1815, three days before the comptroller made this statement, the prices of such issues were 6 per cents, old and deferred, 89; war loans, 87¼; 3 per cents, 55; Louisiana Purchase Loan, 88. By the following October, the 6 per cents had risen to 97, the war loans to 97–97¼, the 3 per cents to 60–61, and the Louisiana Purchase Loan to 98 (*General Shipping and Commercial List*, 14 April, 10 Oct. 1815). In all probability, however, the comptroller was particularly concerned about the large loan that Congress had approved on 3 March 1815, only a month and a few days before the state legislature approved its loan for $1,300,000. Congress authorized the President to borrow almost $18,500,000 to meet the demands on the Treasury arising from steadily maturing short-term loans and treasury notes which had been borrowed or issued during the war (*U.S. Statutes at Large*, 13 Cong., 3 Sess., ch. 87).

This attempt of the state to borrow on the basis of popular subscription, made at a time admittedly "unpropitious," produced results indicating that the doubts of the comptroller and many members of the legislature were, to a considerable extent, unfounded. It is true that ultimately the banks furnished slightly more than half the amount of the loan, but this was far less than many had been led to expect. Under relatively unfavorable circumstances, business and professional men of New York City, who possessed considerable, if not spectacularly large, savings, indicated their willingness to entrust these savings to the state. Among them were bankers such as William Bayard and Charles Wilkes, whose judgment on matters of investment, although not infallible, was based on great familiarity with the money market. These were just two of a total of one hundred and thirty-nine individuals, consisting of merchants, brewers, butchers, bankers, grocers, attorneys, doctors, bakers, sawyers, and carpenters, whose combined savings invested in this loan amounted to almost $650,000.[14] By entrusting their savings, which amounted to only a few thousand dollars each, to the state, these early investors gave grounds for hope that the state might very well be accommodated in the same manner at some future date for the purpose of financing its canals.

The limited success of the loan of 1815 scarcely offered assur-

[14] There were twelve subscriptions between $164 and $450; twenty between $500 and $800; thirty between $1,000 and $1,950; twenty-three between $2,000 and $2,700; twenty-four between $3,000 and $4,850; fourteen between $5,000 and $9,000; and sixteen over $10,000. The two largest subscriptions were for $50,000 each. See "List of Holders of New York State Stock, Resident in the Southern District of This State and Out of This State, on the 31 March 1816, Showing the Amounts Held by Each with the Interest Due and Payable on the First Monday of April 1816," Misc. Canal Papers, NYSL. Names and occupations were checked in *American Almanac: New York Register and City Directory* (New York, 1816) and *Longworth's New York Almanac for 1816–1817.* The percentage of New York residents was extremely high. For example, thirteen of the sixteen in the group that invested $10,000 and above were residents of New York City (NYS, *Ass. Jour.*, 40 Sess., 520).

ance to the Commissioners of the Canal Fund that there would be a favorable public response to the first canal loan two years later. The canal loans, unlike that of 1815, were for projects of internal improvements, and, unfortunately, they revived memories of previous failures in a manner and to an extent that seemed likely to curb the borrowing power of the state for specific projects of this kind. Joshua Forman, a strong supporter of state-constructed canals, privately expressed his embarrassment at being reminded of the failures of General Schuyler and his associates when the question of the Erie and Champlain canals was debated in the Senate; and Samuel Young told Clinton that the record of the Northern Inland Lock Navigation Company proved to be a powerful weapon against the state's project in the Champlain Valley.[15]

The unfavorable history of internal improvements in New York was only one reason for apprehension as the time for offering the first canal loan to the public in June 1817 approached. Seemingly, the time was inappropriate for floating this loan in view of the fact that, as Clinton pointed out, the stakes were very high indeed. "Money is very scarce in this city," Clinton wrote with considerable anxiety to Joseph Ellicott in May 1817. "If this first and small loan should fail, it would have a very pernicious effect on all our future operations." [16]

Clinton's statement implied that there was little hope of borrowing abroad. This conclusion was confirmed two months later by William Bayard's investigation of the foreign money market, which revealed that, at least in Holland, the costs of a loan would be high.[17] The multimillion-dollar foreign loan that the members of the Canal Board in 1812 had blithely predicted could be nego-

[15] Hosack, *Memoir*, 380–381; Samuel Young to Clinton, 20 Dec. 1819, DWC Papers.

[16] Clinton to Ellicott, 10 May 1817, in Severance, ed., *The Holland Land Company*, 125.

[17] Van Eeghen and Co. to William Bayard, 21 July 1817, DWC Papers; "Report of the Commissioners under the Act of April 17, 1816, 17 Feb. 1817," *NY Canal Laws*, I, 269.

tiated without any trouble at all seemed quite out of reach in 1817.[18]

The realization that the Commissioners of the Canal Fund would have to rely on New York City as its principal source of funds must have had a sobering effect even on the most enthusiastic exponents of internal improvements. In January 1817, when the canal commissioners with considerable accuracy estimated that the costs of construction of the Erie and Champlain canals would amount to $7,000,000, the total amount of banking and insurance capital in the state was less than $21,000,000.[19] Only

[18] In May 1817, J. B. Stuart of Albany notified the commissioners that "certain banks in London" had authorized him to offer them a loan of $1,500,000. The indefinite wording of the offer and, more particularly, the fact that nowhere in the letters, documents, or reports of the commissioners is there the slightest reference to this proposal, which would have radically altered the history of the Canal Fund, clearly leads one to suspect that there was more imagination than substance behind it (J. B. Stuart to the Commissioners of the Canal Fund, 29 May 1817, Misc. Canal Papers, Pkg. 550, C44, NYSL; "Report of the Commissioners . . . Act of April 8, 1812," *NY Canal Laws*, I, 86–87).

[19] "Minutes of the Meeting of the Cl. Commers.," Albany, 22 Jan. 1817, XVIII, 24–26, DWC Papers. In all probability, even this estimate was too high. The statement of the comptroller (William L. Marcy) contained the admission in its title that his success in accurately ascertaining the amount of capital actually paid into the banks and insurance companies was limited (NYS, *Ass. Jour.*, 49 Sess., between pp. 418–419). Some years later, Comptroller A. C. Flagg enlarged on the same point, maintaining that, before 1826, banking operations in New York could commence when an amount that varied between 12 and 50 per cent of the capital was paid in, depending upon the provisions contained in the charter of the particular institution. Since, according to Flagg, the banks were rarely required to report their capital, the total could not be determined accurately. Flagg's figures were even higher than Marcy's had been for the period. His estimate for the total banking capital alone in 1815 was $18,215,000, and in 1820, $21,105,000. It need hardly be pointed out that the tendency of bank directors would be to exaggerate the amount of capital at their disposal (NYS, *Ass. Docs.*, 59 Sess., II, Doc. no. 102, 1–6). An important point overlooked by both Flagg and Marcy was the fact that the Bank of the United States went into operation early in the same year that the state authorized the construction of the canals, and its New York branch became an important factor in the business affairs of that city. By July

the success of the first few loans would dispel such doubts as Clinton entertained scarcely a month before the first canal loan was offered to the public.

The reception accorded to the early canal loans verified the fact that there was a large supply of available savings in New York and that it would be entrusted to the state even for the purpose of financing internal improvements. These early loans—those that were offered to the public between 1817 and 1820—were ultimately supported chiefly by individuals of substantial, but not great, savings, whose investments were made in relatively small amounts.[20] During this period, such investors in government securities were virtually restricted to the state loans, because during the same time, the national government made no effort to borrow at all.[21] By the end of 1820, wealthier Americans, consisting of people of importance in business and commerce, became convinced that the loans were safe and profitable and eagerly invested in canal stock. A third great change in the pattern of investment followed almost immediately, when foreigners, particularly Englishmen, for a variety of reasons suddenly began to purchase canal issues as they were offered and to buy up old issues whenever they became available. English investments began suddenly and increased sharply in volume, so that in the last years of construction a larger and larger proportion of each loan was in foreign hands.[22]

1817, the branch bank at New York held $5,391,000 in public deposits, and it had already discounted over $2,747,000 in bills on personal security (U.S. Cong., *House Docs.*, 15 Cong., 2 Sess., Doc. no. 92, m).

[20] See Appendix III.

[21] U.S. Census Office, *10th Census* (Washington, 1880), VII, 430–431.

[22] The conclusions here are based on the following sources: "A List of the Names of Holders of the New York State 6% Stock of a Million Loan and of 5% and 6% Cl. Loans for the Years 1818–1821, for the Quarter Ending 31 Decr., 1821," ". . . for Quarter Ending 31 Decr., 1822," ". . . 31 Decr., 1823"; "Interest Due to the Holders of the New York 6% Stock of a Million Loan, and of Cl. Loans Redeemable in the Years 1837 and 1845, 31 Decr., 1824"; "Yearly Return of Interest Due to the Holders of New York State 5% and 6% Stock (Canal Loans), Quarter Ending 31 Decr., 1829," ". . . for Quarter Ending 31 Decr., 1833"; "List of Loans

Although, in general, between 1817 and 1820, individual investments in canal stock were small and based predominantly on domestic savings, the first canal loan deviated from the pattern that was subsequently set by the ten loans that followed. Not only was a sizable portion of this loan of $200,000 divided between two individuals, but both the men involved were foreigners. David Bevan, director of the Rock Life Assurance Company of London, invested $34,000 in this 6 per cent issue, and John Deacon, director of the Royal Exchange Assurance Company of the same city, invested $40,000. Deacon's investment was so large for the time that not until January 1821 was it exceeded in amount by a local investor when the Commissioners of the Canal Fund offered their tenth consecutive loan to the public.[23]

More characteristic of these early loans was the second of the series, also for $200,000, bearing an interest rate of 6 per cent per annum and redeemable, like all those floated before May 1822, in July 1837. Unlike its predecessor, no large portion of this loan was taken by foreigners or by investors from other states. Similarly, the names of New Yorkers of established wealth were absent from the list of subscribers to this loan. These wealthy individuals clearly preferred the stock of the new Bank of the United States, possibly in part because they could pay for their subscriptions largely with securities of the national government. In any case, their names were conspicuously absent from the lists of subscribers to the canal loans, just as they were conspicuously present on the list of subscribers to the Second Bank of the United States. Conversely, the names of the small businessmen who invested in canal loans seldom appeared on the list of subscribers to the bank's stock.[24]

Redeemable in 1837 and 1845 of 5% and 6% Canal Stock, Signed by Robert White, Cashier, Manhattan Co., 29 Decr., 1836" (henceforth these will be cited as "List of Stockholders," with the appropriate date), Misc. Canal Papers, NYSL.

[23] "List of Stockholders," 31 Dec. 1821; *The Post Office: London Directory for 1821* (London, 1821).

[24] There were, of course, some individuals, such as William James,

Individuals invested in modest amounts in this canal loan of 1818; of its sixty-nine subscribers, fifty-one invested $2,000 or less, and of these, twenty-seven invested sums of less than $1,000. Three individuals and a bank subscribed in excess of $12,000 to this loan. Janet Cheever, thus far unidentified, William James and Laurent Salles, wealthy merchants of Albany and New York City respectively, and the Bank for Savings comprised this small group.[25]

The Bank for Savings in New York City played a conspicuous part during what may be called "the period of the small investor." Judged by the extent of its investments in canal stock, it cannot, of course, be legitimately termed "a small investor"; but it can be considered as such if judged by its depositors, whose small savings it mobilized. This bank was originally founded by busi-

---

Lynde Catlin, and others, who invested in both the canal and the bank loans; but a comparison of the subscription lists indicates that men of established wealth, frequently from families in business for more than one generation, were more interested in the bank speculation. Names such as William Gracie, John G. Costor, Gardiner G. Howland, Brockholst Livingston, James Wadsworth, John Hone, Nicholas Fish, and Nathaniel Prime are found on the subscription list of the bank, and only about 1820–1821 do they appear, if ever, on lists of subscribers to canal loans. This strongly suggests that as a rule investors in the canal loans were businessmen whose careers were just beginning and who, probably, had had less opportunity to participate in federal loans at an earlier time. Important brokers, who either ignored or made only slight investments in canal stock during this period, such as William G. Bucknor, John G. Warren, and LeRoy, Bayard & Company, were actively engaged in the purchase and sale of bank stock. Cf. "List of Stockholders," 31 Dec. 1821, 31 Dec. 1822, 31 Dec. 1823; U.S. Cong., *House Docs.*, 15 Cong., 2 Sess., no. 92.

[25] The Bank for Savings subscribed twice to the same loan. This bank was incorporated in 1819, and it was restricted to investments in state and federal loans under the provisions of its charter. The bank began receiving deposits in July, and by the following Sept., it had begun investing in canal stock and continued to do so steadily on a large scale (NYS, *Laws*, ch. lxii, 42 Sess.; NYS, *Ass. Jour.*, 43 Sess., 237; 44 Sess., 576–577; "List of Stockholders," 31 Dec. 1821). The bank retained its loans for twelve years or more (*infra*, 131, 133–134). Cheever invested $12,400; James, $25,000; and Salles, $34,000.

nessmen and public-spirited citizens who shared in the wide-spread notion that prevailed in the United States, as well as in other countries, that if habits of thrift could be cultivated among "the laboring classes" they would have less need to rely on "the helping hand of others" in times of depression. "The number of poor are increasing on us beyond all calculation," Thomas Eddy wrote in February 1817, observing in astonishment that there were fifteen thousand persons in the city who were "receiving public bounty." The problem of pauperism in New York City was aggravated by the fact that the city was the foremost port of debarkation for immigrants to the United States; and so the founding of a Bank for Savings there seemed, to men like Eddy, especially useful and appropriate.[26]

The bank conveniently gathered the savings of laborers, seamstresses, chambermaids, cooks, clerks, nurses, boot cleaners, preachers of the gospel, and others of comparable income, who individually would never have possessed sufficient funds or information to invest in stock. These small deposits became the basis for the numerous and large investments in canal stock that the trustees of the bank made. By December 1821, this institution held almost 30 per cent of the outstanding canal stock, which included a portion of every loan issued up to that time and represented a total investment of more than a half million dollars of its depositors' savings.[27]

[26] *Second Annual Report of the Managers of the Society for the Prevention of Pauperism in the City of New York* (New York, 1820), 14–15. For a general discussion of the movement for savings banks in England and America, see *Gentleman's Magazine and Historical Chronicle* (London), CXXVIII, 231; *Analectic Magazine* (Philadelphia) IX, 80. There was no sentimentality in Eddy's approach to the problem of poverty. He wrote that he was "tired of assisting [the poor] in their distress & it appears to me more wise, to fix on every possible plan to prevent their poverty and misery by means of employment and establishing savings banks and to do all in our power to discourage the use of spiritous liquors" (Eddy to Clinton, 15 Feb. 1817, DWC Papers).

[27] "List of Stockholders," 31 Dec. 1821, 31 Dec. 1822, 31 Dec. 1823. The bank continued to invest in canal loans after 1820, and before it sur-

By 1818 the state's ability to raise large sums within its own borders for the purpose of financing the canals was clearly demonstrated. Clinton's sudden change from deep pessimism in May 1817 to buoyant optimism by June 1818 illustrated the new-found confidence in the prevailing conditions and in the resources of the domestic money market. "There is money in abundance to loan in our commercial emporium," Clinton informed a projector of the Ohio Canal in June 1818. As far as the governor was concerned, the problems relating to borrowing for the canals were resolved; Clinton assured his correspondent that conditions were such that "the state [could] procure money to any amount even possibly under the rate of 6% per annum," if its finances were properly managed.[28]

Anyone who remembered the low condition of the nation's credit during the war could well have appreciated Clinton's optimism regarding the credit of the state in 1818. That year, in order to retire its "old stock debt," which amounted to $1,880,000 and consisted mainly, although not entirely, of the 7 per cents of 1815, the state borrowed $1,000,000 at the reduced rate of 6 per cent per annum and obtained a premium of 1¼ per cent on this loan.[29] This old loan was retired under these favorable conditions

---

rendered its holdings of almost $1,000,000 of Erie and Champlain canal stock in 1833 at attractive premiums, it was the largest single investor in this type of stock ("List of Stockholders," 31 Dec. 1824, 31 Dec. 1831; NYS, *Ass. Docs.*, 57 Sess., I, Doc. no. 4, "N"; Azariah C. Flagg to Prime, Ward, and King, 1 Aug. 1833, LRC, II, 222–223).

[28] Clinton to W. Steele, 24 June 1818, DWC Papers.

[29] The total stock debt amounted to $1,883,402.50, of which $1,106,-402.50 consisted of the 7 per cents of 1815. According to the comptroller's report, the treasury during 1817 paid $195,247.50 to cancel the first block of the 1815 issue. The second portion of the "old stock debt" consisted of $770,000 worth of 6 per cent stock, which represented a debt to several banks that had been converted by law into stock in 1815 (NYS, *Ass. Jour.*, 41 Sess., 172, 177; NYS, *Laws*, ch. cxli, 38 Sess.). The revenues derived from a somewhat disadvantageous sale of U.S. 3 per cents furnished the state with $575,712.91, which, combined with the proceeds of the "Million Loan" and some of the state's normal revenues, were used to retire the "old stock debt" (NYS, *Ass. Jour.*, 41 Sess., 176; 42 Sess., 399,

at about the same time that the Commissioners of the Canal Fund offered their second issue of canal stock to the public, which was so much regarded as a good opportunity for making a sound investment that subscribers to it were willing to pay $4.52 as a premium on every certificate of $100 of stock that they received.[30] Such was the "exuberance" of the money market in 1818, and so unexpectedly firm was the credit of the state and of the Canal Fund that it was possible for the initial costs of construction of the canals to be met out of predominantly local resources that were sufficient for the purpose.[31]

The period of dependence on the investments of small businessmen and on those of the Bank for Savings drew to a close about the end of 1820. Until that time, the subscription lists for canal loans contained few names of Americans of great wealth. "All rich men are timid," observed Philip Hone, the wealthy merchant of New York City, in 1826; and it was this kind of timidity that characterized the way men of considerable wealth reacted to the canal loans between 1817 and 1820.[32] Even the trustees of the Bank for Savings, men such as Thomas Eddy, John Pintard, William Few, and others, prosperous men but cau-

---

407–408). The "Million Loan" was taken in its entirety by the Bank of the Manhattan Company, as permitted by law (NYS, *Laws*, ch. cclxxxii, 41 Sess., par. v), and then transferred to individual investors. In 1818, more than half of the loan had been transferred to individual investors or to companies, with only a small proportion of the stock ($37,000) going to people outside the state ("List of Stockholders," 31 Dec. 1818; NYS, *Ass. Jour.*, 42 Sess., 401; Clinton to Archibald MacIntyre, 26 May 1818, DWC Papers). By Dec. 1823, three-quarters of the loan had been distributed to individuals, the bulk of the loan, however, still remaining in the hands of New Yorkers ("List of Stockholders," 31 Dec. 1823).

[30] NYS, *Ass. Docs.*, 60 Sess., I, Doc. no. 4, 53.

[31] The cities of New York and Albany succeeded in borrowing fairly large amounts in the period 1817–1818. On 30 June 1817, New York borrowed $100,000 at 6 per cent, and in 1818, Albany borrowed $205,000 at 7 per cent per annum (NYC, *Minutes of the Common Council, 1784–1831* [New York, 1917], XI, 641; NYS, *Laws*, ch. lvi, 41 Sess.; *Report of the Chamberlain of the Corporation of the City of Albany* [Albany, 1822], 11).

[32] Hone to Clinton, 9 Oct. 1826, DWC Papers.

tious as well, who invested the savings of the bank's depositors, avoided risking their own fortunes in the same way.[33] Three and a half years of steady construction, made possible by the savings of income groups less prosperous than their own, persuaded wealthy New Yorkers during a period of economic depression that the state had the financial means and the administrative capacity to complete the canals successfully. It was only then that they came forward with their "risk capital" in order to participate in what had begun to seem like a good investment.

Dramatic evidence of the inventiveness and ingenuity of engineers and contractors in overcoming technical difficulties, along with several other factors, conciliated men of wealth and made them less reluctant to invest in canal stock. Clinton understood the close relationship between the rate of investment and faith in the technical ability of the engineers in charge of the projects; later, in 1823, when offering advice to the governor of Ohio in connection with the Ohio canal project, he stressed the importance of employing "able engineers and skilled contractors" because, as he maintained, only "an undertaking conducted under such auspices will propitiate public opinion and secure the confidence of capitalists who are disposed to embark their funds in the enterprise." [34]

The completion of the middle section, ninety-four miles long, in October 1819, pointed up the efficiency and achievements of

[33] Only William Bayard and Brockholst Livingston among the trustees became interested in canal stock. Bayard's investments were made as a partner of the firm of LeRoy, Bayard & Company. This firm followed the pattern of wealthy investors by making its first purchase of canal stock for $50,000 in 1821, precisely at the time when men of wealth were becoming interested in canal loans. It proved to be an investment of a purely speculative nature, since it was disposed of in less than two years. Previously, the company had invested only $600 in canal loans in spite of Bayard's conspicuous role as a canal enthusiast. Livingston, too, like most men of wealth waited until 1822, when canal stock seemed much more attractive than it had appeared in 1817 ("List of Stockholders," 31 Dec. 1821, 31 Dec. 1822, 31 Dec. 1823).

[34] Clinton to Macajah J. Williams, 8 Nov. 1823, DWC Papers.

the engineers, commissioners, and laborers up to that time. That same month, excited citizens who lived along the line of the canal saw the first waters advance from west to east through the long ditch that connected the Mohawk and the Seneca rivers. The opening of this section was considered an event worthy of celebration, and the governor of the state was on hand to participate in it. On 23 October, Governor Clinton, accompanied by an appropriate entourage of commissioners and friends, boarded a canalboat named "Chief Engineer" in honor of Benjamin Wright at Rome. A military band gave the occasion a festive spirit, a crowd watched the governor's boat depart, and as the governor and his party passed village after village on their way to Utica, they were greeted by the discharge of cannon and the cheers of people who were celebrating an event of great importance to their own communities.[35] According to the governor, the trip fulfilled the commissioners' "most sanguine expectations . . . in the celerity, economy and excellence of its execution." [36] By the following May, the section was opened to navigation, which meant that in less than three years and before the completion of the entire project the state began to receive a return on its investment in the form of tolls. These tolls were hailed by the commissioners as just the beginning of what would eventually result in large revenues.[37]

Construction proceeded at an accelerated pace during 1820. That year gangs of laborers, working at both ends of the middle section, rapidly moved farther apart from each other as they simultaneously lengthened the "ditch" more than fifty miles between the Seneca and Genesee rivers in the west and thirty miles between Utica and Minden in the east.[38] Evidence that this rapid and energetic policy would continue was indicated the following

[35] Watson, *History of the Western Canals*, 79–82. Apparently, navigation did not take place throughout the entire middle section until the following year. Cf. "Annual Report of the Canal Commissioners," 18 Feb. 1820, *NY Canal Laws*, I, 440.

[36] Lincoln, ed., *Messages*, II, 1007.

[37] NYS, *Ass. Jour.*, 44 Sess., 873.   [38] *Ibid.*, 869, 873.

year when contracts were negotiated for operations for a distance of sixty-five miles beyond the Genesee River and for the portion of the route that remained to be constructed in the east up to the Hudson River. Meanwhile, work proceeded on the aqueduct at Rochester, which was designed to carry the canal across the Genesee River on the longest stone bridge built up to that time in America—a feat which provided another example of the readiness with which technical problems of major proportions were being overcome.[39] By the fall of 1822, the Erie Canal was navigable for a distance of two hundred and twenty miles, and the Champlain Canal was open to navigation from Lake Champlain as far south as Waterford.[40]

It was in the midst of this continuous demonstration of spectacular progress, about a year after the middle section was completed, that wealthy Americans began to invest heavily in canal stock. More and more, individual investments amounting to several thousands of dollars each became customary, and those exceeding $10,000 occurred frequently enough so that they ceased to appear unusual. Although lists of stockholders still contained names of people who had invested sums of $1,000 or under, almost invariably such people had purchased their stock during the earlier period when investments were generally made in small amounts. There were some New Yorkers who, during that period, had regularly bought canal stock in moderate amounts and continued to do so in increasing quantities after 1820, accumulating over the years fair-sized holdings. Among such early backers of the projects were businessmen like William and Frederick C. Havemeyer, the sugar refiners; Lewis and Thomas C. Hammersley, dealers in hardware; Peter and George Lorillard, tobacco merchants; and Lynde Catlin, the banker. These more venturesome spirits were joined by other wealthy businessmen of New York City about 1821, when canal stock seemed more

[39] Blake McKelvey, *Rochester, the Water-Power City, 1812–1854* (Cambridge, Mass., 1945), 91.
[40] NYS, *Ass. Jour.*, 46 Sess., 495, 505.

attractive as an investment and safer than it had appeared two or three years earlier. The Aspinwalls and Stephen Allen invested savings that had accumulated as a result of their successful mercantile activities; Robert Lenox and Harmon Hendricks, also merchants but at the same time shrewd investors in urban real estate, became owners of canal stock for the first time. Men of this kind could easily afford to invest several thousand dollars at a time, and did so.[41]

The attractions of the canal stock were also felt beyond the borders of the state, so that an increasing number of non-New Yorkers began to participate in their purchase. Langdon Cheves of South Carolina, the president of the Second Bank of the United States, invested $45,000 in 1821. Gardiner Greene of Boston, one of the richest men in that city at the time of his death, suddenly accelerated his purchases of canal stock in 1821 in much the same way that other businessmen were doing. A. Y. Nicoll of New Jersey, who had bought small portions of several of the early issues, waited until 1822 before he began investing in larger sums.[42]

Even more dramatic evidence of the shift in the pattern of investment that occurred about 1820–1821 was the fact that well-known brokers and brokerage houses that had scrupulously avoided the canal issues between 1817 and 1820 also became active buyers and sellers of this stock during this period. The middle-

---

[41] Joseph A. Scoville (Walter Barrett, pseud.), *The Old Merchants of New York City* (New York, 1863–1866), I, 12, 116, 341; II, 65, 235, 328–329, 332, 337–338; IV, 148, 208. For sketches of the Lorillards and Havemeyers see *DAB*. See also "List of Stockholders," 31 Dec. 1821, 31 Dec. 1822, 31 Dec. 1823, 31 Dec. 1824; William N. MacBean, *Biographical Register of Saint Andrews' Society of the State of New York* (New York, 1922), I, 173–174.

[42] John Belton O'Neall, *Biographical Sketches of the Bench and Bar of South Carolina* (Charleston, 1859), I, 133–139. See also sketch of Cheves in *DAB*. For Nicoll's New Jersey residence see NYS, *Ass. Docs.*, 46 Sess., II, Doc. no. 89, 53. See also Thomas L. V. Wilson, *The Aristocracy of Boston: Who They Are and What They Were* (Boston, 1846), 20; "List of Stockholders," 1821–1824.

men of the investment world, whose profession it was to lure idle capital into avenues of investment, were now convinced that the New York canal stock was a salable commodity among people of large savings both at home and abroad. For example, William G. Bucknor and LeRoy, Bayard & Company took $50,000 each of the stock of the loan of July 1821, in order to dispose of the certificates quickly and at a profit. Previously Bucknor had ignored the canal issues, and LeRoy, Bayard & Company, despite Bayard's known enthusiasm for the canals, had taken only $600 worth of the stock of the loan of June 1817. During 1821, the firm of Prime, Ward, and Sands also made its first sizable purchase of canal stock. This firm, which after reorganization as Prime, Ward, and King played a leading part in buying and selling New York canal stock at home and abroad, had prior to 1821 invested in this way only $1,700; in 1821, however, it bought $85,000 worth of the certificates.[43]

It was merely a question of months before John Jacob Astor also found the canal issues irresistible, although he had overlooked their existence completely for a period of more than four years. By 1822 not only did Astor begin to buy large blocks of stock as they were issued, but he also made a considerable effort as well to buy up portions of older loans as they became available in the market. By the end of the year Astor's total holdings of New York stock amounted to more than $213,000, which he, like Bucknor and the firms LeRoy, Bayard & Company, and Prime, Ward, and Sands, disposed of just as soon as it seemed profitable to do so.[44]

It is not surprising that the interest of wealthy Americans in

[43] Bucknor and Prime, Ward, and Sands were listed as "Brokers of the New York Exchange Board" in 1817 (Scoville, *The Old Merchants of New York City*, II, 128). Within a year of his purchase, Bucknor sold all but $100 worth of his holdings of canal stock. LeRoy, Bayard & Company sold its entire investment within two years. In 1822, Prime, Ward, and Sands held $98,000 worth of stock, which was diminished by progressive sales to slightly above $10,000 by 1824 (cf. "List of Stockholders," 31 Dec. 1821, 31 Dec. 1822, 31 Dec. 1823, 31 Dec. 1824).

[44] "List of Stockholders," 1821–1824.

canal stock should have increased considerably in the midst of the depression of 1819–1822. Generally this depression was disastrous both for business and for agriculture; evaluated narrowly, however, in terms of making possible the swift and economical completion of the canals, the depression provided the state with unanticipated advantages of a considerable sort. By 1820, its impact was felt sufficiently to enable the canal commissioners to negotiate contracts at prices that were from 30 to 40 per cent lower than those that had prevailed during previous seasons for comparable jobs.[45] While farmers of the Genesee Valley declared that the fall in farm prices was "without a parallel" in the past, threatening their very survival, the governor and the legislature agreed that the existing economic conditions provided a "favorable opportunity" and "great advantages" for completing the canal.[46] Members of the legislature considered "the cheapness and abundance of labor" and "the low rate of interest at which money could be obtained" as justification for allowing the Commissioners of the Canal Fund to borrow record-breaking sums, so that complete advantage might be taken of the favorable market for manpower, money, and materials.[47]

[45] "Report of the Canal Commissioners," 12 March 1821, *NY Canal Laws*, II, 7; Lincoln, ed., *Messages*, II, 1044–1045.

[46] "Extract from an Address Delivered before the Genesee Agricultural Society, at Their Cattle Show and Fair held at Batavia, on the 18th of October, 1820. By Samuel N. Hopkins, Esq., President," in Mathew Carey, *Essays*, 419. The severity of the depression may be judged by the fall in commodity prices between January 1817 and December 1820. The price of wheat, so important in New York State as an export, fell from $2.72 to $.68 a bushel; potash, from $200 to $112.50 a ton; cotton, from $.26 to $.14 a pound; hogs' lard, from $.185 to $.103 a pound (Arthur H. Cole, *Wholesale Commodity Prices in the United States, 1700–1861* [Cambridge, Mass., 1938], 178–181, 191–194; NYS, *Laws*, ch. xxxvi, 44 Sess.; Lincoln, ed., *Messages*, II, 1045).

[47] NYS, *Laws*, preamble, ch. xxxvi, 44 Sess. The vote on the bill authorizing expenditures of $1,000,000 in excess of what the commissioners were normally permitted to borrow ($600,000) was 23-6 in the Senate and 79-32 in the Assembly (NYS, *Sen. Jour.*, 44 Sess., 39–40; NYS, *Ass. Jour.*, 44 Sess., 396).

The governor and the members of the legislature correctly assumed that during this period of depression there would be a great demand for a safe investment that might well reduce the cost of borrowing to finance the canals. This conclusion was widely held; in the press it was frequently repeated that in periods of great depression there was an "immense capital" available for investment. American capital was described as "lying dead" and causing "embarrassment among capitalists" who had no alternative but to begin "loaning money at 5% per annum." The high price of stocks in the American market, it was said, could be attributed partly to the "demand in Europe as well as in the United States for things in which money may be safely and profitably invested." [48] The great demand for canal stock that existed during the last half of 1820—a period described by John Quincy Adams as the nadir of the depression—was reflected in the high premium of 8 per cent that the Bank for Savings paid for the privilege of lending $263,000 to the state at an interest rate of 6 per cent per annum.[49] The anticipated fall in the interest rate occurred early in 1821, justifying the enlarged borrowing policy that the legislature had authorized. The demand for canal stock persisted throughout the year and enabled the Commissioners of the Canal Fund to borrow $1,400,000 at the reduced rate of 5 per cent per annum in a series of loans that brought attractive premiums as well.[50]

[48] *Niles' Weekly Register* (Baltimore, 1821), XX, 34, 209, 231 (17 March, 2 June, 9 June 1821).

[49] NYS, *Ass. Docs.*, 60 Sess., I, Doc. no. 4, 53; "List of Stockholders," 31 Dec. 1822; Charles Francis Adams, ed., *Memoirs of John Quincy Adams* (Philadelphia, 1875), V, 409.

[50] NYS, *Ass. Docs.*, 60 Sess., I, Doc. no. 4, 53.

VI

The Explosion of Foreign Capital

ECONOMIC recovery, first felt toward the end of 1821, gained momentum during the spring of the new year. Congressman Churchill C. Cambreleng noted that the "general revival of trade" was "absorbing the capital of the country" and was responsible for "an advance in the market rate of interest." [1] Prices of canal stock in the market and the interest rate on new canal loans were directly affected by this new state of affairs, with the former experiencing a gradual decline until midyear, when the 6 per cent interest rate was necessarily restored for a new loan of $600,000. Actually, the decline in the market price of the canal stock ended at a point which was considerably higher than where it had been three years earlier, indicating that the reputation of the issues had been considerably enhanced with the passage of time. It was approximately at this time—during the second quarter of 1822— and under these conditions that English investors made their first large-scale purchases of canal stock.[2]

[1] *Annals of Cong.*, 17 Cong., 1 Sess., 1331.

[2] One list of stockholders, signed by Robert White, cashier of the Bank of Manhattan Company, who was also transfer officer of the Canal Fund, designated the residence of each stockholder. This list was dated 29 Dec. 1836. On the basis of two additional lists used together it was possible to classify stockholders in such broad geographical categories as "New

There were many reasons why Englishmen should have been susceptible to the attractions of New York canal stock. By this time more than half of the Erie Canal was navigable, a fact that strikingly demonstrated that all the major problems involved in the enterprise—problems of finance, engineering, labor, and administration—had been successfully resolved and that the completion of the major canal was only a matter of time. Moreover, since the projects had won the approval of Americans of great wealth, such as John Jacob Astor and Prime, Ward, and Sands, men or firms with English business connections, English businessmen could not fail to be convinced that the canals offered the possibility of a sound investment. But there were reasons even more basic than these. Englishmen had long-standing familiarity and, frequently, highly favorable experience with investments in canal stock at home. In addition, the projects had received much commendatory publicity in the English press. Most important of all was the fact that there was a surplus of exportable capital in England, for which opportunities for investment were eagerly being sought.

Without question, canals and investment in canal stock were far less of a mystery to Englishmen than they were to Americans. The great canal boom in England was an integral part of the industrial revolution of the eighteenth century; the result of this boom was a network of canals that wrought necessary improve-

---

Yorkers," "residents of other states," and "foreigners." The information contained in these lists facilitated the identification of many of the investors of the early 1820's, especially of foreigners who were less likely to transfer their stock. Further identification of stockholders was established by use of the following: *American Almanac: New York Register and City Directory* (New York, 1816); directories published by Longworth for New York City under slightly different titles for the years 1817–1825; *Dictionary of American Biography; Dictionary of National Biography from the Earliest Times to 1900* (London, 1921–1922); Scoville, *The Old Merchants of New York City; The Post Office: London Directory for 1821* (London, 1821); "List of Stockholders," 31 Dec. 1822, 31 Dec. 1823, 31 Dec. 1829; residence of holders of canal stock derived from "List of Stockholders," 29 Dec. 1836.

ments in the transportation facilities of the industrial areas of Lancashire and Yorkshire. England's most important rivers—the Thames, Severn, Humber, and Mersey—were linked by canals, and such developing centers of industrial activity as Liverpool, London, Birmingham, Manchester, and Leeds were given needed access either to seaports or to sources of raw materials. The construction of England's system of artificial waterways continued through the first quarter of the nineteenth century, and there was continuing interest in the canals not only because of the improved means of transportation that they afforded but because they also provided an opportunity for profitable investment.[3]

In 1821–1822, just prior to the time when Englishmen became interested in investing in New York canal stock, English journals contained numerous accounts of projected canals or of those under construction. Articles dealing with technical problems of hydraulics, canal engineering, the annual statistics of freight carried on the inland waterways, and the propulsion of canalboats appeared regularly. More important, however, the journals listed declared dividends and the prices of canal stocks at regular intervals.[4] When Englishmen first began investing in New York canal stock, some stocks of English canal companies were paying huge dividends and their prices in the market had soared to fantastic heights.[5]

[3] W. T. Jackman, *The Development of Transportation in Modern England* (Cambridge, Eng., 1916), I, 376–377.

[4] *Monthly Magazine; or, British Register* (London), LI, 490, 586; LII. 26, 129, 132, 171, 268, 459, 556–557; *Gentleman's Magazine,* CXXXI, 356; CXXXIII, 80.

[5] Some dazzling prices for canal stocks were regularly reported in the journals in 1821–1822. Coventry canal shares, originally £100 a share, sold in Aug. 1822 for £1,060 to £1,070 a share. The dividend on this stock for the year was £44. Trent and Mersey stock, par value £100, sold in Jan. 1821 for £1,800 per share. The price for Oxford canal stock, par value £100, was quoted at £710 to £740 and paid a dividend of £32. Leeds and Liverpool stock, par value £100, was quoted at £300 in Jan. 1821 and paid a dividend of £10. Details on profitable and unprofitable issues may be

While the press kept Englishmen informed of the progress and profits in inland navigation at home, it turned its attention as well to canal projects abroad. Laudatory stories reprinted from American newspapers told of the past progress and the future prosperity that the New York canals would bring to the state, in language optimistic enough to have been written by Governor Clinton himself. A writer in the *Gentleman's Magazine*, for instance, declared that "the junction of the American Lakes with the Atlantic Ocean, calculated to improve prodigiously the commerce of New York, goes on nobly to its completion." [6] The *Times* of London informed its readers that the canals would make New York City the "London of the New World"; [7] and Frances Wright, having returned from a trip to America where she had seen the "big ditch" under excavation at Utica, reported in the published account of her travels that the canal's "consequences" would be "truly grand, affording a water-highway from the heart of this great continent to the ocean." The feminist and future equal-rights advocate had been impressed by the generous way in which nature had endowed the new republic with rivers and lakes and predicted that it would be only a short time before "states now in embryo" would pour their produce eastward, through all the avenues of transportation, natural and artificial, that would be open to them.[8]

---

found in Jackman, *The Development of Transportation*, I, 421–426; Thomas Gray, *Observations on a General Iron Railway; or, Land Steam Conveyance* (London, 1825), 155; L. T. C. Holt, *The Inland Waterways of England* (London, 1950), 56. Generally the journals seemed more interested in reporting returns on the more profitable issues, which undoubtedly helped mislead the public. As a contemporary observer pointed out, canal enthusiasts normally "collected the names of a few canal and river navigations that pay well (and few they are indeed when compared with those that pay ill . . .)" so that "from reading their works, a stranger would conclude that all were alike beneficial" (John Sutcliffe, *A Treatise on Canals and Reservoirs* [Rochdale, 1816], iv).

[6] XCII, Pt. II, 363.   [7] 3 Sept. 1822.

[8] Frances Wright Darusmont, *Views of Society and Manners in America . . . by an Englishwoman* (London, 1821), 179, 258–259. A large por-

An article that appeared in the financial column of the *Times* of London in September 1822 took an optimistic view of the program of canal construction undertaken by the state of New York. Its optimism is understandable; the article had originally appeared in the Albany *Argus* and reflected the hopes and enthusiasm of the editor of that paper. The article asserted that the state could complete the canals by depending exclusively on its own resources and without placing an undue strain on the economy of the state. Moreover, readers of the *Times* were informed that the entire canal debt could be retired within a period of twenty-five or thirty years merely by using the duties that the state collected at the Onondaga saltworks and the canal tolls that would be collected on the shipment of such salt to market.[9] The reference to the growing "salt town" of Syracuse in connection with the expected profits that the canal would yield could not have failed to impress potential English investors, many of whom were familiar with the fact that the salt industry was partially responsible for the development of the canal system in the Midlands. Manufacturers of salt in Cheshire were among the outstanding supporters of the Mersey and Trent Canal. This great artery cut across the narrow waist of England, linked the Irish and North seas, and made water-borne transportation possible between Liverpool and Hull; it turned out to be a most profitable venture in itself and of inestimable value to the salt industry.[10]

Neither familiarity with canals, however, nor previous profitable investments in canal stock, nor confidence in the safety and profit of New York State's canal loans could have lured English capital to New York if it could have been invested as safely and as profitably at home. By 1819 English bankers, in fierce com-

tion of the book, including the section containing observations on the canal, was republished in the *Monthly Magazine*, Jan. 1822, vol. LII, pt. II for 1821, pp. 615, 620. There was also an edition published in New York in 1821.

[9] 6 Sept. 1822.

[10] Jackman, *The Development of Transportation*, I, 364.

petition with each other for opportunities for investment at home, were anxiously looking to the continent and to North and South America for profitable opportunities for investment abroad. Joseph Lowe, a contemporary English economist writing in 1823, explained the rapid growth of interest in foreign investment in terms of circumstances that developed after Waterloo. "One of the chief features in the transition from war to peace," Lowe wrote, was "the increase in disposable capital" in Britain. This surplus capital, he pointed out, found its way into foreign investment because "the interest of money is always highest in the least advanced communities, and capital has consequently a tendency to move thither, not rapidly . . . but progressively." [11] Here was the chief reason for the sudden interest of English investors in New York canal stock, one fully appreciated by New Yorkers who were aware that English investment in their canals constituted just a small detail of the much larger story of English investment overseas.[12]

The initial large-scale impact of English capital on New York State's Canal Fund occurred in May 1822. The rapid movement of English capital overseas that year seemingly contradicted Lowe's assertion that such a movement into relatively underdeveloped areas proceeds "not rapidly . . . but progressively." Even Lowe conceded that 1822 was "remarkable for the ex-

[11] Joseph Lowe, *The Present State of England in Regard to Agriculture, Trade, and Finance* (London, 1823), 401, 404.

[12] Existing financial conditions in Great Britain were understood in New York as easing credit facilities in the United States and elsewhere. "There is a vast disposable capital in Great Britain," Governor Clinton pointed out in 1823, adding that because the British government required no loans "in a period of peace . . . the greatest borrower is consequently out of the market." For this reason, he informed Canal Commissioner Williams of Ohio, "the monied men of Europe" were able to accommodate "France, Austria, Russia and some of the governments in South America with extensive loans." For the same reasons, he maintained that Ohio's need for credit would be accommodated and, he might have added with justice, that the state of New York to some extent had already been accommodated (Clinton to Micajah Williams, 8 Nov. 1823, DWC Papers).

tent of such transfers."[13] The canal loan of May 1822 was for
$600,000, bore an annual rate of interest of 6 per cent per
annum, and was awarded originally to the Mechanics and Farmers Bank and the New York State Bank, both of Albany, at a
premium of 1¼ per cent.[14] Almost immediately this loan went
through a process of fragmentation in which the banks and
subsequently John Jacob Astor, the English firm of Thomas
Wilson and Company, and Swinton C. Holland, one of the
Baring Brothers' partners, were instrumental in transferring a
large proportion of it to investors in Great Britain.[15] Later that
year, Wilson and Company and Holland participated conspicuously in placing almost half of the total of two loans amounting
to $550,000 with English investors in the short period of three
months. A smaller 5 per cent loan showed the same propensity
of its immediate predecessors to gravitate toward the London
money market; and in this case, after fifteen months, the bulk
of the loan was also held chiefly by Englishmen.[16]

As English interest in canal stock continued to mount, English
investors were less content to wait for new loans to be offered
to the public. Whenever new issues appeared, they of course

[13] Lowe, *The Present State of England*, 401. It was within a year after
the first heavy British investments were made in canal stock that this influx
of British capital became clearly recognized in New York as a phenome-
non of some proportions. In this connection, the opposition of Senator
John A. King to a special tax on foreign property within the state is re-
vealing. King pointed out that "the system of public improvements" that
was under construction required "constantly large advances of money";
and he declared that it was far more advisable for the state to "invite and
encourage the investment and circulation of capital within its limits" than
to discourage it by taxing the property of foreigners. This was a policy
which, in the senator's opinion, would "clip the wings by which [New
York] . . . soared so far above her sister states" (NYS, *Sen. Jour.*, 46
Sess., 282; Albany *Daily Advertiser*, 16 April 1823).

[14] NYS, *Ass. Docs.*, 60 Sess., I, Doc. no. 4, 53.

[15] Holland was a partner in the firm of Baring Brothers, but in these
operations he was acting on his own (Edgar S. Holland, *A History of the
Family of Holland of Mobberley and Knutsford* [Edinburgh, 1902], 70).

[16] Cf. "List of Stockholders," 31 Dec. 1822, 31 Dec. 1823.

took large portions for themselves, but they did not fail, at the same time, to take advantage of whatever opportunities arose to relieve Americans of their holdings of earlier issues. John Deacon, Thomas Cotterill, and Swinton C. Holland made modest efforts in this direction during 1822, but it was only by the following year that Baring Brothers, having made its first investment in a canal loan, led all others in an aggressive effort to buy up portions of older loans in the open market. In addition to investing in three of the four loans floated by the Commissioners of the Canal Fund in 1823, Baring Brothers succeeded, at the same time, in gaining possession of varying amounts of seven older issues that reached as far back as the loan of July 1818. These investments ranged in amount from $500 in the loan of October 1819 to $171,000 in that of August 1823. By the end of 1823, the firm had in its possession $241,000 of various issues of New York State canal stock, which increased to a total of $322,923.30 by 1824.[17]

Increasingly after 1823, the transfer officer's list of subscribers to the canal loans contained names of foreign investors. Included among the names of many individuals, now unknown, who invested a few thousand dollars each were those of prominent financiers, businessmen, landowners, and banking firms. Samuel Jones Loyd, of the firm of Jones and Loyd of London, a man with a long career in banking and finance behind him, invested the large sum of $122,000 in canal stock in 1823, increased this amount to $150,000 the following year, and retained his stock for at least ten years, if not more. Peter Lord King, a wealthy landowner, who had written on the related subjects of money and banking and therefore could pass as an authority in the field of finance, demonstrated his confidence in the canal issue by buying his first block of stock for $4,000 in 1823; by 1824, he had increased this amount to $28,500 and, according to available records, held $40,500 in 1829, which he did not relinquish

[17] "List of Stockholders," 31 Dec. 1821, 31 Dec. 1822, 31 Dec. 1823, 31 Dec. 1824.

until 1837. James Cropper, of the firm of Cropper, Benson, and Company of Liverpool, a man with long experience in Anglo-American trade who combined his interest in speculation with his enthusiasm for internal improvements, also invested in New York canal issues. But the future director of the Liverpool and Manchester Railroad did not lock his certificates up in his vault, as apparently King and Loyd did, in order to collect interest every quarter; Cropper repeatedly bought and sold various issues in differing amounts, as did many large-scale foreign speculators through whose hands increasing numbers of certificates passed before they came to rest in the possession of someone of non-speculative inclinations.[18] Several banking concerns to which the English people looked for financial leadership were very active as investors or as brokers in connection with the canal issues. Among these firms, besides the house of Baring, were Smith, Payne, and Smith and Gowan and Marx of London; Galton, Galton, and James and Lloyds of Birmingham.

Foreign funds for the construction of the canals also came from Canada, the West Indies, Switzerland, Bermuda, Scotland, Spain, France, and, in the case of one investor, China. England, however, was the major source of the foreign capital which found its way to the Canal Fund. The trade and manufactures that accounted for the accumulation of wealth in London, Birmingham, Manchester, Bristol, and Liverpool also provided the major portion of surplus foreign capital that was invested in the canals of New York.

Between June 1817 and November 1824, a total of $7,411,-

[18] For sketches of King, Loyd, and Cropper, see *DNB;* William E. Axon, *The Annals of Manchester* (London, 1886), 156; Clement Jones, *Pioneer Shipowners* (Liverpool, 1935), 16–21; the Rt. Hon. Lord Overstone (Samuel Jones Loyd), *Tracts and Other Publications on Metallic and Paper Currency* (London, 1857); Peter Lord King, *Thoughts on the Effects of the Bank Restrictions* (London, 1804). See also "List of Stockholders," 31 Dec. 1822, 31 Dec. 1823, 31 Dec. 1824, 31 Dec. 1829, 31 Dec. 1831, 31 Dec. 1833, 29 Dec. 1836; NYS, *Ass. Docs.,* 59 Sess., I, Doc. no. 4, "T"; 62 Sess., II, Doc. no. 26, 36.

770.99 was borrowed in order to finance the construction of the Erie and Champlain canals.[19] This amount, extremely large for its time, was raised by means of twenty-four separate loans. The earliest loans were for modest amounts; between 1817 and 1820 only one out of a total of nine exceeded the sum of $200,000, while five others were for sums of less than that amount. Early in 1821, the rate of borrowing was abruptly increased to allow the Commissioners of the Canal Fund to take full advantage of the lowered costs of borrowing that the depression made possible. This meant that the rate of borrowing was doubled within a year, having been increased from a total of $693,500 in 1820 to $1,400,000 in 1821. Once the rate of borrowing was accelerated, the increased rate of construction that took place required that it be maintained.[20]

The contrast between the amounts borrowed beginning June 1817 and through October 1819, when the middle section was completed, and from May 1822 through July 1824—periods of approximately equal length—is striking. During the first period, a total of $800,000 was borrowed; during the second, $4,068,-270.99.[21] But the importance of the first sum cannot be measured in quantitative terms alone, for it made possible the construction of the middle section, which provided the visible proof that the internal resources of the state were sufficient to permit the completion of a large segment of the entire project without resorting to outside support to any appreciable extent. It served to demonstrate the technical competence of surveyors, engineers, and

[19] *NY Canal Laws,* II, 293; NYS, *Ass. Docs.,* 60 Sess., I, Doc. no. 4, 53–54. There is a discrepancy between these two sources of $1.08. The commissioners borrowed in addition $270,000 in July 1825 on a short-term basis, which was reimbursed in 1826 (NYS, *Sen. Jour.,* 50 Sess., 399).

[20] NYS, *Ass. Docs.,* 60 Sess., I, Doc. no. 4, 53–54. The *annual* rate of borrowing was, for 1817, $200,000; 1818, $200,000; 1819, $400,000; 1820, $693,500; 1821, $1,400,000; 1822, $1,350,000; 1823, $1,600,000; and 1824, $1,568,270.99.

[21] Compiled from NYS, *Ass. Docs.,* 60 Sess., I, Doc. no. 4, 53–54.

contractors and in this way helped to banish the fears of those who had felt that the technological problems involved were insuperable. Moreover, the successful completion of the middle section, accomplished on the basis of this relatively small sum, was partly responsible for the widened support that the canal stock won immediately afterward.

The period 1817–1825, during which the state borrowed to pay for the construction of the Erie and Champlain canals, appears in retrospect to have been a favorable one for raising the more than $7,400,000 that was required. During this time the Commissioners of the Canal Fund never encountered serious difficulty in borrowing the sums necessary; nor did they ever find it necessary to exceed the 6 per cent annual rate of interest on their loans. The thirteen loans that were offered at the 6 per cent per annum interest rate were negotiated at par or above, with two of them bringing premiums as high as 8 per cent. Generally, the 5 per cent loans were received favorably also; and although on occasion they encountered a certain amount of resistance in the money market, this resistance was never great enough to raise questions about the basic soundness of the investment. Thus, in June 1823, the Commissioners of the Canal Fund were unable to market a 5 per cent loan for a half-million dollars on more favorable terms than a discount of 6½ per cent, but this situation was of brief duration.[22] By the final year of construction on the Erie Canal, when the Champlain Canal was already completed and both were earning impressive tolls, four loans amounting to a total of more than $1,500,000 and bearing an interest rate of 5 per cent per annum brought premiums that varied between 8$\frac{1}{100}$ and 10$\frac{62}{100}$ per cent.[23]

[22] NYS, *Ass. Docs.*, 60 Sess., I, Doc. no. 4, 52–53.

[23] *NY Canal Laws*, II, 175. Under two separate acts, the national government borrowed $10,000,000 at an interest rate of 4½ per cent. Both loans were redeemable in Jan. 1832 (*U.S. Statutes at Large*, 18 Cong., 1 Sess., ch. 140, 192; U.S. Census Office, *10th Census* [Washington, 1880], VII, 358–359).

By 1824, despite the large influx of foreign funds, the bulk of the canal debt was still in American hands.[24] During the next five years, the steady movement of stock certificates overseas continued, so that by 1829 foreign ownership of canal stock exceeded the amount owned by Americans by several hundred thousand dollars.[25] The following six-year period revealed that foreign investors tended to hold on to their certificates more tenaciously than did Americans. As a result of continuous redemptions between January 1833 and December 1836, the Erie and Champlain canal debt, by the latter date, had shrunk to a sum of $3,444,000, of which $2,896,000 was held by foreigners while only $548,000 remained in the possession of Americans.[26]

The greatest risk in financing the Erie and Champlain canals was assumed by New Yorkers of moderate means who were already on the road toward achieving modest success and respectability as businessmen, merchants, and bankers. Sharing this risk, unknown to themselves, were the working people whose small deposits were accumulated in the Bank for Savings and invested by the trustees in canal stock. These funds made possible the construction of the middle section of the Erie Canal, which, in part, served to attract Americans of larger means, who had shunned canal stock during the early years. Rapid progress in construction, together with the evidence of generous domestic support of the projects, made the canals a source of interest to English capitalists who, at the time, had more funds than they could use at home and were in search of profitable investment

[24] A total of $3,940,000 represented investments of Americans, chiefly New Yorkers. More than $2,400,000 comprised investments of foreigners, largely British. The remaining creditors, whose holdings totaled about $1,071,000, could not be identified as to residence ("List of Stockholders," 31 Dec. 1824).

[25] "List of Stockholders," 31 Dec. 1829.

[26] Computed from "List of Stockholders," 29 Dec. 1836. Almost a year earlier, as of the first week of Jan. 1836, the distribution of the canal debt was as follows: foreigners, $3,365,000; inhabitants of New York State, $933,000; inhabitants of other states, $51,900; total, $4,349,900 (NYS, *Ass. Docs.*, 59 Sess., I, Doc. no. 4, 10).

opportunities abroad. Under these circumstances, there was a large influx of English capital into New York State in the form of investments in canal stock.

It is highly doubtful if the influx of English capital was an indispensable factor in making possible the completion of the canals. English investment in canal stock began to be important only about 1822, when large portions of the projects were already completed, when there was a steadily mounting income from tolls, and when the element of risk as far as the investor was concerned had been considerably diminished. Without doubt, the availability of English capital helped to lower the costs of borrowing. However, had the state been restricted to such sources of capital as it had relied on until 1822—that is, had it been required to rely mainly on American sources, consisting largely of investments of New Yorkers—the projects still would have been brought to a successful completion, although perhaps in a somewhat longer time and at a slightly higher cost.[27]

[27] It is interesting to note that after the War of 1812 the possibility of another war with England and the need for access to the Canadian frontier under such circumstances were offered as additional reasons in support of the construction of the canals. At the same time, the necessity to divert American produce from being exported down the St. Lawrence was stressed as well. Paradoxically, large amounts of English capital were invested in the projects designed ostensibly to avoid such contingencies (Albany *Daily Advertiser*, 14 June, 18 Nov. 1816; Albany *Gazette and Daily Advertiser*, 2 April 1817).

Part Three

THE CANAL FUND AS A FORCE

FOR DEVELOPMENT

VII

Diffusing the Canal Fund's

Revenues

THE official opening of the Erie Canal, with its fanfare, speeches, discharge of cannon, and festive procession across the state led by the governor's barge, took place in 1825. New Yorkers had reason to celebrate: the construction of the great artery that joined the waters of the lakes with those of the Hudson River was a technical achievement of considerable magnitude. It was a financial achievement as well, and evidence of this began to appear as early as 1821, when the first revenues from tolls collected on the partly completed canal began to flow into the Canal Fund. By 1825, year of the official opening, the more than $500,000 received from tolls alone exceeded by $100,000 the amount necessary to pay the interest on the outstanding canal debt.[1]

Prosperity, however, raised the immediate problem of what was to be done with the surplus revenues. When the legislature

[1] The various sources of revenue yielded: tolls, $521,344; vendue duty, $253,452; salt duty, $71,223; sales of land, $2,370; loans, $270,000 (NYS, *Ass. Docs.*, 60 Sess., I, Doc. no. 3, "U"; NYS, *Ass. Jour.*, 49 Sess., 997).

considered the matter in 1826, the answer seemed simple enough. The commissioners were authorized to invest in the public stocks of the United States and of the cities of Albany and New York or to retire outstanding canal certificates provided that these could be purchased on favorable terms.[2]

The commissioners soon discovered that the national government and the cities had little to offer them by way of investment opportunities, and the creditors of the Canal Fund were so well satisfied with their investments in canal stock that they refused to part with their certificates. The annual reports of the canal commissioners detailed the increased amounts of produce and passengers carried through the canals; reports of the Commissioners of the Canal Fund showed a mounting income from tolls, salt duties, and auction duties. If such information were not enough to persuade investors in canal stock that their certificates were worth retaining, the quoted price of canal stock carried in the newspapers no doubt helped to do so.

With all the authorized avenues of investment closed, the commissioners reported that the revenues remained "in the depositing banks producing nothing." Because the commissioners, as "faithful guardians of the fund entrusted to their management," were enjoined by law to make the Canal Fund as "productive" as possible, Comptroller William L. Marcy approached bankers of Albany and Troy in 1826 to determine what they would offer for deposits of the revenues of the Erie and Champlain Canal Fund.[3]

Little did the comptroller realize when he negotiated with the banks in 1826 that he was taking the first step in the creation of a mechanism which would introduce the revenues of the Canal Fund into the channels of business, so that eventually their influence in the economy would be felt from one end of the state to the other. This process of involvement with the banks began as

[2] NYS, *Laws*, ch. cccxiv, 49 Sess.

[3] NYS, *Ass. Docs.*, 56 Sess., I, Doc. no. 4, 20–22; 58 Sess., I, Doc. no. 4, 15–16; NYS, *Ass. Jour.*, 42 Sess., 396–397.

a modest effort in the Albany-Troy area to earn a return on the revenues of the Canal Fund; soon it embraced the banks in towns along the line of the canals and gradually spread to include many banking institutions as distant from the canals as Ogdensburg in the north and New York City in the south. Without exaggeration, the Commissioners of the Canal Fund could truly say by 1834 that the revenues of the fund were "diffused through every department of business." [4]

The process of "diffusion" began when the Bank of Troy and the Farmers Bank of the same city agreed to pay the Canal Fund 5 per cent per annum for the privilege of dividing its surplus revenues; the following year, on the basis of competitive bidding, the New York State Bank and the Mechanics and Farmers Bank, both of Albany, supplanted the Troy banks as the "depository Banks" for the Canal Fund, despite the fact that they offered only 3½ per cent for the revenues. [5] This arrangement marked the beginning of an enduring relationship between the two banks in Albany and the Canal Fund, whose resources would soon constitute an impressive proportion of their total deposits. The low return paid on the deposits of the Canal Fund resulted directly from the commissioners' insistence that they be permitted to draw "at sight." In 1827, however, such an advantage was clouded by the more apparent fact that a 3½ per cent return on their revenues was low, and the commissioners, therefore, felt justified in seeking out "opportunities to improve the productiveness of the large sums coming into their hands, and constantly in bank at this low rate of interest." [6]

The commissioners were handicapped in their efforts to make more advantageous arrangements for investing the surplus revenues of the Canal Fund because their opportunities, clearly, were restricted to banks. [7] Many bankers urged them to consider "time deposits" at higher rates of return than the depository

---

[4] NYS, *Ass. Docs.*, 58 Sess., I, Doc. no. 4, 18; 57 Sess., I, Doc. no. 4, 19.
[5] *Ibid.*, 56 Sess., I, Doc. no. 4, 1, 20–21; 58 Sess., I, Doc. no. 4, 15–16.
[6] *Ibid.*, 58 Sess., I, Doc. no. 4, 15–16.   [7] *Supra*, 115–116.

banks paid, but such proposals the commissioners felt they were bound to reject because they were not legally empowered to place the revenues of the fund beyond their own control for any length of time. Even if such legal authorization were theirs, it is doubtful that the commissioners would have hastened to enter into this kind of relationship with banks in 1827. New to the responsibility of administering the large sums that were accumulating in their hands, they moved slowly out of a genuine fear of involvement with banking institutions whose "solvency and good management" they admittedly had no way of judging.[8]

Progressive increase in the use of the canals produced, of course, greater revenues and kept the question of their disposal constantly before the commissioners. Despite the disbursement of more than a million dollars for interest payments, repairs, maintenance, and retirement of canal stock owned by the General Fund of the state, the commissioners reported a surplus of more than $563,900 at the end of the fiscal year 1829. Even the directors of the depository banks were alarmed and asked that they be "relieved of a portion of the deposits on hand." [9] By 1829, Silas Wright, the new comptroller, quite correctly concluded that the best solution to the problem of the mounting surplus revenues possible under the law and within reach of the commissioners would be an arrangement providing for their distribution among banks outside of Albany. In reply to his inquiries, twenty-five banks along the canals furnished information on which the commissioners based a plan for broadening the distribution of the Canal Fund's revenues.[10] The plan provided for seasonal contracts between the commissioners and banks near collection points on the canals. On the basis of these contracts, collectors would deposit tolls and salt duties in the banks and the banks had "free use" of the deposits for fifteen

[8] NYS, *Ass. Docs.*, 56 Sess., I, Doc. no. 4, 20–22.
[9] *Ibid.*, 53 Sess., II, Doc. no. 152, 6, 26–27.
[10] *Ibid.*, 56 Sess., I, Doc. no. 4, 22–23.

days beyond the end of the month during which they were made. At the end of that period, the banks could request the commissioners to draw for the total sum, or the commissioners were free to draw on the deposit whenever they wished. However, if the banks chose to retain the deposit, they could do so by paying an annual rate of 4½ per cent interest for the privilege.[11]

By such a plan, the commissioners hoped to stop the overwhelming flow of revenues to the depository banks in Albany. In addition, Comptroller Wright anticipated that drafts on the depository banks for expenses incurred in maintaining the canals and servicing the debt would progressively diminish the amount of deposits in those institutions.[12] The plan, however, did not work out immediately as the comptroller hoped. For the first seven or eight months of 1831, there was a lull in the demand for funds in the less-developed areas of New York. Local banks retained only $315,000 of $800,000 in canal tolls and salt duties deposited with them by the state's collectors; as a result, the rest of the revenues migrated to Albany, where they increased the Canal Fund's account in the Mechanics and Farmers Bank and the New York State Bank to a total of $1,500,000.[13] Within the next two years, however, the normal character of the western country reasserted itself in a feverish demand for money, so that banking institutions along the canals were willing, and indeed anxious, to retain the collectors' deposits. By the end of 1833, revenues belonging to the Canal Fund were deposited in seventeen banks along the line of the canals in sums ranging from $6,000 to $184,000.[14]

---

11 *Ibid.*, 55 Sess., I, Doc. no. 5, 10; Silas Wright to David Boyd, 5 March 1832, LRC, II, 5. The commissioners justified granting the banks "free use" of the revenues for the stated period "because of the difference of exchange, the expense of agencies, and the risk of transmission" involved in the arrangement for the banks.

12 Silas Wright to Lynde Catlin, 15 April 1831, LRC, I, 404–405.

13 NYS, *Ass. Docs.*, 55 Sess., I, Doc. no. 5, 11–12.

14 *Ibid.*, 57 Sess., I, Doc. no. 4, "L."

Despite the anxiety of the banks located along the line of the Erie and Champlain canals to retain deposits in 1832, 1833, and thereafter, the immediate impression created after the commissioners' plan went into effect in 1831 was that it had failed. Presumably, the legislature shared in this belief, since it was in 1831 that it authorized the commissioners to make time deposits in banks. This decision represented a considerable change in the administration of the Canal Fund which may be attributed to the prevalent belief that the problem of the mounting surplus was acute and required a sharp change in customary policy to achieve an immediate solution. The commissioners referred to the time deposits that the legislature authorized as "loans" which they were permitted to make "to any safe incorporated monied institution" in the state. The advantages that the banks gained as a result of this policy was clear, since the commissioners would be required to notify them of their intention to draw on such "loans" sixty days in advance. Doubtless this legislation gave the banker who operated on the basis of limited resources and a narrow margin of security an additional amount of protection which he valued enough to pay for. This was especially true of the country banker whose leniency in renewing notes blurred the difference between the definition of short- and long-term loans and made him especially vulnerable to sudden withdrawals.[15]

The commissioners made their first loan under the terms of the act of 1831 to the National Bank of New York City. Even before an agreement between the bank and the commissioners was reached, Comptroller Wright had predicted, in a letter to Albert Gallatin, the bank's president, that its request for a loan would be favorably entertained. The large amount of canal revenues in the depository banks in Albany, where they were draw-

[15] The act authorized the commissioners to "deposit" the revenues; the word "loan" is not used in the act. Nevertheless, contracts for loans with various banks read, "Resolved, that this Board will loan, in the nature of a deposit," etc. (NYS, *Ass. Docs.*, 57 Sess., I, Doc. no. 4, 56–57; 58 Sess., I, Doc. no. 4, 17).

ing a low rate of interest, Wright explained, made it necessary
for the National Bank only to offer the commissioners sufficient
"inducement" for the contract to be successfully consummated.
Apparently in June 1831, at a time when the money market was
"easy," the offer of an interest rate of 4 per cent per annum,
exceeding only by ½ of 1 per cent the rate that the depository
banks paid, was inducement enough.[16] The contract for a loan
of $150,000 was completed in August, and on 1 October each
of the depository banks in Albany paid $75,000 to the National
Bank of New York.[17]

Gallatin's seemingly unseasonable contract for a loan from
the Canal Fund proved to be a fortunate move for the National
Bank. The small institution over which the ex-Secretary of the
Treasury presided was the only one that borrowed from the
Canal Fund before 30 September, the end of the fiscal year. By
that time, however, conditions in the money market began to
change rapidly with the reappearance of the more normal condition of a credit stringency. As a result, during the latter part
of September and the first two weeks of October, a number of
banks applied to the Commissioners of the Canal Fund for loans
and indicated their readiness to pay an annual rate of 4½ per
cent interest for them, notwithstanding the 4 per cent arrangement with the National Bank. In the brief period of six weeks,
banks applied to the commissioners for a total of $1,100,000
in loans. Even the National Bank was sufficiently pressed to request another loan, which the commissioners refused, with the
explanation that they preferred to distribute their money "in
moderate sums to solvent institutions." [18]

The commissioners showed marked reluctance to enter upon
the large-scale lending policy that the prevailing condition of
the money market made possible; and while in early October the

[16] Silas Wright to Albert Gallatin, 18 July 1831, LRC, I, 476.

[17] Silas Wright to Gallatin, 29 July 1831; Philip Phelps to Gallatin, 11
Aug. 1831: LRC, I, 482, 484; Misc. Canal Papers, Pkg. 915, C44, NYSL.

[18] Silas Wright to Samuel Flewelling, 14 Oct. 1831, LRC, I, 409; NYS,
Ass. Docs., 56 Sess., I, Doc. no. 4, 25.

banks were overwhelming them with requests for loans, the commissioners, in turn, were intensifying their efforts to do what they could to redeem outstanding certificates of stock. With surplus revenues of more than $2,000,000 at their disposal, the commissioners instructed Robert White, transfer officer of the state and also cashier of the Bank of the Manhattan Company, to offer liberal premiums to stockholders as an inducement to them to surrender their stock.[19] The commissioners were anxious to be relieved of the "fearful responsibility . . . of investing and managing $2,000,000," and throughout 1831, in their letters to the transfer officer, they indicated their desire to reduce the surplus by retiring outstanding stock.[20]

Clearly they preferred to "buy in" their stock, rather than to "bank" their money, but the prices "offered and asked," although occasionally showing sharp rises and falls, generally maintained high and relatively stable levels. In 1831, the commissioners commented on the fact that the canal revenues deposited in the New York State Bank and the Mechanics and Farmers Bank would produce a cumulative loss of 10½ per cent for the Canal Fund over a period of seven years if these revenues remained in the banks and were not used instead to retire the 5 per cents of 1837. This reasoning was based on the unwarranted assumption that the stock could be purchased at par. On the contrary, the price of the canal issues of 1837 oscillated between 12½ and 14 per cent above par, which meant that the 3½ per cent interest that the depository banks paid on the canal revenues was a more desirable arrangement for the Canal Fund than purchasing the outstanding 5 per cents at the prevailing rate.[21] Repeatedly, the commissioners noted in their reports that stocks "could not be bought at a reasonable rate," that they were not available on terms "advantageous to the in-

[19] Silas Wright to Robert White, 4 Oct. 1831, LRC, I, 495–496.

[20] Silas Wright to Robert White, 4 Oct., 14 Oct. 1831, LRC, I, 495–496, 500.

[21] NYS, *Ass. Docs.*, 54 Sess., II, Doc. no. 102, 4–6.

terests of the Canal Fund," and that, in their judgment, it was "inadvisable to embrace" the limited opportunities and the high expense involved in the purchase of whatever stock was available.[22] The high prices that prevailed in the market for the canal stocks, the comptroller declared, explained the commissioners' decision to lend a total of $500,000 to the Commercial Bank of Albany, the Bank of Utica, the Bank of America, and the Phoenix Bank.[23] If the value that investors attached to their canal stock was too great to allow them to part with their certificates, the commissioners could at least take advantage of a favorable money market by entering it as lenders in order to earn a higher rate of return on their money than the depository banks in Albany paid. The comptroller informed the transfer officer, that

your account of the rise of stocks has discouraged us in hope of being able to make purchases to any extent at prices which will be as favorable to us as the terms upon which we can invest the money. We have, therefore, just closed our actions upon propositions from various banks for loans of portions of this fund, and we offer half a million at 4½% with liberty to draw for it upon a notice of 60 days. It will undoubtedly all be taken, and if so, we shall not be anxious to purchase as the difference upon these investments will be but half a percent against us. . . . In the meantime, I do not wish you to press for purchases unless it is of the 1837 stock and those not at prices beyond those fixed in my last.[24]

At times, the comptroller patiently explained to importunate borrowers that the commissioners had come perilously close to retaining in their possession the bare minimum necessary to pay the interest charges on the debt, the cost of repairs, salaries, and other incidental expenses.[25] Frequently, the comptroller in-

[22] NYS, *Ass. Jour.*, 52 Sess., 770; NYS, *Ass. Docs.*, 53 Sess., II, Doc. no. 152, 6; 54 Sess., II, Doc. no. 102, 5–6.

[23] The Bank of America and the Phoenix Bank were located in New York City.

[24] Silas Wright to Robert White, 14 Oct. 1831, LRC, I, 500.

[25] The required amount was $750,000. See NYS, *Ass. Docs.*, 56 Sess., I, Doc. no. 4, 8; Silas Wright to Cornelius Heyer, 23 March 1832; Wright to Robert Campbell, 10 Aug. 1832: LRC, II, 13, 60–61.

formed bankers interested in loans that the commissioners would resume lending only when expected revenues from current tolls replenished reserves in the depository banks. Sometimes, as in the late summer of 1832, when the money market was particularly tight and banks along the line of the canals exercised their privilege of retaining the revenues deposited with them, the comptroller bluntly declared that "nothing could be done to satisfy the many applicants for loans" since the commissioners "had not funds at their command." [26]

Not a single private investor saw fit to offer his stock for redemption at the transfer office before February 1832.[27] As a result, bankers who made attractive offers to the Commissioners of the Canal Fund came increasingly into possession of the fund's accumulating revenues, borrowing as they did in 1832 in response to the tightness of the money market that prevailed that year. The Farmers Bank of Troy, evidently especially hardpressed for funds, consented to pay an interest rate of 5 per cent per annum on a loan of $50,000, indicating that the market favored the commissioners and that borrowing banks had no choice other than to submit to the climbing interest rate. More frequently than ever, the comptroller had to turn away applicants for loans, many of whom, in their anxiety to be accommodated, were prone to lose sight of the fact that the essential function of the commissioners was not that of lending money to banks but of managing the finances of the Canal Fund so that all its obligations could be met and the canals maintained in operation.

During 1833, the Canal Fund made loans to eight additional

[26] Silas Wright to P. G. Shields, 9 Aug. 1832; Wright to David C. Judson, 9 Aug. 1832: LRC, II, 58, 59; NYS, *Ass. Docs.*, 56 Sess., Doc. no. 4, 15.

[27] NYS, *Ass. Docs.*, 56 Sess., I, Doc. no. 4, 13; 68 Sess., V, Doc. no. 175, Statement no. 2. There was a short-term issue amounting to $270,000, bearing 6 per cent interest per annum, and taken in part by the comptroller for the School Fund, by the Health Office of New York, and by the New York State Bank and the Mechanics and Farmers Bank in 1825. It was repaid on 1 Oct. 1826.

banks that had never received such loans before, bringing to $1,641,000 the total amount of loans outstanding. Particularly striking was the fact that the addition of new banks and the consequent modest enlargement of the total amount on loan under provisions of the act of 1831 took place at a time when the commissioners were feverishly engaged in redeeming large amounts of outstanding stock. Undoubtedly, some of the old recipients of canal revenues were drawn upon to accommodate the new banks; nevertheless, it is clear that income from revenues was high enough to make possible both the redemption of stock and the additional loans to banks. The beneficiaries of the new distribution included four banks in "canal" counties: one in Albany, two in New York City, and the Ogdensburg Bank, situated far off to the north on the St. Lawrence River, a bank which repeatedly had petitioned for, but now for the first time received, a share of the surplus revenues of the Canal Fund.[28]

No essential change in the relationship of the Canal Fund to the banks took place during the period preceding 1837. By 1836, the banks reached the peak in their indebtedness to the Canal Fund for this period; they owed it slightly more than $3,600,000, which was an amount almost equal to one-half the original cost of the canals and constituted a surplus over and above the high costs of maintenance and the large expenditure of more than $3,000,000 incurred from 1833 on in redeeming the outstanding debt. By 1837, the Canal Fund had contracts with fifty-two banks in the state, and of these, only two paid less than 5 per cent per annum for their loans.[29]

On the surface, it appears as if the revenues of the Canal Fund had been scattered throughout the state; actually, a large proportion of them gravitated to such points of great commercial activity as New York City, Albany, Troy, Utica, Syracuse,

[28] Silas Wright to H. B. Gibson, 28 Dec. 1832, LRC, II, 79–80; NYS, *Ass. Docs.*, 56 Sess., I, Doc. no. 4, 2; 57 Sess., I, Doc. no. 4, 2.

[29] NYS, *Ass. Docs.*, 60 Sess., I, Doc. no. 3, 36; 61 Sess., I, Doc. no. 5 (no. 28).

Lockport, Rochester, and Buffalo, where money was in greatest demand and where it could be used with the greatest profit.[30]

Banks that first opened their doors for business between 1832 and 1837 frequently benefited from a loan or from a deposit of the Canal Fund which must have added significantly to their resources during their early months of operation. The commissioners granted a total of $589,006 in loans to eleven banks whose declared aggregate capital amounted to $3,050,000 during the year immediately following their incorporation.[31] But whether or not particular banks were old institutions or had been recently established, the loans and deposits that the commissioners granted to them undoubtedly represented important additions to their resources and to the resources of the communities that they served. "The resources of this country are not half-developed," declared the Rochester *Advertiser* in 1833, in a plea for more banking capital in both Rochester and Buffalo. "Rochester is the Manchester of the West. Give her capital. Her enterprise will ensure the result." [32] In the absence of an increase in banking capital, the Canal Fund instead swelled the resources of the Bank of Rochester, an institution capitalized at $250,000, by maintaining an average annual deposit at that bank of $69,717 in the period 1831–1837, plus an average annual loan of $95,660 for the years 1833–1837. Considering the clamor for increased credit facilities in Rochester, such additions to the loanable resources of the community were welcome. Similarly, the Canal Fund maintained its loan to the Wayne County Bank of Palmyra at the level of about $28,600 for the years 1831–1837, while the average of its deposits in the same bank for 1831–1837 amounted to $21,638 for the entire period.[33] The accumulating revenues of the Canal Fund also entered the channels of business

[30] See Appendix II for geographical distribution.

[31] Compiled from Appendix I.

[32] 26 Nov. 1833, quoted in McKelvey, *Rochester, the Water-Power City*, 174.

[33] See Appendixes I and II.

through the agency of the larger banks in the cities of Troy, Albany, and New York. The average loan of the Canal Fund to the Canal Bank of Albany for the period 1832–1837 was $113,625; it was $139,595 for the Merchants and Mechanics Bank of New York City and $44,300 for the Farmers Bank of Troy. Comparable averages for deposits in banks for smaller communities such as Lockport and Geneva in 1831–1837 were $49,994 and $39,532 respectively; for the Bank of Whitehall, the level of deposits of the Canal Fund in 1832–1837 averaged $43,718 for the period.[34]

The commissioners had reluctantly resorted to the banks in the absence of other means of disposing of or investing their surplus revenues. They granted that they "knew of no other equally profitable mode of investing [their] funds," but they were not without misgivings concerning the course that they had taken. By 1831, the significance of their lending activity was brought home to them when they realized that local bankers in business along the canals did "in some measure" govern the extent of their accommodations to their customers on the basis of the amount of money belonging to the Canal Fund that they held.[35] Almost imperceptibly, it seemed, the commissioners' responsibility, originally concerned only with the financial administration of the canal, had expanded, and it began to appear as if they were, in part at least, responsible for the stability of the economy. They became increasingly conscious of the importance that bankers attached to the loans and deposits of the Canal Fund;

[34] Appendixes I and II.

[35] Silas Wright to A. B. Johnson, 11 April 1831, LRC, I, 396; NYS, *Ass. Docs.*, 56 Sess., I, Doc. no. 4, 14. The Common School Fund lost $50,000 as a result of the failure of the Middle District Bank in 1829 (Lincoln, ed., *Messages*, II, 295). The commissioners feared such failures of banks holding their loans and deposits, notwithstanding what appears to be their strict investigation beforehand of the institutions with which they contracted and the periodic examination of most of these banks by the bank commissioners (NYS, *Ass. Docs.*, 58 Sess., IV, Doc. no. 305, 4–5; Wright to George Newbold, 30 Sept. 1831, LRC, I, 493).

these sums, they realized, which seemed so large at the time, with their approval were being "diffused . . . through every department of business." Were they inducing "overtrading"? were not the deposits and the loans of the Canal Fund a source of "false" credit likely to delude borrowers into misinterpreting the true condition of the money market? [36]

The commissioners' responsibility seemed even more onerous in 1832 before they were able to cancel any of their outstanding stock. What would happen, they wondered, on 1 July 1837, when the banks would necessarily be called upon to return $3,500,000 to the Canal Fund in order to cancel 5 and 6 per cent issues of stock due on that date? There might be no danger in drawing such a large amount from the banks at one time if the period when this large sum was needed was one of "ease and plenty." In that case, they predicted, their calls on the banks would "be met without distress and disaster" on the part of the banks' customers. "Should a scarcity of money prevail," however, the commissioners conjectured, the "heavy amount" that they would require to redeem the outstanding stock "might draw too largely upon the disposable means of the banks for the entire safety of the community." [37] Having demonstrated rare foresight regarding what turned out to be a year of crisis in the history of the Canal Fund as well as in the annals of the American economy, the commissioners had little to offer the legislature by way of recommendation. If the legislature thought proper, the commissioners suggested, it might set a maximum limit on their loans to banks; obviously the commissioners did not press too hard for such action. They saw the dangers that might well arise as a result of the increasingly intimate relationship of the Canal Fund to the banks, but they knew of no other equally profitable investment for their surplus revenues. Despite the fact that the legislature failed to act, the commissioners felt that they had been wise to raise the question; it served to warn the banks that

[36] NYS, *Ass. Docs.*, 57 Sess., I, Doc. no. 4, 19; 58 Sess., I, Doc. no. 4, 18.
[37] *Ibid.*, 56 Sess., I, Doc. no. 4, 14; IV, Doc. no. 305, 4–5.

they would be drawn on heavily in 1837 and that they would do well to prepare for the withdrawals in advance.[38]

The commissioners accurately estimated the possible dangers that could arise in 1837 when the first large-scale redemption of canal stock was scheduled to fall due. Their only hope to avert the anticipated risks—the possible strain on the banking system and even a fairly serious dislocation of economic activity in the state—lay in arranging for progressive redemption of outstanding stock between 1832 and 1837. But as late as January 1833, the commissioners saw no evidence that the creditors of the Canal Fund were likely to alter the pattern of investment behavior that had characterized them for a period of fourteen years. During that time, many certificates held by private investors had changed hands in the open market, but not one had been offered to the transfer officer for redemption and cancellation. Moreover, the possibility of "buying in" their certificates, it seemed clear, would become increasingly remote since President Jackson's determination to retire the national debt would only accelerate the flow of investment capital into the money market, and as a result, prices of the canal stocks would be likely to rise.[39]

When, however, on 28 January 1833 the brokerage house of Prime, Ward, and King, heavy dealers in American stocks overseas, offered the transfer officer $30,000 worth of the issue of 5 per cents of 1837 for redemption and cancellation, it was evident that the market for New York canal stocks was rapidly changing.[40] The offer was made on terms that the commissioners could accept, and it was soon followed by similar offers from the same house, as well as from the Albany Savings Bank.[41] Redemption had become an actuality, and the commissioners were determined to make the most of it.

What had opened this alternative avenue of investment for

[38] *Ibid.*, 56 Sess., IV, Doc. no. 305, 4–5.

[39] *Ibid.*, 56 Sess., I, Doc. no. 4, 13; 68 Sess., Doc. no. 175, Statement no. 2.

[40] A. C. Flagg to Prime, Ward, and King, 28 Jan., 2 Feb. 1833; Flagg to Robert White, n.d.: LRC, II, 85, 86, 99.

[41] NYS, *Ass. Docs.*, 57 Sess., I, Doc. no. 4, "N."

the revenues of the Canal Fund? Why did the opportunity for progressive retirement of canal stock appear early in 1833, to the relief of the commissioners who had already begun to look forward with trepidation to the date of maturity of the first issues?

A circular that the commissioners distributed the following August for the purpose of persuading creditors of the Canal Fund to surrender their certificates for redemption and cancellation contained a simple explanation of the revolution that had taken place in the market. A creditor who retained his stock beyond 1833, the commissioners pointed out, did so at a loss. If such a holder of the issues of 1837, the commissioners noted, reinvested the principal of his canal loan plus the premium that he received on redemption, he would earn more, even at the relatively low rate of 4 per cent, than if he held his canal stock until the date of maturity.[42] This was a persuasive argument; indeed, it was the most persuasive of all and accounted for the steadily increasing movement for redemption that began in 1833. The commissioners re-enforced this argument by declaring it a "moral certainty" that they would redeem their stock at par and on schedule by 1 July 1837; they pointed to the surplus revenues that offered such assurance and to the provision in the state Constitution that prohibited a reduction in tolls on the canals until the original debt was canceled.[43]

For a long time, the commissioners had been aware that creditors of the Canal Fund, and especially those who held large blocks of stock, retained them because they anticipated great difficulty in finding alternative investment opportunities. In 1833, however, the commissioners were able to call the attention of Prime, Ward, and King to the loan of $1,000,000 that they were about to float for the purpose of financing the Chenango Canal. The commissioners expressed the hope that the brokerage house would purchase issues of 1837 abroad "whenever the foreign

[42] *Ibid.*, 57 Sess., I, Doc. no. 4, 18–19.
[43] Constitution of 1821 of the State of New York, Art. VII, Sec. 10.

market makes it for your interest to do so," and they suggested that the offer of the Chenango stock would encourage those foreigners who held large blocks of stock to sell. Prime, Ward, and King, the commissioners declared, could persuade the holders of the Erie and Champlain issues of 1837 to bid for the Chenango loan, "knowing that if they get it, we will purchase the old stock from them, and the effect will be . . . to exchange short for long stock and relatively to get as good a premium as they pay." [44]

The commissioners used the same kind of persuasive arguments with the Bank for Savings, which previously had rejected proposals that it offer its stock for redemption on the grounds that it would be extremely difficult to reinvest the large sums that its holdings represented. In 1833, however, the bank was willing to offer for redemption $600,000 worth of its Erie and Champlain canal stock, declining at the same time the commissioners' offer of the Chenango loan in favor of an issue of Pennsylvania canal stock which seemed at the time more profitable. [45] Obviously, expanding opportunities for large investors in internal improvements stock were no longer confined to New York.

To a great degree, the kind of opportunities for large-scale

[44] NYS, *Ass. Docs.*, 57 Sess., I, Doc. no. 4, 15–16; NYS, *Laws*, ch. xxxii, 56 Sess. This act provided for the construction of the Chenango Canal and authorized a loan of $1,000,000, which was raised piecemeal. See NYS, *Ass. Docs.*, 60 Sess., I, Doc. no. 4, 56.

At the end of 1833, the total amount of Erie and Champlain canal stock held by foreigners was $4,103,000; held by Americans, $1,420,000. Foreigners held $1,420,000 of the 5 per cents and 6 per cents of 1837; Americans, $855,000 of the same issues (NYS, *Ass. Docs.*, 57 Sess., I, 21; Flagg to Prime, Ward, and King, 1 Aug. 1833, LRC, II, 222–223).

[45] Unsigned, probably A. C. Flagg, to John Pintard, 22 April 1833, LRC, II, between 118 and 119; NYS, *Ass. Docs.*, 57 Sess., I, Doc. no. 4, 16. The Chenango loan did not, of course, go begging. William B. Astor held $78,000 worth of the Chenango issues of 1833 and 1835, and English investors, such as E. & R. Ellice, Overend, Gurney & Company, Baring Brothers, and others, were large holders of Chenango stock by 1836 ("Loan of Feb. 1833 and April 1835. 5% Stock Chenango Canal," Misc. Canal Papers, NYSL).

investment that the trustees of the Bank for Savings were able to find beyond the borders of New York State may be attributed to the success of the Erie Canal. The "canal era" was initiated in New York; the "canal fever" spread from the Empire State not only because of the Erie Canal's catalytic effect on the local economy, which was quickly understood in other states, but because merchants of Baltimore, Boston, and Philadelphia immediately appreciated the great advantage that the city of New York had gained in the western trade as a result of the construction of the main-line canal. State legislatures absorbed, in great measure, the sense of rivalry for control of the western trade that was first generated in the seaboard cities. These legislatures, in imitation of New York, authorized comparable schemes of internal improvements, which, in turn, gave rise to an orgy of borrowing that contributed to the enlargement of investment opportunities such as those that the trustees of the Bank for Savings had found in Pennsylvania.[46] With the opening up of such opportunities within and outside of New York State, the commissioners' difficulties in retiring the stock issues of 1837 were considerably eased.

Once redemption began in 1833, it proceeded rapidly. By the

[46] For rivalry among the seaboard cities for the western trade and the impact of the Erie Canal in stimulating support for public works within other states, see Reginald C. McGrane, *Foreign Bondholders and American State Debts* (New York, 1935), 5, 63, 102; Walter S. Sanderlin, *The Great National Project: A History of the Chesapeake and Ohio Canal* (Johns Hopkins Univ. Studies in Hist. and Pol. Sci., LXIV, no. 1; Baltimore, 1946), 83, 191; Oscar and Mary F. Handlin, *Commonwealth: A Study of the Role of the Government in the American Economy: Massachusetts, 1774–1861* (New York, 1947), 184–185; Louis Hartz, *Economic Policy and Democratic Thought* (Cambridge, Mass., 1948). This is not to minimize the amount of debt incurred in southern states for purposes of banking; however, in 1838, debts incurred for banking purposes equaled approximately one-half of the total indebtedness of states that originated in efforts to finance internal improvements, including canals, railroads, and turnpikes (B. U. Ratchford, *American State Debts* [Durham, 1941], 88, Table 7).

spring of that year, the commissioners viewed the possibility of "buying in" their stock as almost limitless and controlled solely by the demands that they could make on the banks.[47] They warned the "depository banks" that they could expect to be drawn on for large amounts "within a short period" and that they could anticipate that the Canal Fund's account with them would be sharply reduced. They asserted, too, that deposits and loans made to banks throughout the state would also be drawn on in order to furnish the cash necessary to reimburse creditors of the Canal Fund. Their demands on the banking system, they declared, would be controlled only by considerations of "inconvenience" that customers of such institutions might suffer if the rate of withdrawal proved to be too rapid. The commissioners warned the brokerage house of Prime, Ward, and King to notify them of their purchases of stock in Europe well in advance in order to be sure that the transfer officer would have the cash necessary to retire the stock that they turned over to him.[48] By May, John Ward and Company, a Wall Street firm dealing in canal stock, learned that redemption of a quantity of stock that the company had on hand would be delayed as a matter of "convenience" to the commissioners. This was another way of saying that the commissioners had run out of cash and that further redemption had to await expiration of the sixty-day notification period required before the commissioners could draw on their loans to banks.[49] Between the end of January 1833 and the middle of June, the commissioners' accounts in the depository banks were reduced from more than $600,000 to $95,000, even though at the same time some of the banks receiving collectors' deposits had been drawn on also for the same purpose of reimbursing creditors of the Canal Fund.[50] Two

[47] NYS, *Ass. Docs.*, 56 Sess., IV, Doc. no. 305, 4, 5.

[48] Flagg to Prime, Ward, and King, 5 April 1833, LRC, II, 108.

[49] Flagg to John Ward and Co., 10 May 1833, LRC, II, 137.

[50] NYS, *Ass. Docs.*, 57 Sess., I, Doc. no. 4, 16, 19–20n; Flagg to Robert White, 24 May 1833, LRC, II, 151–152.

payments to the Bank for Savings representing a total of $400,000 accounted mainly for the sharp reduction in the Canal Fund's balances with the depository banks; for the purpose of redeeming a third block of stock of $213,000 held by the same institution, Comptroller Flagg was forced to turn to the banks along the canals and to draw the total deposits of tolls for the month of May.[51] Flagg explained to Ashbel Kellogg, cashier of the Bank of Salina, that the offer of the Bank for Savings had been "unexpected"; since the bank had not warned the commissioners of its intention to offer its stock for redemption, they had made no provision to inform banks that required sixty-day notification that they would be drawn on.[52] This meant that about $1,500,000 of their loans were immobilized and accounted for the large demands that they were making on the banks which were not protected in their contracts by a sixty-day notification clause.

Redemption proceeded so rapidly through June 1833 that the comptroller found it necessary to urge three banks in New York City to waive the sixty-day requirement so that he could pay the quarterly interest on the canal debt that fell due on 1 July.[53] Nevertheless, the commissioners hastened onward in their effort to retire more of the outstanding stock. They continued their negotiations with the Bank for Savings for the remaining $393,000 of Erie and Champlain canal stock in its possession. Despite the fact that this stock consisted of a 5 per cent loan that was redeemable in 1845, the commissioners were so eager to retire it that they arranged to pay for it in longer issues of stock that had been floated to finance two short feeder canals, the Oswego and Crooked Lake canals, and in stock of the Delaware and Hudson Canal Company, which the Canal Fund

[51] Flagg to Banks Receiving Deposits, 27 May 1833, LRC, II, 154-155.
[52] Flagg to Ashbel Kellogg, 28 May 1833, LRC, II, 148.
[53] Flagg to S. Flewelling, G. Newbold, and J. Delafield, 24 June 1833; Flagg to Prime, Ward, and King, 5 Feb. 1834: LRC, II, 182, 324; NYS, *Ass. Docs.*, 57 Sess., I, Doc. no. 5, 10-11. See Flagg to George Newbold, 30 Sept. 1834, LRC, II, 486, for conclusive evidence that the banks granted the comptroller's request.

had previously taken as an investment.[54] This was a hard bargain that the trustees of the Bank for Savings drove with the commissioners. Comptroller Flagg believed that the bank should have paid a premium of 1 or 2 per cent for the Crooked Lake canal issue, which ran until 1850, five years beyond the stock for which it was being exchanged. Secretary of State John A. Dix called the trustees of the bank, otherwise known as stable and respected citizens of New York, "a damned pack of sharpers" for squeezing 2 or 3 per cent out of the Canal Fund and even objected, "on principle," to turning over the issues which matured in 1846 and 1847 to the bank at par. Both men finally agreed to the terms that the bank offered because, as Flagg said, they were "afraid to lose the opportunity of the whole purchase" and because they were anxious to cancel the debt.[55] The commissioners persuaded themselves that they had not suffered a total defeat at the hands of the trustees of the Bank for Savings. They took comfort in the realization that they paid "the sharpers" for their 5 per cents of 1845 valued at 17 or 18 per cent above par in the market with $213,000 worth of Crooked Lake Canal stock that they had bought for the Canal Fund at par originally.[56]

By the end of the fiscal year 1833, the commissioners had redeemed almost $1,500,000, if the $393,000 worth of stock held by the Bank for Savings and exchanged for longer issues is included. Through the period ending in 1837, there was not a year when the commissioners failed to redeem at least $500,000 in stock. Redemptions exceeded $3,000,000 by the end of 1836, with about $2,225,000 of the stock "bought in" consisting of issues maturing in 1837 and an additional $800,000 consisting of issues

[54] The commissioners had available for this transaction $200,000 worth of D. & H. stock, redeemable in 1847, $120,000 of Crooked Lake canal stock, redeemable in 1850, and $80,000 of Oswego canal stock, redeemable in 1846 (Flagg to John Pintard, 22 June 1833, LRC, II, 182).

[55] Flagg to John Pintard, 28 June, 29 June 1833; Flagg to Robert White, 29 June 1833: LRC, II, 189, 192–193; John A. Dix to Flagg, 27 June 1833, Flagg Papers, NYPL; NYS, *Ass. Docs.*, 57 Sess., I, Doc. no. 4, "N."

[56] Flagg to William C. Bouck, 18 July 1833, LRC, II, 211.

payable in 1845.[57] Doubtless the banks were more subject to withdrawals as a result of the willingness of creditors of the Canal Fund to surrender their stocks; and perhaps, to some extent, the possibility of redemption accounted for the higher rate of 5 per cent per annum that the banks were required to pay for loans from the Canal Fund. Certainly at times the fact that creditors of the fund were eager to be repaid the principal of their investments made it necessary for the comptroller to draw on the banks receiving deposits of tolls as soon as he was legally entitled to do so.[58]

The purchasing of outstanding issues proceeded through 1837 with only a few sudden halts in times of crisis.[59] Despite the commissioners' general willingness to buy and their success in retiring more than $3,000,000 worth of the outstanding issues by the end of 1836, what stands out most markedly is the fact that the income of the Canal Fund was, at the same time, large enough so that its revenues could continue to be funneled by means of the banks into the economy and remain a significant source of credit within the state.[60]

[57] NYS, *Ass. Docs.*, 57 Sess., I, Doc. no. 4, "N"; 58 Sess., I, Doc. no. 4, "O"; 59 Sess., I, Doc. no. 4, "T"; 60 Sess., I, Doc. no. 3, "T."

[58] The comptroller often explained the commissioners' refusal to lend to banks as resulting directly from the large outlays made for the redemption of canal stock that accounted for a shortage of funds in their possession (Flagg to Fourteen Bankers, 27 Nov. 1833; Flagg to William Moore, Flagg to Watts Sherman, 2 Jan. 1834: LRC, II, 307, 325–326).

[59] *Infra*, 163–165, 191–192.

[60] In this connection it is pertinent to note that, in spite of the high rate of redemption, revenues of the Canal Fund in possession of the banks, as reported for the end of fiscal years (30 Sept.) between 1834 and 1838, ranged from $3,300,000, to $3,650,000, with the exception of the year 1837. In 1837, the amount deposited and lent was $2,799,000. In some of these years, the sums given include deposits and loans for the Chenango, Black River, and Genesee Valley canals. See NYS, *Ass. Docs.*, 58 Sess., I, Doc. no. 4, "L"; 59 Sess., I, Doc. no. 4, "S"; 60 Sess., I, Doc. no. 3, "S"; 61 Sess., I, Doc. no. 5 (no. 28); 62 Sess., Doc. no. 26, 26.

VIII

A Bank for Development

THE eagerness of the Commissioners of the Canal Fund to retire the outstanding debt and to disengage the fund as much as possible from its connection with the banks found little sympathy with people of an enterprising spirit and slight resources. Bankers, businessmen, millers, railroad promoters, farmers, salt manufacturers, and others in New York were quick to sense the importance of the Canal Fund; they appreciated the fact that the revenues of the fund swelled the available resources of the banks and provided, therefore, additional financial support for expanding agriculture and business.

There was abundant evidence that sources of credit were insufficient to meet the needs of New Yorkers during these years. In 1829, the Committee on Banks and Insurance Companies of the Assembly of New York judged that the basic problem of an economic nature facing New Yorkers could be solved by expanding banking capital in the state. The committee cited the record—"the increased business, the accumulated wealth, and the extensive commercial prosperity of the State; . . . the mighty strides which the western part has taken . . . the rich, enterprising and intelligent population of that region . . . [the state's] internal improvements, the genius, industry and enterprise of her population"—all this, in the committee's estimation, held great promise for the future, if sources of capital were expanded.[1]

Young men, insurance companies, and moneylenders in New York were wise to go west in the 1830's. There was a frontier for all three in the state. The New York Life Insurance and Trust Company had discovered it in the late twenties, and by 1832, its investments in the area already exceeded $1,200,000. The adventurousness of this company in turning its attention to western New York at an early day cannot be attributed to light-headedness on the part of its Board of Trustees. Some of the most sophisticated men in the world of banking, trade, and finance ornamented this board. John Jacob Astor and Nathaniel Prime, known in the money markets of London, Paris, and New York; Peter Remsen, former president of the Bank of the Manhattan Company, and the merchant, Robert Bowne, both conspicuous in business circles of New York City; and Erastus Corning, hardware merchant, then railroad promoter in Albany —these were some of the men who turned their attention, in a collective way, to the investment possibilities in western New York.

In 1832, the insurance company sent Nicholas Devereaux, a "westerner" from Utica, to survey conditions in the canal counties as far as Buffalo, in order to evaluate the security of the company's investments in that area and to determine whether it should continue making loans there on bonds and mortgages. Devereaux was also assigned the duty of instructing the company's agents on standards that they would be required to maintain in the future in examining property offered as security for the loans they recommended.

Nothing of economic importance escaped the notice of Devereaux in performing his duty as eyes and ears of the insurance company. He noted the expanded population, the growth of cities and towns, and the fertility of the soil. The increased number

[1] NYS, *Ass. Jour.*, 52 Sess., 440–441.

of buildings, flour mills, and "manufactures" impressed him, and he commented on the "high state of agricultural improvement" which he related to the section's new "easy access to market." Devereaux concluded that only a "few other sagacious capitalists," along with the New York Life Insurance Company, adequately appreciated the opportunities that western New Yorkers offered to lenders. He judged that capitalists neglected that area because they "always found ready employment" for their money in New York City; Devereaux praised the "sagacious" few who "disposed of their funds at a higher rate of interest in the country," and he complimented especially his own company for its judgment and boldness in carrying its lending activities in the west on a "liberal and extensive scale." [2]

Devereaux's picture of the insurance company and a handful of moneylenders on the lonely frontier of investment in western New York was an exaggeration. Had he examined the lists of stockholders in some of the local banks in the canal counties— the Madison County Bank, the Bank of Oswego, the Wayne County Bank, the Bank of Genesee, the Lockport Bank, the Bank of Buffalo, the Bank of Ithaca, and the Yates County Bank, for example—he would have been impressed by the number of easterners, New Englanders as well as New Yorkers, who were exploiting the growing possibilities of the west as an area of financial investment.[3] Whereas the activities of the land speculator were more visible and more spectacular, the growth of the creditor relationship between east and west was relatively quiet and hidden but perhaps equally as important in the development of the west. Isaac Bronson, a New York moneylender, is a good example of a "sagacious" capitalist who understood the opportunities for investment that existed in western New York, where customers for loans on "improved fertile and productive farms"

[2] NYS, *Ass. Docs.*, 56 Sess., III, Doc. no. 209, 15–17, 24, 27–28.
[3] A large number of New Yorkers owned shares, for example, in the Bank of Monroe at Rochester, but the overwhelming proportion of its stock was held by citizens of Connecticut and Massachusetts (NYS, *Ass. Docs.*, 56 Sess., II, Doc. no. 89, 8–44).

abounded. Bronson discovered in 1830 that a lender who ventured no farther west than Little Falls had ventured far enough to reap a tidy profit.[4] His reputation spread along with his money, so that in the fall of 1831, when money grew "tight," a number of westerners and northerners called his attention to the possibilities presented by the new conditions, promising him "a considerable amount of excellent investments" and a field free of competition for such loans.[5]

That same year, however, banks throughout the canal country began to receive the deposits of the Canal Fund and, shortly thereafter, its loans, as authorized by the act of 1831. In effect, the Commissioners of the Canal Fund joined the insurance company and individual moneylenders such as Bronson and contributed to the expansion of the credit facilities of the area. The act of 1831 was highly appreciated by the inhabitants of these western communities. The vote in the Assembly on the act disclosed a sectional cleavage, suggesting that the eastern and southern parts of the state were becoming increasingly creditor-conscious while the northern and western parts were debtor-oriented. Representatives of the Hudson River counties opposed the act. From the county of Richmond in the south to Washington and Rensselaer counties in the north, a vote of 18-13 was cast against the act, while assemblymen from New York City voted 7-3 in opposition to it. By way of contrast, the representatives from an unbroken stretch of sixteen counties, either embracing or flanking the line of the Erie Canal and extending from the headwaters of the Mohawk River westward, upheld the act by a vote of 24-4.[6] These were the counties

---

[4] Isaac Bronson to Andrew A. Finch, 21 July 1830, Bronson Papers, Martin Collection, NYPL.

[5] Charles Butler to Isaac Bronson, 14 Sept. 1831, Bronson Papers; McNall, *Agricultural History of the Genesee Valley*, 210–211.

[6] NYS, *Ass. Jour.*, 54 Sess., 835–836. Hudson River counties are Richmond, Kings (no vote cast), New York, Rockland, Westchester, Putnam, Orange, Ulster, Dutchess, Greene, Columbia, Albany, Rensselaer. The Erie canal counties were Oneida, Madison, Oswego, Onondaga, Cayuga, Seneca, Wayne, Ontario, Monroe, Orleans, Livingston (no vote cast),

where the canal provided a tremendous impetus to economic development and where the opening of any new source of credit was a matter of importance.

Assemblymen from these areas reflected the prevailing popular interest in retaining the revenues of the Canal Fund in their communities as a means of broadening the basis of local credit. The commissioners, in turn, appreciated this interest and explained their policy of selecting banks close to the collection points in these terms as well as in terms of a concern for the safety of the revenues. Proximity to the point of collection reduced "the risk of transmission" of the revenues from the collectors to the banks, but in addition, the commissioners pointed out, local farmers and merchants "must . . . be most deeply interested in the disposition of the deposit of tolls." Such farmers and merchants readily understood that the local bank "in some measure [would] . . . govern its accommodations" to its customers on the basis of the revenues of the Canal Fund that it had in its possession. Moreover, the commissioners could see a kind of simple justice in depositing the tolls in the local bank, for it could be "assumed that the bank nearest to the point where any portion of the revenue is collected is most likely to be called upon for accommodations by payers of that revenue." [7]

Bankers who sought loans and deposits from the Canal Fund or wished to retain those that they already had always insisted that their community's need for credit justified, or almost obliged, the commissioners to act favorably on their petitions. Inhabitants of the state who were fully aware of the importance of the canals in the economy were awakened to the importance of the Canal Fund as well. As the fund's revenues increased, so did the demand for their use. No longer could the commis-

---

Genesee, Niagara (no vote cast), Erie, Tompkins, Yates. The Champlain canal counties, including those bordering on the lake, were Saratoga, Washington, Warren, Essex, Clinton, Rensselaer, and Albany; exclusive of the last, these voted 5–3 in favor of the act, whereas Albany county voted 2–1 against it.

[7] Silas Wright to Alexander B. Johnson, 11 April 1831, LRC, I, 396.

sioners reach decisions solely with reference to the costs of operations and the debt management of the canals; their responsibility extended to the public just as soon as the influence of the Canal Fund extended to the marketplace, and they had no choice but to take this new factor into consideration.

The commissioners' concern for the marketplace and for the buyer and seller in it governed their conduct, for instance, toward the Bank of Monroe in Rochester in 1833 and the Cayuga County Bank at Auburn in 1834. The commissioners had intended to draw on their deposits in the Bank of Monroe in the spring of 1833 in order to accommodate other banking institutions that had not yet shared in the revenues of the Canal Fund. They delayed doing so out of consideration for the bank and its customers who, they expected, would be able to "dispose of their flour in New York City" and put the bank "in funds without much inconvenience" by the month of May.[8] The following spring, the comptroller informed George B. Throop, cashier of the Cayuga County Bank, that although the commissioners planned to draw on the banks they would do so with due regard for the impact of their actions on the local economy. "For the first sixty days, we intend to draw as lightly as possible upon the depositing banks," Comptroller Flagg informed Throop. Flagg explained to the cashier that the commissioners had decided to favor the bank in this manner "in order to facilitate, so far as this forebearance will do it, the measures of the bank in getting the produce of the country to market." [9]

An incident that occurred in Buffalo in 1841 illustrates how local bankers and businessmen shared a common concern for the way that the Canal Fund was administered. A rumor had spread that revenues from tolls collected at Black Rock and customarily deposited in the Commercial Bank and the Bank of

[8] A. C. Flagg to Abraham Schermerhorn, 10 April 1833, LRC.
[9] Flagg to George B. Throop, 31 March 1834, LRC, II, 366.

Buffalo would be transferred to a bank in Lockport. First to protest the possibility of such a change was Israel Hatch of the Commercial Bank of Buffalo. Hatch hotly denied the allegation that businessmen "did not receive the usual business facilities from the banks here." He offered to collect testimonials from major business firms in Buffalo to the effect that the two banks had furnished them with requisite accommodations. He asserted that the bank commissioner, Bates Cooke, could testify on the basis of his inspection of the books of the Commercial Bank that it had discounted "from 100 to 150 thousand dollars" of "produce bills . . . principally to pay canal tolls, charges and advances on produce going on the canal to market." [10] Philo Durfee, who was one of the foremost millers in the area, backed Hatch in his opposition to any possible transfer of the canal revenues to Lockport. Durfee's opinion reflected the interest of a man engaged in large-scale enterprise who had an intimate knowledge of the business community. Millers like himself, Durfee noted, relied on the Commercial Bank for credit, and the bank, in turn, relied in considerable measure on the Canal Fund. Durfee explained the relationship of the millers, the bank, and the fund when he observed that

the millers at this place generally receive their facilities from the Commercial Bank of Buffalo for paying their tolls and to a great extent for carrying on their business of manufacturing and the bank is materially aided in the business by the deposit that it receives from the collectors here.

Durfee envisioned great difficulties for the millers of Buffalo if the commissioners carried out their alleged intention of transferring the canal deposits to Lockport. He predicted that

should the money paid here for tolls be placed in bank at Lockport, it would soon create such a balance at Buffalo as to compel them to

[10] Israel Hatch to John A. Collier, 20 April 1841, General Correspondence of the Comptroller, NYSL (hereafter cited as GCC).

discontinue affording us the facilities we do much need. You will readily perceive the inconvenience for the miller here to do his bank business and keep his bank up at Lockport 25 miles distant.[11]

Perhaps Durfee exaggerated for effect; in any case, he apparently felt that the commissioners would not be surprised to learn that where the millers borrowed was in part determined by the bank in which the commissioners decided to deposit the tolls collected on the canal.

As in Buffalo, so in other communities the Canal Fund's relations with the banks demonstrated that the fund's revenues had become an important force in local economic life. Lockport, for instance, was a town that the Erie Canal had created. The imposing set of locks, a major achievement of the canal engineers, was regarded as one of the wonders of the Western world by the 1830's. Here the Lockport Bank grew with the town, and by 1833, the bank had benefited as a result of the deposits that it had received from the Canal Fund. When, however, the commissioners began to draw steadily on the bank throughout the winter of 1834–1835, so that the Canal Fund's balance in the institution was reduced in less than a year from $75,000 to about $40,000, Lot Clark protested in behalf of the bank about the adverse effect that the commissioners' policy was having on business in the area. Clark understood the business of the area well; with politicians and bankers, he had come to Lockport to speculate in lands at the foot of the locks, where land values would be directly affected by hydraulic privileges based on the overflow waters of the canal that could be purchased from the state. Clark declared that the commissioners' steady withdrawals from the bank "render it necessary for us to push our customers to their inconvenience. We must therefore ask you if convenient to hold up for a while—we would

[11] Durfee claimed that he manufactured and shipped 62,000 barrels of flour on the Erie Canal in 1840 (Durfee to John A. Collier, 16 April 1841, GCC).

like to keep our deposits at $60,000. That sum we can use to the advantage of the bank and the public." [12]

Clark went on to indicate that there was more at stake than the interests of private business, although he did not deny that these were present; he insisted that the use of the canal at Lockport would diminish if the commissioners did not reverse their policy. "Nearly every dollar of canal tolls paid here," Clark explained, "are by loans from us, and when the state draws off too fast, we have to hold up and thereby diminish the amount of tolls." [13] Unsubtle as Clark's appeal to the commissioners was, it had the merit of clearly indicating the importance that officials of the Lockport Bank attached to the revenues of the Canal Fund for both the bank and the community that it served.

Two years later, exactly one day before the force of the Panic of 1837 compelled the banks of New York City to suspend specie payments, Washington Hunt, speaking for the Lockport Bank, was effusive in his gratitude to the commissioners for a loan that they had recently granted to the bank. "We feel under many obligations to you," Hunt wrote to the comptroller. The loan, he declared, "could not have come at a better time. I intend nothing unreasonable when I enquire if you cannot consistently provide us with $10,000 more from the same source." [14]

In the light of prevailing conditions, Hunt's eagerness for additional revenues from the Canal Fund is easily understood. By the time he wrote to the comptroller, Hunt noted that the banks of Buffalo had already suspended specie payments and had "produced a general distrust of the soundness of other institutions." Panic was in the air, and Hunt was worried by the number of billholders that appeared at the bank and demanded specie. For this reason, the banker declared, "a bank was wise

[12] Lot Clark to Flagg, 22 July 1835, Townsend Papers, NYPL.
[13] *Ibid.*   [14] Washington Hunt to Flagg, 9 May 1837, GCC.

to be well fortified" under the circumstances. "Fortunately, our circulation is small," Hunt confided to the comptroller. "I trust that we shall get through safely under any circumstances, but we really need the additional amount which I have named to relieve us from apprehension." [15]

Banks in Syracuse and Salina had long-standing accounts with salt manufacturers at the state-owned salt springs. The salt manufacturers leased their sites from the state, and for many years, the manufacture of salt was a major industry in the area of Syracuse. One measure of the importance of the industry is the total sum of salt duties collected between 1817 and 1836, which amounted to $2,055,000. These duties, along with auction duties and income from tolls, had been allocated by the legislature to the Canal Fund and constituted a guarantee to investors that the interest and principal on the state stocks that they subscribed to would be paid. A large portion of the salt duties were deposited in the Bank of Utica, the Onondaga County Bank, the Bank of Salina, and possibly others.

From 1833 and thereafter, the Commissioners of the Canal Fund made deposits in the Bank of Salina. In 1839, M. W. Bennett, cashier of the bank, protested that the terms of the new contract, defining the conditions on which the commissioners would continue to deposit the revenues of the Canal Fund with the bank, placed the bank at such a disadvantage that it would be prevented from accommodating the salt manufacturers as it had done in the past. Apparently, the commissioners proposed to reduce the amount of deposits that the bank had been accustomed to receive from the Canal Fund. In stating his objections, Bennett declared:

We have so long been in the practice of affording the salt manufacturers all the facilities in our power, that we dislike to be placed in a position which will compel us to discontinue doing their business to the extent we have done, which we must do if the duties collected here are taken to foreign institutions.[16]

[15] *Ibid.*   [16] M. W. Bennett to Bates Cooke, 5 June 1839, GCC.

Later that year, when the comptroller notified the bank of the commissioners' intention to draw $21,000, Bennett again protested in terms of the consequences that such a move would have for the manufacturers of salt. Bennett's protest had as much to do with his concern for the future business of the bank as with the needs of the rest of the business community despite the fact that he was not as frank as Clark of Lockport had been to say so. He responded to the commissioners' stated intention to draw on the bank by pointing out that the bank had been "discounting for the salt manufacturers and to that class of men exclusively in order to prevent their being driven to stop the manufacture." Failure to persuade the commissioners to refrain from drawing on the bank would leave it with "no alternative but to make sacrifices to pay over our debts," with obvious unfortunate consequences for the salt manufacturers. Most of them, Bennett predicted, under such circumstances, would "have to stop about two months earlier than usual unless some bank or banks will discount the paper taken in payment for salt." [17]

The fact that the banks depended on the Canal Fund for credit was apparently understood as well by the salt manufacturers in Salina as it had been by the millers of Buffalo. Amos P. Granger, also of the Bank of Salina, explained to Comptroller Bates Cooke that manufacturers of salt applied to the bank for accommodations and were "very generally denied, in consequence of which a very serious embarrassment pervades this important branch of industry." Granger, however, pointed out that the manufacturers did not blame the directors of the bank for denying them the credit they needed; instead, they directed their criticism at the Commissioners of the Canal Fund. Granger explained to the comptroller that

it is here generally understood that in consequence of the frequent and unexpected drafts of the Comptroller on the bank of Salina for its public deposits, that institution is compelled to withhold its fa-

[17] M. W. Bennett to Bates Cooke, 19 Sept. 1839, GCC.

cilities which it would otherwise cheerfully grant in aid of an interest in which so many of our citizens are concerned and from which the State derived so large a revenue.[18]

The comptroller's reply to this letter must have been a sharp one, for, in less than a week, Bennett, the cashier of the bank, explained in an apologetic tone that the allegations against the Commissioners of the Canal Fund were the work of unnamed "officious intermeddling politicians" and he denied vigorously that any of the directors of the bank had accused the commissioners of having "unnecessarily drawn for funds from this bank." If anything, Bennett declared, the bank had publicized the liberality of the commissioners to the community. He explained to the comptroller that

your willingness to let the amounts falling due 1st Sept. and 1st October remain with us has been frequently spoken of by our bank as liberal on your part and as evincing a disposition to aid us to furnish all the facilities to the manufacturers that was possible. We have faithfully carried out the suggestions we made to you and have done all in our power to aid the salt folks.[19]

During the following year, Hamilton White, cashier of the Onondaga County Bank, requested the comptroller to exercise restraint in drawing for the revenues of the salt duties that were deposited in the bank. The reasons he offered were much the same as those that Bennett and Granger of the Bank of Salina had expressed when they pointed out to the commissioners the dependence of the salt manufacturers on the bank and the bank's dependence on the Canal Fund. White, too, was solicitous about the welfare of the salt manufacturers. The manufacturers, declared White, "require very large discounts at the opening of the salt business"; they depended on the banks of Syracuse, and, he added, "the banks of this town, while they endeavor to make money, at the same time I believe use all

[18] Amos P. Granger to Bates Cooke, 3 Oct. 1839, GCC.
[19] M. W. Bennett to Bates Cooke, 7 Oct. 1839, GCC.

exertions to aid the business of the country." [20] Early in the
year, White had apparently petitioned for a deposit of the
Canal Fund's revenues in his bank to supplement the salt duties
that it regularly received. The commissioners refused White's
request, which had been couched in terms of the benefits that
the desired deposit was likely to yield not only to the salt manufacturers of Syracuse but also to the farmers of the surrounding countryside. The comptroller indicated that the commissioners' funds were committed but that they always made an
effort to aid the economic groups for whom White sought the
loan. Comptroller Cooke wrote:

While I accord most readily in your views of the necessity of aid
to be extended to the agricultural and salt manufacturing interest,
I have to regret that the Commissioners of the Canal Fund have it not
in their power to make you a loan, or deposit with your bank any
part of the monies designated for the redemption of Erie and Champlain Canal stock." [21]

In 1839, President Whittelsey of the Bank of Monroe warned
that the demands of the Commissioners of the Canal Fund,
if acceded to, threatened the successful completion of the
Tonawanda Railroad. Whittelsey's accusation came in response
to a sight draft that the commissioners had drawn on the bank,
notwithstanding the fact that the contract between the commissioners and the bank was based on the act of 1831 and required the commissioners to notify the bank sixty days in advance of its intention to draw. The commissioners obviously
had erred, but the error gave Whittelsey an opportunity to
discharge some of his aggressions against them, at the same time
that he rejected the draft. The president, of course, insisted on
the preliminary notice that the contract between the bank and
the commissioners provided for; with regard to the money in
question, Whittelsey explained that the bank had "gone on"
and "discounted for the accommodation of the public." Elabo-

[20] Hamilton White to Bates Cooke, 19 Aug. 1840, GCC.
[21] Bates Cooke to Hamilton White, 21 March 1840, LRC, V, 230.

rating on his objections to the premature demand of the commissioners, Whittelsey explained that "it is inconvenient for a country bank at this season as you well know to meet such sudden demands, and it is injurious to the community as they must either press their debtors at a bad season of the year, or curtail discounts which are now much wanted to enable them to meet such drafts." [22]

The commissioners' unjustified demand gave Whittelsey an opportunity to review the bank's connection with the Canal Fund over a period of years and brought him around to the subject of the Tonawanda Railroad. Whittelsey pointed out that prior to February 1838 the bank held almost $200,000 of the revenues of the Canal Fund. He explained that the commissioners had deposited $50,000 in the bank, when he and Jonathan Child, an enterprising businessman in Rochester, had applied for a deposit in behalf of the bank. Whittelsey candidly declared that he and Child were "large stockholders in the Tonawanda Railroad Company," and he revealed that "a large portion" of the revenues that the commissioners had deposited in the bank was, in turn, borrowed by himself and Child "to enable us to carry out what was deemed an important improvement." By July 1837, $30,000 of the $50,000 that Whittelsey and Child had persuaded the commissioners to deposit in the bank was repaid to the Canal Fund, and the remaining $20,000 was converted into a loan under terms of the act of 1831. This was the loan on which the commissioners, unwittingly, had attempted to draw. Their action, Whittelsey declared, failed to take into consideration the fact that "the Bank of Monroe . . . aided in building our railroad and has done it from patriotic motives and to their own injury." Surely, Whittelsey implied, here was an example of the highest kind of "public spirit" that a financial institution was capable of demonstrating, and the commissioners, out of appreciation for the public serv-

[22] Frederick Whittelsey to Bates Cooke, 8 Feb. 1839, GCC.

ices that the bank had rendered in aiding the railroad, would be justified in treating the institution with greater leniency and understanding than it had done in the past. Aside from the Canal Fund, the state itself had an obligation to the bank for what it had done by way of public service. In this connection, Whittelsey pointed out that the bank "held demands against the railroad which should be paid and which we hope to get the aid of the legislature to enable us to pay," a hope which was fulfilled by 1838.[23] Reverting to his general theme, the president of the bank expressed his annoyance with the commissioners. These officials, in Whittelsey's view, failed to understand fully the total effect of their demands on the Bank of Monroe. He protested that "the bank has paid hugely of its debt to the Canal Fund and of its other debts in the whole to the amount of about $300,000. They wish to do some business and the community want them to do it." [24]

Whittelsey's conclusion was inescapable: the commissioners' decision to draw on the deposits or loans held by the Bank of Monroe endangered the business of Rochester and was hostile to the best interests of the Tonawanda Railroad, a project that was conceived in the spirit of the most unselfish public interest.[25]

The Commissioners of the Canal Fund frequently discussed in their reports the "diffusion" of their revenues "through every department of business" and noted the seemingly obvious fact that the only reason the banks sought loans and deposits from the fund was so that they could relend the money to individuals.[26] They pointed out that "the banks can use this money

[23] NYS, *Ass. Docs.*, 66 Sess., I, Doc. no. 10, 30.

[24] Whittelsey to Cooke, 8 Feb. 1839, GCC.

[25] The Tonawanda Railroad, which ran parallel to the Erie Canal and eventually competed with it for traffic, was thus built in part on credit supplied by the Canal Fund. In addition, the railroad received $100,000 in "special stock" from the state. This form of aid constituted, in effect, a loan of the state's credit to the corporation (NYS, *Ass. Docs.*, 66 Sess., I, Doc. no. 10, 30; NYS, *Laws*, ch. cc, 62 Sess.).

[26] NYS, *Ass. Docs.*, 58 Sess., II, Doc. no. 74, 23.

profitably so as to afford to pay interest, in no other way than by loaning it to individuals, as they do their own capital." [27]

By 1832, the commissioners could explain the increased circulation of banks outside of the city of New York, as compared to the previous year, by attributing it "in part to the use of capital belonging to the Canal Fund, in part to the establishment of new banks, and partly to a general overtrading in the country, somewhat encouraged by the facilities afforded by those banks." The commissioners then evaluated the effect of the Canal Fund on the banks of the state and concluded that

the magnitude of the Canal Fund is now such as to have an important influence over the banking concerns of the State, so long as the present mode of its investment is continued. It may be considered as an addition to the bank capital of the state of about two millions, which will be annually accumulating. Deposits from this Fund, in the first instant, were distributed among three of the banks in the city of New York, and fourteen in other parts of the state, which report to us; and nearly all the institutions, particularly in the country, directly or indirectly participate in the use of the capital which it affords. The circulation of the last year has been more than could have been sustained without the aid of that Fund, and more perhaps than prudent operators should have hazarded upon such a reliance.[28]

By 1835 it appeared that the commissioners' prediction with regard to the growing "influence" of the Canal Fund "over the banking concerns of the State" was not to be dismissed lightly. Statistics collected by the bank commissioners, whose duty it was to inspect the books of safety-fund banks and to report on their condition, indicated that in the case of numerous banks the Canal Fund constituted a significant part of their holdings on the basis of which their business activities expanded. The picture varied from bank to bank; the canal revenues seemed more important for some banks than for others. One way of

[27] *Ibid.*, 56 Sess., II, Doc. no. 69, 12–13.
[28] *Ibid.*, 55 Sess., II, Doc. no. 70, 7–8.

judging how important the revenues of the Canal Fund were to the business of the banks is to observe, on a percentage basis, the relationship of canal loans to the amount of loans and discounts that the banks were extending at the same time to their customers. Obviously, as both the commissioners and the bankers pointed out, the banks borrowed from the Canal Fund in order to lend to their customers. In the case of the Schenectady Bank, its canal loans equaled 6 per cent of its loans and discounts; the Farmers Bank, 8 per cent; the Essex County Bank, 9 per cent; the Madison County Bank, 11 per cent; the Wayne County Bank, 12 per cent; the Canal Bank, 14 per cent; the Bank of Troy, 15 per cent; the Bank of Whitehall, 18 per cent; the Merchants and Mechanics Bank, 22 per cent. It is interesting to observe that the five banks that protested diminution of loans from the Canal Fund had considerable reason for doing so. Canal loans to the Commercial Bank of Buffalo equaled 8 per cent of its loans and discounts in 1835; the Bank of Salina, 15 per cent; the Bank of Monroe, 19 per cent; the Lockport Bank, 22 per cent; the Onondaga County Bank, 29 per cent.[29] Lot Clark, therefore, was amply justified when he insisted that if the commissioners drew heavily on the Lockport Bank the bank, in turn, would have to "push" its customers to their inconvenience. Similarly, Frederick Whittelsey correctly linked the resources of the Canal Fund placed at the disposal of officials of the Bank of Monroe with their capacity to "do some business." The same may be said of Hamilton White's declaration that the banks of his town "endeavor to make money," a statement

[29] Computations are based on the figures derived from the *Annual Report of the Bank Commissioners*, 23 Jan. 1836 (NYS, *Ass. Docs.*, 59 Sess., II, Doc. no. 80, 18–36). There is considerable reason for questioning how accurately the commissioners' figures reflected the actual amount of loans and discounts made by the banks. It was common knowledge that banks restricted, and even called in, their loans prior to the inspection of the commissioners and reversed the process as soon as the commissioners had completed their work and departed.

striking for its frankness. Equally striking, too, was the fact that, in order to do so, White's own bank had to lean heavily on the resources of the Canal Fund.[30]

By 1836, the involvement of the Canal Fund with the banks provided the legislature with a means of resisting demands to increase the number of banks and the amount of banking capital in the state. Legislators could point to the "accumulation of Canal Fund monies in the hands of the banks" and could echo the opinion of the commissioners that their loans and deposits had "enlarged the ability of banks to discount upon nearly so much additional capital." "It is only by use of them now," the commissioners declared in connection with the Canal Fund revenues, "that the banks are enabled to sustain the large amount of their discounts." [31]

[30] *Supra*, 144–145, 148–151.
[31] NYS, *Ass. Docs.*, 59 Sess., Doc. no. 80, 12. In terms of the effect on the economy, it must, of course, be remembered that by this time transfer of the deposits of the national government from the Second Bank of the United States to the so-called "pet banks," some of them in New York City, was of far greater significance than were the loans and deposits of the Canal Fund.

IX

The Panic of 1834

THE commissioners' power to administer large funds, to deposit large revenues in banks and to withdraw them, to issue stock and to redeem it, inevitably meant that the question of politics would be raised in connection with their activities. The commissioners were frequently accused, in their dealings with the banks, of shaping their decisions with an eye to political considerations.

Historically, it is clear that banking and politics were closely associated in New York. Well beyond the first quarter of the nineteenth century, the legislative fate of numerous bank charters in New York State was determined on the basis of the political affiliations of the banks' directors.[1] It was not unusual for politicians to support a bill for the incorporation of a bank in a credit-short community in order to strengthen the appeal of their party with the voters. Apparently, this was one of the reasons why the Chautauqua County Bank was incorporated in 1831. Ostensibly, the bank was chartered in order to meet the need for credit that lumbering, the manufacture of potash and pearlash, and local trade created, and to avoid the necessity for local borrowers to deal with banks in Buffalo or distant Canan-

[1] J. D. Hammond, *History of Political Parties*, I, 329–339.

daigua or Catskill. But, as the historian of the county points out, it was chartered, too, to meet the need of Democrats "with a view to advance the interests of the party in the county." [2] However, the Democrats were not alone in making use of the close connection that existed between banking and politics. The election of 1834 in Buffalo found Democratic and Whig banks warring against each other for the purpose of immediate political gain.

We Whigs are busy and I believe we are well organized for the battle. . . . The Jackson bank here will doubtless do something for the Tory cause but in the course of next month we shall retaliate. —We shall make a first debut with from $10,000 to $20,000 and continue operations until they are satisfied that Jacksonianism cannot flourish in our city—the Jackson bank for the last week fell in debt to our other banks over $15,000 last week, and it will continue to increase as their money gets out. [3]

Under such circumstances, it is not surprising that the commissioners were subject to political pressure from interested partisans. In 1830, for example, when the officials of the National Bank of New York feared that subscription to its stock would not be "filled up," William James, Jr., wrote to the Comptroller Azariah C. Flagg, reminding him of his previously expressed "strong desire" to have the bank "filled up" and declaring that all that was needed to attract subscribers to invest in the bank's stock was a visible demonstration of state patronage. The only thing wanting, said James, "to assure our getting filled up . . . is what our friends can accomplish . . . *giving us the state patronage as far as this city is concerned.*" James called this "a reasonable expectation . . . one perfectly proper in itself and such as we should expect from our friends." Certainly, if there were no legislation that barred patronage from a Democratic administration to a Democratic bank, James

---

[2] Obed Edson, *History of Chautauqua County, New York* (Boston, 1894), 328.

[3] Weed and Pratt to I. & J. Townsend, 24 Oct. 1834, Townsend Papers.

pointed out, and "it is in the power of the government to do their business with any institution they please, then we would naturally expect *that patronage* and could it be known that such a result would follow, we would fill the bank in two hours." [4]

Despite the fact that the first loan that the commissioners made went to the National Bank in 1831, it seems unlikely that the commissioners' decision to make this loan was the result of political influence. The National Bank, it will be remembered, applied for its loan in a period when money was "easy"; no other bank applied for a loan from the Canal Fund at the time. In addition, when money grew "tighter" and several other banks applied to the commissioners for loans under the act of 1831, these banks were accommodated whereas the second application of the National Bank was rejected. [5]

At times, the commissioners were accused of abusing their powers for political ends. The *American Railroad Journal and Advocate of Internal Improvements* in 1834 declared that the commissioners refused to redeem about $2,000,000 worth of canal stock held abroad and did so for insidious political reasons. This charge was false, as the commissioners' well-known desire to retire the debt demonstrated, but it was made nevertheless. [6] The *Railroad Journal* declared that the large sum "is held by the commissioners of the fund, just as the public deposits are held by the president [Jackson] as a fund to be used and transferred at pleasure, to reward this or punish that bank, according to the more or less political subserviency of its directors." [7] When, that same year, the commissioners announced their intention to borrow $900,000 to finance the construction of the Chenango Canal, Whigs once again denounced the Demo-

---

[4] William James, Jr., to A. C. Flagg, 1 May 1830, GCC. (Italics are James's.)

[5] *Supra*, 121.

[6] III, pt. 1, 197; *supra*, 129–136. The commissioners were willing to halt redemption only in times of crises (*infra*, 162–164, 191–193).

[7] III, pt. 1, 197.

cratic administration for its financial policies. Subscribers to the loan, they indicated, had to pay collectively $900,000 within ninety days of the date of subscription, whereas the commissioners would not spend the revenues that the loan brought in for at least two years. Meanwhile, these critics emphasized, "the people" would have to meet the regular interest payments on this loan which had obviously been floated prematurely in order to realize purely political objectives through economic means.

Such are the juggling tricks of the money changers at Albany, to . . . put money in the pockets of their friends at the expense of the people. An understanding as we are assured has already been made and these Chenango Canal loans are to go into certain country banks.[8]

The commissioners—as tools of the Democratic party, the reigning "Regency" in Albany—according to the Whigs, were fleecing the people for the benefit of bankers whose politics were also Democratic.

Thus, while those banks, the political machines of the Regency, are dividing their 10, 12, and 14% per annum, their capital and their dividends are thus to be increased by the people of the state. Such is the operation of the Canal Fund. . . .

The banks borrow . . . the millions of canal fund revenues at an interest of 4 and 5% and use the whole in banking—shaving the people with their own money and pocketing their 10 and 14%.[9]

The commissioners rejected the charge that the Chenango loan had been raised prematurely. They explained that the contractors found the prevailing low price of labor and raw materials an inducement to accelerate the pace of operations on the canal; for this reason, they had hastened to float the loan because they anticipated that the money would be "required during the summer and fall of 1834." The commissioners readily admitted that all the revenues from the loan were not used

[8] New York *Commercial Advertiser,* 4 April 1834.   [9] *Ibid.*

immediately, and their failure to explain why this was so did not, of course, allay the suspicions of their critics.[10]

The absence of sufficient evidence makes it difficult to sustain the charge that the commissioners allocated their deposits and loans among the banks in a way that was designed to produce maximum political advantage for the Democratic party. By contrast, the evidence is clear and abundant that during the Panic of 1834 the commissioners asserted their powers in behalf of local bankers, many of whom were Democrats. These bankers felt free to communicate with the comptroller on the subject of the policy of the commissioners in connection with the problems that the panic created. It is notable, however, that not a few Whig bankers agreed with the Democrats that the commissioners might try to mitigate the severity of the impact of the panic in the state by use of the powers at their disposal.

Although this manifestation of bipartisanship that emerged in a part of the banking community is a matter of interest, of larger significance is the fact that the goals of the commissioners, of Democratic bankers in New York, and of the Democratic administration in Washington were exactly the same. Their combined purpose was to fend off the attack that the Bank of the United States made on the economy in order to secure an extension of its charter from an unwilling administration.

The panic ensued after the Bank of the United States began a sudden and sharp cutback in its discounts in October 1833 and repeated the process in January 1834.[11] The bank's spokes-

[10] The commissioners pointed out that the transaction produced no loss for the Canal Fund, since the unused portion of the loan was deposited in the banks at an annual interest of 5 per cent, the same rate of interest that the state paid on its stock. They noted, too, that the premium on the loan of $58,000 was also banked, but this was not a satisfactory answer for critics who accused them of being in collusion with bankers (NYS, *Ass. Docs.*, 58 Sess., I, Doc. no. 4, 25).

[11] Walter B. Smith, *Economic Aspects of the Second Bank of the United States* (Cambridge, Mass., 1953), 161, 163, 167. The bank reduced its discounts by $6,000,000 in Oct. 1833 and followed this with a further reduction of $3,000,000 in Jan. 1834.

men justified this change in policy on the basis of the national administration's announced intention to dispense with its services as a depository for federal funds; they maintained that the bank had no choice but to contract its discounts and loans before the Treasury of the United States acted. This decision was sound in principle although it was unnecessarily ruthless as applied in practice. A reduction of loans and discounts was justified under the circumstances but not to the extent where it equaled almost twice the amount of the account that the Treasury eventually terminated.[12] Obviously, the bank's policy was shaped less by considerations of sound banking practice than by the more basic concern of its directors for the institution's survival.[13]

Early in 1832, Congress had passed a bill providing for an extension of the charter of the bank, which President Jackson promptly vetoed. The question of the bank became an issue in the presidential campaign of that year, and when Henry Clay, the Whig candidate who supported rechartering the bank, was defeated by President Jackson in the election, the administration interpreted the results of the election as the final judgment of the people on the question of the bank. It was this judgment that Nicholas Biddle, president of the bank, sought to set aside by contracting the credit facilities that the bank customarily provided. Contraction led to panic, and panic to hardship; this was Biddle's method of forcing Congress to act again on the issue of a national bank and of pressuring the President by means of the cries of distress that would arise from the people.

[12] Ardent defenders of the bank maintain that the institution's responsibility to its depositors and the unpredictable behavior of the Treasury Department in its day-to-day relations with it dictated the severe policy of contraction that the bank initiated in Oct. 1833. The deposits of the federal government were not "withdrawn" in the technical meaning of the term; they were disbursed and not replaced (B. Hammond, *Banking and Politics*, 420).

[13] Nicholas Biddle, president of the bank, admitted that it persisted in its policy of contraction even when it "was entirely beyond reach of any mischief of the treasury" (Smith, *Economic Aspects*, 161, 163, 167).

"Nothing but the evidence of suffering abroad will produce any effect on Congress," Biddle declared, intent on carrying the struggle to its bitter end, no matter what the cost would be for the economy as a whole. "All the other banks and all the merchants may break," wrote Biddle at the height of the panic, "but the Bank of the United States shall not break." [14] Meanwhile, banks and brokerage houses were closing their doors, prices of stock were toppling, and there was a visible increase of unemployment in the cities.

With a Democratic administration in Albany, it was hardly likely that the Commissioners of the Canal Fund would sit idly by watching the "banks . . . and . . . merchants . . . break." The Democratic cause, its hostility to the Bank of the United States, was the same in Albany as in Washington. Personal ties with the national administration strengthened those of a partisan kind, if such strengthening were at all needed. Ex-Governor Martin Van Buren of New York was now Vice-President of the United States; the former Comptroller Silas Wright had become a powerful voice for the administration in the Senate of the United States. The Canal Fund's resources were, of course, no match for those of the Bank of the United States; but what the commissioners were able to do with the resources that they had and with the Canal Fund that they managed, they did. Their procedures were entirely in harmony with the general policies of the national administration and won the approval, as well, of many local bankers in New York. These bankers were absolutely bent on destroying the Bank of the United States, their major competitor. Their views on the dangers that the mammoth bank posed to the economy, on the causes and the course of the panic, and on arrangements that the national government might make with state banks after the deposits were removed from the great bank coincided with those of the leaders of the Democratic party in the state. Al-

[14] Reginald C. McGrane, ed., *The Correspondence of Nicholas Biddle* (Boston, 1919), 219, 221.

though many of these bankers were Democrats, Whigs like George Newbold and the directors of the Bank of America joined them in a common opposition to the Bank of the United States.[15]

The policy that the commissioners fashioned specifically for the purpose of meeting the crisis caused by the panic was not a spectacular one. They decided, simply, to allow the Canal Fund's revenues to remain where they would do the most good at a time when the Bank of the United States seemed to be doing its best to dry up all sources of credit. This meant that, wherever possible, loans and deposits would remain with the banks, and only expenditures that could not be avoided, such as interest payments and maintenance charges, would constitute reasons for calling on the banks for funds.

This policy was a complete reversal of the one that had prevailed since the early part of the year. For more than six months, the commissioners had persisted in a policy of steady redemption of its stock, and during the first week of August, the commissioners had made it clear, through the comptroller, that they expected to continue to redeem as much of the outstanding stock as they possibly could. This was the impression that Comptroller Flagg clearly conveyed in his correspondence with the brokerage house of Prime, Ward, and King. Because this house dealt largely in stock owned abroad and because long periods of time frequently elapsed between the actual purchase of such stock and its delivery to the transfer officer in New York, Flagg outlined in advance for the convenience of the firm the likely policy of redemption that would prevail and stated the prices that the commissioners were willing to pay for stock up to and including April 1834. The comptroller committed himself without reservation to making large purchases of stock abroad through the first quarter of 1834. He explained that, since the retirement of about $1,000,000 worth of the stock held by the Bank For Savings two months earlier,

[15] B. Hammond, *Banking and Politics*, 357, 392, 415–416.

there were "very few large lots of the Erie and Champlain stock" left in the country. "In order to make redemption to any considerable amount during the coming year," the comptroller wrote, "we must look to the foreign market." Before the panic broke, Flagg made no effort to hide the commissioners' eagerness to continue to "buy in" canal stock. The commissioners would buy from anyone, anywhere, and Flagg warned Prime, Ward, and King not to expect to serve the commissioners as their sole purchasing agent in Europe. "Our prices will be known," wrote the comptroller, "and if others offer us stock at those prices, we shall purchase whether procured at home or abroad." [16]

When the Bank of the United States contracted its discounts and panic ensued, the commissioners responded to the changed conditions by reversing their announced policy. Instead of drawing on the banks and buying stock in Europe and America, as Flagg had declared they would, the commissioners abruptly abandoned the purchase of all stock and resumed lending to banks. Even before the full force of the panic was felt, the commissioners were extending loans to banks in Troy, Utica, Palmyra, and elsewhere, indicating that their policy had changed completely in a brief period of six weeks.[17] In February 1834, the comptroller explained the commissioners' policy for the duration of the panic to Nathaniel S. Benton, a banker of Little Falls. "We have in a great measure discontinued the purchase of stock," Flagg declared, "in order to relieve the banks from any drafts at this time." [18]

Flagg, personally, had never been very enthusiastic about the policy of lending to or depositing in banks the revenues of the Canal Fund, and he saw, during these difficult months of 1833–1834, evidence that seemed to corroborate some of his deep-

[16] Flagg to Prime, Ward, and King., 1 Aug 1833, LRC, II, 222–223.

[17] Flagg to J. S. Fenton, 10 Sept. 1833; Flagg to A. B. Johnson, 21 Sept. 1833; George W. Newell to S. K. Stow, 18 Oct. 1833: LRC, II, 259, 267, 279.

[18] Flagg to N. S. Benton, 24 Feb. 1834, LRC, II, 343.

seated misgivings about the wisdom of the Canal Fund's intimate relationship with the banks. He told Benton that some
banks were in difficulty just because they had loans from the
Canal Fund. Such "banks which have them are so extended on
account of having the loans that it would be inconvenient [for
them] to be drawn upon at this time." When Benton urged
the commissioners to grant loans to country banks that had
none in order to enable them to accommodate customers that
they were turning away in great numbers, the comptroller's
reply reflected the commissioners' understanding of the serious
strain on the banks and the dangers that might ensue if any of
the deposits or loans were disturbed. Flagg explained:

We have $2,800,000 in all the banks: of this there is half a million in
New York, about the same in Troy, and $400,000 in Albany—and
the country banks have $1,400,000 or thereabouts. The loans are in
thirty-six banks and pretty well spread over the state. I should be
glad if portions of the loans to some of the country banks were in the
hands of those who had none. But it would be hazardous at this time
to attempt an equalization. We have the interest on the debt, $80,000
or $100,000 to pay on the first of April, and we shall draw upon
Troy and New York for this sum. For the spring repairs, about
$70,000, we are drawing upon the country banks. *In all other re-
spects we desire to let the money remain where the pressure found
it.*[19]

Flagg explained to Silas Wright, former comptroller and his
predecessor in office, what the policy of the commissioners had
been from the worst days of the panic until July, by which time
the Bank of the United States had reversed its policy, expanded
its discounts, and permitted the business community to breathe
freely once more. "We have purchased very little stock since
January . . . and shall not purchase much in these times: The
money-changers, of course, are very sensitive on this point,

[19] *Ibid.* (italics are mine); A. Cutler to I. & J. Townsend, 4 March 1834;
S. C. Jones to I. & J. Townsend, 19 March 1834: Townsend Papers.

and wish us to stop short; we are disposed to keep quiet and favor them as much as we can." [20]

In spite of Flagg's contempt for the "money-changers," he saw many of the issues of the day just as they did. Robert White, cashier of the Bank of the Manhattan Company, heartily endorsed the policy that the commissioners adopted toward the banks during the panic. "Under the present warfare carried on by the bank and its presses and incendiary publications," White declared, the commissioners would do well to avoid "calling on the banks for either *deposits or debts*." [21] This recommendation fully accorded with the accepted policy of the commissioners for the duration of the panic.

The cashier of the Bank of the Manhattan Company and the comptroller agreed that the Bank of the United States abused and oppressed local banks in New York. White called on the national government to aid its "friends," the state banks, by abruptly ending its patronage of the national bank. He explained the financial crisis to Flagg in a letter in July 1833:

Money has become very scarce and no one can satisfactorily account for it. There is no export or demand for specie from abroad. The branch [of the Bank of the United States] here draws specie from the banks weekly. Yesterday the state banks were called on for $200,000 and the same course will be pursued until the administration protect their friends and take the power from their enemy. Let the deposits be withdrawn and they are as harmless and dependent as any little Bank in the country.[22]

Flagg agreed so completely with White that he could not resist the temptation to reinforce the banker's argument with additional data. As he viewed the situation, he saw that businessmen, and especially importers, could pay their large revenues to the federal government only because of the facilities

[20] Flagg to Silas Wright, 14 July 1834, Flagg Papers.
[21] Robert White to Flagg, 22 Feb. 1834, NYHS. (Italics are White's.)
[22] Robert White to Flagg, 6 July 1833, Flagg Papers.

that they derived "for doing so from the state banks." Such revenues amounted annually to about $15,000,000, the comptroller declared, and once paid, they immediately came under the "control and management" of half a dozen men, officials of the Bank of the United States, "who have no feelings or sympathy in common with the men who are called upon to pay this revenue." Flagg judged the "movement . . . in relation to the removal of the deposits on the part of the [national] government" as the quintessence of justice, because the avowed purpose of the "mammoth bank" was "to cripple the local banks and to dry up the very business from which the government derives its revenues." [23]

When Flagg suggested a plan providing for an arrangement whereby the state banks would take over the services that the Bank of the United States had performed for the government since 1816, his plan paralleled closely the ideas entertained by eminent state bankers on the same subject. Flagg urged co-operation among state banks, normally rivals in business, for the purpose of demonstrating that by their joint efforts they could perform all the functions of the Bank of the United States, thereby making the national bank unnecessary and destroying a major argument of supporters of the bank, who contended that the institution was indispensable to the national economy.[24] Thomas Ellicott, of the Union Bank of Maryland in Baltimore, in a letter to George Newbold, president of the Bank of America in New York City, drew the broad outlines of a plan similar to Flagg's. Ellicott wrote:

[23] Flagg to Robert White, 11 Aug. 1833, Flagg Papers. The competition between the branches of the Bank of the United States and the local banks was reflected in the contrasting rates of interest on their loans. The branch banks lent at a maximum interest rate of 6 per cent and thereby incurred the hostility of local Safety Fund banks that were permitted by law to charge 7 per cent. There were branches in New York City, Utica, and Buffalo (B. Hammond, *Banking and Politics*, 392).

[24] Flagg to Robert White, 11 Aug. 1833, Flagg Papers.

It strikes me that the banks in Boston, New York and Philadelphia and Baltimore who receive the public monies ought to confer together and unite in setting a system upon which they can cooperate with each other in realizing the wishes of the Treasury Department . . . to consider how far by uniting together they can become the primary banks of the government for the management of the whole fiscal concerns of the treasury.[25]

Ellicott agreed with Flagg on the desirability for such cooperation among the state banks and agreed, too, that a major objective of his proposal was to "satisfy the public that the Bank of the United States can never be necessary." [26]

Men like George Newbold and Robert White, "anxious to enjoy the golden harvest growing out of the use of the national deposits," could not wait patiently "the death of their great rival for the fruition of their hopes." [27] Thanks to Andrew Jackson they did not have to wait longer than 1 October, after which the federal deposits in their possession mounted rapidly.[28] Such men, however, were embarrassed by the fact that the receipt of the deposits by state banks coincided with the onset of the panic. They felt compelled, therefore, to speak out on the causes of the panic lest it be attributed to the increase of the deposits of the national government in state banks. When they did, they explained the prevailing economic difficulties in much the same way that Flagg and his fellow Commissioners of the

[25] Thomas Ellicott to George Newbold, 15 Oct. 1833, Newbold Papers, NYHS.

[26] Thomas Ellicott to the president or cashier of the Bank of America, 29 Oct. 1833, Newbold Papers.

[27] J. D. Hammond, *History of Political Parties*, II, 434.

[28] At the end of the third quarter, neither bank had any federal funds deposited with it; at the end of the fourth quarter, over $2,000,000 of federal funds were deposited in the Bank of the Manhattan Company and almost $1,500,000 in the Bank of America (Statement of Cash to the Credit of the Treasurer of the United States in the Several Banks, 30 Sept., 31 Dec. 1833, U.S. Cong., *Exec. Docs.*, 23 Cong., 2 Sess., Doc. no. 110, 52–53, 114–115).

Canal Fund had. Newbold maintained that the constant agitation of the removal question by partisans of the bank had created a feeling of uncertainty and a loss of confidence among businessmen and disrupted the course of business activity. The purpose of this agitation, he declared, was to keep the question of the renewal of the charter of the United States bank before the people, and he insisted that "it is one of the principal causes and perhaps the greatest of the present difficulties and embarrassments in the commercial community." Newbold flatly declared that the "money stringency" and the resultant hard times was Biddle's way of forcing on the nation renewal of the charter of the bank, and he had little doubt that Biddle's maneuver would end in failure.[29]

The reasons for condemning the bank were the same for Newbold as they were for Secretary of State John A. Dix or for the comptroller, Azariah C. Flagg. Because Newbold was a Whig and one among many other Whigs in New York who opposed Biddle's policy, it might be expected that the Democrats would have valued the display of bipartisanship and have attacked the bank as a foreign, out-of-state, institution, rather than as one supported by the opposition party.[30] But the temptation to make political capital out of the situation was too great. Comptroller Flagg accused the Whigs of crying up the panic in order to bring about a recharter of the bank. "The federal merchants cry distress to accommodate the aristocracy and get a charter," wrote the comptroller; and like Newbold, he was convinced that the cry was a piece of calculated strategy designed to help them achieve their objective. "They may carry their distress manufacture as far as they please; our folks will bear it until the getters-up of the panic will rue the day they enlisted," continued the comptroller. Then, like the banker, he

---

[29] George Newbold to Thomas Cumming, 17 Jan. 1834, Newbold Papers.

[30] For Newbold's political affiliation, see B. Hammond, *Banking and Politics*, 415–416.

turned his attention to the group that he felt was hit hardest by the panic. "All the men who have done a fair business are easy and safe," he explained, but "for the speculator and monopolist, the times are hard. Although intended for evil, the pressure will have a post-salutary and purifying effect." Among other things, he pointed out, the pressure "is a cure for stock gambling." [31]

At times it appeared as if Secretary Dix could not make up his mind if a pressure and panic existed at all. Acknowledging that a pressure existed seemed to Dix like an admission that the national government had committed a gross error in severing its connection with the Bank of the United States and was responsible, therefore, for the panic that had overtaken the country. Denying that a keen stringency existed in the money market must have seemed like flying in the face of the truth, but Dix discovered that even this argument, with proper qualifications, could be advanced with impunity. Within a period of less than a week, Dix both affirmed and denied that a "pressure" existed; but in both instances, he managed to reach conclusions which bankers like White and Newbold approved and with which his colleague, Comptroller Flagg, could readily agree. When he admitted that a "pressure" existed, he, like Flagg, pointed out that it was "probably confined to those who have been engaged in engrossing something or other . . . dealers in stock, who have been caught with large quantities on their hands, and to engrossers who have extended themselves upon credit." [32] When the secretary of state was taking the opposite view and wrote to Martin Van Buren that "we are under the influence of nothing in the shape of panic or pressure here," he denounced those of the opposition who cried havoc and condemned stock speculators again, as Newbold and Flagg had done.[33]

[31] Flagg to Silas Wright, 14 July 1834, Flagg Papers.
[32] Dix to Silas Wright, 11 Feb. 1834, Flagg Papers.
[33] Dix to Martin Van Buren, 16 Feb. 1834, Flagg Papers.

Dix was willing to recognize that the speculative element could be found in his own party. There is no shortage of evidence that the same element existed in the Whig ranks also. Philip Hone, former mayor of New York, an eminently successful merchant and Whig, made frequent entries in his diary at this time concerning the relationship of the removal of the deposits and the prevailing "pressure." He held that their removal was an "unadvised and arbitrary step of the president," that it "occasioned a collision between the branches of that institution and the state banks . . . producing an awful scarcity of money with immediate distress and melancholy forebodings to the merchants and others who require credit to sustain them." "Stocks have fallen prodigiously," Hone continued. "Money cannot be obtained at 7% on bonds and mortgages. . . . My share of the punishment amounts to $20,000 which I have lost by the fall of stock." [34]

Interestingly enough, Hone viewed the struggle as one that raged between the national bank and the state banks. The ex-mayor of New York City was careful to indicate that Jackson men were not the exclusive supporters of the local banks. Hone referred to "others," presumably Whigs, who like Newbold and the members of the Board of Directors of the Bank of America had sufficient reason to go along with the "whole army of Jackson men" in opposition to the Bank of the United States.[35] Democrats, then, were not the sole beneficiaries of the policies that the commissioners adopted in response to the panic. Whig and Democratic bankers alike had felt the sting of Biddle's whip, and they appreciated help no matter what the source.

[34] Philip Hone, Diary, VII, 288, 340–341, MS, NYHS; Philip Hone, *The Diary of Philip Hone*, ed. by Allan Nevins (New York, 1927), I, 106–107.

[35] *Supra*, 162. Amos Kendall declared that "every director of the Bank of America was a whig and opposed to General Jackson's administration . . . yet the Bank of America was foremost in yielding its support to the proposed measures of the government" (*Autobiography of Amos Kendall* [Boston, 1872], 381).

Along with Democrats, such Whig bankers relished the prospect of the impending demise of the Bank of the United States that the policy of the national administration promised. Jabez Hammond, a temperate and judicious observer of New York politics at the time, maintained that anti-Jackson men held a majority of the stock of the banks of New York but that "nearly all of these citizens either directly or indirectly supported" the President in his firm stand against rechartering the Bank of the United States.[36] A coincidence of interest of this kind meant, too, that a large number of bankers, Whigs and Democrats alike, in New York could approve the determination of the Commissioners of the Canal Fund to assist the banking and business community to ride out the storm that had originated in Philadelphia.

[36] J. D. Hammond, *History of Political Parties*, II, 350. For a brief description of the arrangement which was enacted into law to aid the banks in 1834 on the basis of the credit of the state, but which was never actually resorted to, see Ivor D. Spencer, *The Victor and the Spoils: A Life of William L. Marcy* (Providence, 1959), 80–82.

X

The Great Fire of 1835

THE demand for public aid following the fire of 1835 in New York City scarcely needed justification. The gutted appearance of the city, the suffering, and the enormous losses that were obviously sustained appealed to the charitable instincts of most men. Beyond this, the tradition of state intervention in the economy seemed to assure to the stricken community assistance originating in Albany. Businessmen in New York clamored for help with so much vigor and persistence that the state, the municipal, and the national governments responded with measures designed to restore the favorable conditions of economic development that had prevailed before they were altered so drastically by the fire.

Almost immediately, the administration in Albany considered to what extent the large resources of the Canal Fund could be employed as an instrument of economic recovery. With justice, the administration entertained high hopes that the Canal Fund, by shifting some of its loans and deposits to banks in the city, might contribute considerably to the city's recovery, and it determined to take action along these lines.

The objections to these plans that developed in the Chenango Valley and elsewhere were rooted in local economic considerations that demonstrated the widespread understanding of the Canal Fund's potentialities in furthering economic development. Inhabitants of such areas did not lack sympathy as much as they lacked capital. They undoubtedly approved of aid to the city but balked at a form of aid that could be furnished only at their expense. In response to such objections, the state administration was forced to compromise on its original plan, to curtail the amount of aid that it finally granted to the city, and even to disguise the methods that it employed in diverting some of the Canal Fund's resources into the city.

The fire that swept through the heart of the commercial and mercantile area of the city of New York on the night of 16 December 1835 burned with an awesome ferocity and lit up the skies so brightly that the glow was seen seventy-five miles away in Poughkeepsie. The flames roared through fifty-two acres of the business district, consuming warehouses, stores, offices, and some residences. They drove firemen before them, who surrendered block after block of business and residential buildings to destruction. Volunteer firemen poured into the city from Newark, Brooklyn, Jersey City, Elizabethtown, and Philadelphia and joined forces with New Yorkers who labored through the night into the next day using water and explosives in order to extinguish the flames. Merchants made vain efforts to rescue their goods, but usually with no success. A group of young men struggled to save from destruction the statue of Alexander Hamilton, erected earlier that year in front of the Merchants' Exchange, but they also failed. Almost as a symbol of the hopes of the city's business community, the statue was enveloped by the flames and destroyed.

The destructiveness of the fire recalled the burning of Moscow in 1812 and the Great Fire of London in 1666. The city was left in "one conspicuous heap of smouldering ruin," declared one newspaper, and losses were estimated at between $18,000,000 and $20,000,000. Messages of sympathy poured into the city from points as distant as London and as close as

Brooklyn. A meeting in Albany, called to demonstrate upstate sympathy for the stricken community, was told that the fire would have far-reaching effects on trade, commerce, and business throughout the entire nation. At a similar meeting held in Boston's Faneuil Hall, the fire was described as a "national calamity." [1]

The outcry of the city's officials and businessmen for public relief began even before the smoke had completely cleared and was directed toward the state and national governments. It was an outcry that centered, however, on the plight of the business community, which found itself faced with a sudden, almost incredible change in its prospects. In a matter of months, following the panic, the pace of business in New York had quickened, producing a sense of optimism among businessmen and a feeling of dawning prosperity that promised to multiply opportunities both for individuals and for the community as a whole. But what a change had taken place by 17 December! "What blighted prospects! What disappointed hopes!" commented Philip Hone in his diary. The ruin of merchants and manufacturers, his own losses and those of his son, evoked in this urban aristocrat a sense of esteem for himself and his class. Businessmen were ruined, he felt, because they customarily bore such great responsibilities; far more fortunate were the poor by comparison, for if they "were burned out and exposed to the inclemency of the biting blasts of winter, a good fire, a warm bed, and plenty to eat and drink as temporary relief would make them as well off as before. 'Take nothing from nothing and nothing remains.' " [2]

Relief for business, therefore, as far as leading citizens of the city were concerned, outweighed all other considerations when

[1] Hone, *Diary*, I, 345–355; New York *Commerical Advertiser*, 17, 18 Dec. 1835; NYS, *Ass. Docs.*, 59 Sess., I, Doc. no. 7; New York City, Bd. of Assts., *Docs.*, II, Doc. no. 58, 451–523; U.S. Cong., *House Docs.*, 24 Cong., 2 Sess., Doc. no. 25, 1; Alexander J. Wall, "The Great Fire of 1835," *Quar. Bull. N.-Y. Hist. Soc.*, XX, 3–22.

[2] Hone, Diary, XI, 159–160, MS.

the community turned to the state and the national government for aid. City officials, bankers, brokers, manufacturers, and merchants, who met on 19 December for the purpose of mapping a course of recovery, operated on the basis of this assumption.

None of the leaders of the community who attended the meeting had to be told that immediate action was urgent. They organized themselves rapidly and efficiently into committees and subcommittees, drafting men of stature and recognized leadership from among themselves to present their claims for aid in Washington and Albany. Albert Gallatin and Louis Mc-Lane, both ex-Secretaries of the Treasury who were by this time conspicuous in the business community, along with the merchant and mayor of the city, Cornelius Lawrence, as well as others, were assigned to the committee for soliciting aid in Washington. What these gentlemen were supposed to accomplish in Washington, Philip Hone, ex-Governor Throop, and others were expected to do in Albany.

The business community believed that the state and the national government had both the capacity and responsibility to assist it along the road to recovery. Mayor Lawrence, speaking for the committee seeking aid from Washington, pointed to the large economic power that the national government exercised through its control of the tariff and to the resources of the national treasury as evidence that it had the means at its disposal to ease the burdens of New York's businessmen and especially of its importers. Concentrating on assistance for the city's importers, who customarily posted bonds in lieu of immediate payment of duties, the mayor likened the city to a "suffering debtor" who turned to his more "fortunate creditor," the national government, in his hour of need. Lawrence asked that the government grant importers additional time to pay their duties and recommended, somewhat later, that the Treasury return to importers such duties as had been collected on goods destroyed in the fire. That the "creditor" was indeed fortunate was no secret; it was common knowledge that the national debt had disappeared beneath an avalanche of revenues. Under these circumstances, the mayor seized the opportunity to redefine the nature and purpose of the government of the United States. The national government, Lawrence explained, was "a large capitalist, with an overflowing treasury . . . whose duty it is to promote the welfare and prosperity of the people." [3]

Importers like Moses Taylor were satisfied with the mayor's presentation of their case. "An extension of time is not what is required by our merchants, but what they feel to be due them," Taylor declared, and he insisted that it would be a "mere act of justice" for the Treasury to return duties that merchants had paid on goods destroyed in the fire.[4]

Suggestions for aid by the national government appeared in other, more controversial forms. Congressman C. C. Cambreleng urged that local banks in New York City be permitted to retain deposits of the national government for a minimum period of twelve months in order to allow the banks to expand their accommodations to their customers. In this way, the Congressman proposed to hasten the resumption of normal business activity. Cambreleng's proposal took on a bipartisan cast when Daniel Webster, who was highly esteemed by the Whig merchants of New York City, advanced a suggestion along the same lines.[5] Bipartisan or not, Secretary of the Treasury Woodbury rejected the plan. He called it "prejudicial" to the banking policies of the administration and especially undesirable because it "compromised the dignity and character of a great nation" by advocating the use of treasury funds "for the purpose of either building up or increasing the credit of any institution." [6]

By his suggestion, Cambreleng succeeded momentarily in re-

[3] U.S. Cong., *House Docs.*, 24 Cong., 1 Sess., II, Doc. no. 33, 1–4, 8.
[4] Moses Taylor to Gideon Lee (Congressman), 28 Dec. 1835, Letterbooks, IV, Moses Taylor Papers, NYPL.
[5] *Cong. Globe*, 24 Cong., 1 Sess., III, 54.
[6] New York *Evening Post*, 7 Jan. 1836; Reuben Whitney to George Newbold, 7 Jan. 1836, Newbold Papers.

kindling the old antagonisms involving the Bank of the United States that had smoldered since the Panic of 1834. Supporters of the bank denounced his proposal as a subtle device for "recognizing the legality of the control assumed by the President over the deposits." On the contrary, declared the sympathetic *Journal of Commerce*, Cambreleng was "honestly and generously laboring to serve the city." He was "mixing up his nasty politics" in the urgent matter of relief, retorted Philip Hone in anger. Politics, for the moment, obscured the larger issue. "If party rancor had burned in this fiendish manner either at Albany or Washington, no measure of relief would have been adopted at either place," the *Journal of Commerce* commented.[7]

Despite John C. Calhoun's warning against establishing a precedent that would make the national government the "general insurer for all losses, whether of an agricultural, commercial, or manufacturing community" and against granting to New York City "precedence" over other ports of the Union, Congress passed two acts for the benefit of the city's importers. It authorized the Treasury to remit duties on imports that had been destroyed in the fire, and it extended the period of time in which importers were required to pay their duties.[8]

Just as Mayor Lawrence looked on the national government as an affluent "capitalist" capable of commanding the necessary resources for the promotion of the welfare of the people, so

[7] New York *Evening Post*, 7 Jan. 1836; New York *Journal of Commerce*, 17 Feb. 1836; Hone, Diary, XI, 154, MS.

[8] *Cong. Globe*, 24 Cong., 1 Sess., 98, 102; *U.S. Statutes at large*, 24 Cong., 1 Sess., ch. 42; 25 Cong., 2 Sess., ch. 174. Importers were quick to avail themselves of the assistance which these acts provided. By Dec. 1836, the collector of New York Port recorded that importers had renewed more than a million dollars' worth of bonds. Merchants who had suffered damage in the fire accounted for more than $900,000 of these renewals. The remainder represented renewals by bondholders whom Congressman Graves of Kentucky had sought to deny any government aid at all. These were importers who had suffered no direct injury from the fire and for whom aid could be justified only on the grounds that they could use additional credit to help replenish the total supply of imports in the city. See U.S. Cong., *House Docs.*, 24 Cong., 2 Sess., II, Doc. no. 49, 2.

citizens of Utica were impressed by the "CREATIVE ENERGIES OF THE STATE," which they urged might be effectively employed for the "relief of the suffering citizens of New York City." At a public meeting, these citizens, whose commercial ties with the "great emporium" were many, recommended several measures for state aid to the city. They urged "liberal appropriations to improve [the city's] commercial facilities, the extension and creation of loaning, trust and banking privileges, or a judicious loan of the credit of the State to [the city's] monied institutions and suffering citizens." [9]

Ex-Governor Throop justified proposals of this kind, arguing that they constituted part of a long tradition that reached back to the earliest days of the state. In the past, Throop correctly declared, the legislature had assisted individuals and companies engaged in "laudable enterprises"; in depression years—1786, 1792, 1808—he noted, the state had made direct loans to farmers. Hence, the ex-governor concluded that the state's obligation to aid the city, in keeping with its established traditions, was inescapable. He declared that

if pecuniary embarrassments brought upon the country by an adverse course of business; if inability to conduct to a successful issue individual enterprises tending to the public benefit have been deemed adequate inducement to the legislature to grant the arm of the treasury to their relief; we should not entertain a doubt that the same power will extend similar aid to this city.[10]

Philip Hone, chosen to head the Committee on State Relief, prepared himself for the assignment by touring insurance com-

[9] The capitalized portion appears in the original (NYC, Bd. of Assts., *Docs.*, II, Doc. no. 58, 500–502).

[10] NYC, Bd. of Assts., *Docs.*, II, Doc. no. 53, 408. Apparently, this kind of reasoning was widespread. The New York *Commercial Advertiser* of 19 Jan. 1836 declared that "it is as much the interest and duty of government to extend its succour towards such of its citizens as have been subjected to some great and unparalleled disaster as it is to promote the sciences, advance agriculture, promote manufactures, or protect commerce."

panies and interviewing their officers. Hone's purpose was to establish the true conditions of the companies as far as he possibly could, to determine how and to what extent their assets could be distributed to necessitous businessmen, and, in addition, to ascertain in what manner the companies could be assisted to remain in business and provide the community with sufficient protection so that it could resume its normal business activities in an atmosphere of confidence.

There was no question that the companies had exceeded by far all reasonable limits in issuing insurance, but Hone's committee steered clear of this sensitive subject. On the contrary, when the committee reached Albany, it urged, instead, that the time was ripe to assist the city by assisting the insurance companies. The committee recommended legislation that would facilitate the distribution of the assets of insolvent companies and would authorize the city to borrow so that it could assume the bonds and mortgages in which the companies had invested. It proposed additional legislation that would enable companies to resume business as soon as they acquired new capital; but, fearful that such an arrangement would not provide the city adequately with insurance coverage, the committee also recommended that all laws prohibiting foreign insurance companies from conducting business in the state be repealed.[11]

Governor Marcy, Comptroller Flagg, and Secretary of State John A. Dix convinced Hone and his committee that the administration was "disposed to do everything consistent with its duty for the relief of the sufferers in New York." [12] Hone's judgment of the administration's intentions was confirmed by Governor Marcy's message to the legislature in which he approved all the committee's recommendations except the one that favored lifting prevailing prohibitions against the operations of foreign insurance companies in New York State. The governor

[11] A more detailed account of the committee's recommendations may be found in NYS, *Ass. Docs.*, 59 Sess., I, Doc. no. 3, 5–8.

[12] Hone, Diary, XI, 156–157, MS.

found the committee's reasoning for assisting the companies persuasive; he stressed that businessmen were afflicted with a "peculiar uneasiness" when forced by circumstances to conduct their activities without sufficient insurance coverage, as the committee maintained. Marcy urged, too, as did the committee, the necessity for "an increase of capital or of bank accommodations . . . to enable the commercial community to sustain, in a proper manner, the pressure caused by their heavy losses." [13]

"An excellent paper," Hone, the Whig, declared in describing the message of the governor to the legislature. "There is no shrinking from Responsibility," the ex-merchant asserted; "the measures of relief to be adopted are exactly what they ought to have been." Hone's wholehearted approval is understandable; most of the recommendations that appeared in the governor's message were his own. [14]

The legislature indicated its agreement with the governor's recommendations by enacting them into law. Arrangements for facilitating the distribution of the assets of insolvent companies, for enabling companies to resume business after collecting new capital, and for authorizing the city to borrow in order to assume bonds and mortgages held by the insurance companies quickly received legislative approval. [15]

No contemporary New Yorker would have maintained that the state's "creative energies" had been thoroughly exploited, however, without resorting to the revenues of the Canal Fund.

[13] Lincoln, ed., *Messages*, III, 586.

[14] Hone was author of the "Communication of the New York Committee" as his diary indicates; and the language that the governor used in his message corresponds closely to Hone's original wording. It may be noted, incidentally, that Hone had suffered considerable loss as a stockholder in an insurance company (Hone, Diary, XI, 172–179, 156–157, MS).

[15] NYS, *Laws*, chs. iii, xxiv, 59 Sess. The city of New York was authorized to float a fire loan of $6,000,000. Actually, the city borrowed a little over $1,000,000 and assumed that amount of bonds and mortgages. This transaction, constituting a kind of experiment in municipal banking from the city's point of view, proved to be a profitable one as well as a useful source of relief to the community.

Even Hone probably had the Canal Fund in mind when he recommended to the governor that the "public deposits" be made the basis for expanding the resources of the banks of New York. It is not surprising, therefore, that within a week of the fire the comptroller informed Robert White that the Commissioners of the Canal Fund were in the process of formulating a general policy with respect to the "recent great calamity to the citizens of New York." Flagg declared that the commissioners proposed to "make every arrangement in their power to relieve the city from embarrassment" and would use the credit of the state for expanding the resources of the banks in New York City. The comptroller based his plan on the marketability of the state's canal stock and explained his proposed procedure in his letter to White.

The Commissioners can issue $860,000 of 5% canal stock redeemable in 1845, at a premium of 8% and would deposit the money with banks in New York at 4½% interest payable quarterly if they were bidders, until the same should be required for the Chenango Canal, say 12 to 15 months for the whole. They must, however, as you are aware, advertise two weeks and accept the best offer.[16]

That a bank-conscious generation should have considered relief in terms of increased accommodations by banks is understandable and may scarcely be regarded as an idea originating exclusively with the commissioners. Cambreleng and Webster, for example, had advanced such a proposal based on the surplus revenues of the national treasury; Philip Hone seemed vaguely in agreement that some such means should be tried, and Governor Marcy, in his message to the legislature, acknowledged that much pressure existed for aid of this kind to the city.

The governor's recommendation to the legislature for expanding the accommodations of banks in New York City was essentially an elaboration of the plan that Flagg had outlined in his letter to White. Noting that about $1,000,000 of the surplus revenues of the Canal Fund was already lent to or de-

[16] Flagg to Robert White, 22 Dec. 1835, LRC, III, 287.

posited in banks in the city, Marcy proposed to double this amount by issuing the stock for the Chenango loan in addition to stock already in the possession of the commissioners and lending the proceeds of these loans to the banks. Thereafter, Marcy pointed out, only legislation authorizing the safety-fund banks to regard the canal loans and deposits as "so much increase of capital and to discount on it as such for the time that they may retain the loan" would be necessary to enable the banks to increase their accommodations to the public. The governor estimated that the banks in the city might increase their loans and discounts to the extent of three, four, or possibly five million dollars by means of the plan that he suggested, but he proposed to leave the question of the amount of the increase for the legislature to determine.[17]

Marcy's proposal to divert the revenues of the Chenango canal loan to the banks of New York City was as bold as it was politically dangerous. For years, politics in the Chenango Valley had centered around the proposed canal from Binghamton to Utica; old political allegiances were frequently disregarded as voters, more interested in internal improvements than in partisan loyalty, flocked to the polls to vote for a genuine canal "enthusiast." [18] When, therefore, by 1836, construction of the Chenango Canal was under way but proceeding at a cost that far exceeded the original estimates, it seemed unlikely that residents of the valley would look on quietly as the revenues of the $860,000 Chenango canal loan were diverted to city banks for the purpose of relief.[19]

[17] Lincoln, ed., *Messages*, III, 586–587.

[18] Francis Granger, a Whig, founded his political career in the Chenango Valley on such "enthusiasm" and lured many Democratic votes in this normally Democratic area to his support. When Marcy was gubernatorial candidate of the Democratic ticket in 1833, the Democrats of Chenango County pledged their support to him only after he had committed himself in favor of the canal (J. D. Hammond, *History of Political Parties*, II, 336–337, 416, 422).

[19] Whitford, *History of the Canal System*, I, 683.

It took no special political insight for Governor Marcy to avoid committing so egregious a political error as slighting the Chenango canal interest, and this explains the statement in his message which indicated that his plan could be implemented "without producing any inconvenience to the pecuniary affairs of other parts of the state." [20]

Relief for the city would not impede the progress in constructing the Chenango Canal, according to Marcy's plan, because it provided that revenues from tolls collected on the Erie and Champlain canals were to be used temporarily for the purpose while proceeds of the Chenango loan were diverted to the banks in the city. Would the inhabitants of the Erie canal counties, however, speaking through their representatives in the legislature, relinquish the use of the canal tolls any more readily than residents of the Chenango Valley were prepared to surrender the revenues of their canal loan to the New York banks? Marcy had words of assurance, insufficient as they turned out to be, for these counties also. The city's "embarrassment," he explained, "caused by the disaster will only be temporary," thus suggesting the conclusion that the diversion of the revenues of the Erie and Champlain canal tolls to the Chenango Canal would, therefore, be only temporary also.[21]

There were two reactions to the governor's proposal; both in some measure involved an interpretation of Marcy's concept of "temporariness." The first regarded the immediate financial problem raised by the fire as only incidental to the larger and long-range question of a shortage of capital and credit in the city and the state. The second, which prevailed in the Erie canal counties, was more concerned with the matter of the enlargement of that canal and how the governor's plan would affect this vital interest.

Preston King, Democratic representative in the Assembly from St. Lawrence County, was especially concerned with the

[20] Lincoln, ed., *Messages*, III, 586–587.   [21] *Ibid.*

more general question of the shortage of capital, rather than
with the immediate needs raised by the fire.[22] King, assuming
that the governor's plan would allow the banks to expand their
capital and, hence, their loans for a period of three years, raised
the question concerning the difficulties that would arise at the
close of the three-year period when the banks would be forced
to curtail their accommodations. King thought it was "a dangerous mode of increasing bank capital, authorizing as it did
discounts on money not paid in, but borrowed." He proposed,
instead, that the banks apply to the legislature "in direct form
on direct application" for a permanent increase of capital. There
was danger involved in the governor's proposal, King felt, and
he judged that the plan involved no consideration for the "public
Safety." [23] Luther Bradish, from the same county, although a
Whig, supported the Democratic governor and spoke in answer
to King's objections. Bradish believed that King completely mis-
understood the gravity of the emergency that confronted the
city. He pointed out that the business community had to replace
capital that had been destroyed in the fire, which was a considerable problem in itself. Bradish also observed that the community would be required to maintain business operations
beyond the following 4 March without the services of the
branch bank of the Bank of the United States, whose affairs
would be wound up on that date as a result of the expiration of
the charter of the parent bank. This additional complication,
Bradish maintained, was one that people like King failed to consider with sufficient seriousness in assessing the community's
financial position. Cessation of the branch bank's operations in
the city, Bradish declared, would deprive its merchants and
manufacturers of $7,000,000; "a large amount of banking capital"

[22] New York *Post*, 22 Jan. 1836. Hone had considered the importance
of introducing new capital into the state and had recommended to the
governor that laws "subjecting the property of non-resident mortgagees
to taxation" be repealed in order to do so (NYS, *Ass. Docs.*, 59 Sess.,
I, Doc. no. 3, 5–8).

[23] New York *Post*, 22 Jan. 1836.

would be lost, he noted, "at a moment when the city was least able to bear such a withdrawal." [24]

Assemblyman Cutting, a Democrat from New York City, joined Bradish in his support of the governor, declaring that he favored a temporary increase "of the capacity of existing banks to accommodate the business community" as the governor had suggested, because he believed that this was "the readiest and most efficient mode of alleviating the present suffering conditions of the metropolis." In Cutting's opinion, schemes such as King's, designed to create new capital, or increase old capital, or even incorporate new banks, made no sense under the prevailing circumstances. Cutting declared that such proposals were tantamount to making "additional requisitions for capital" upon a community already suffering from the lack of it. "It would be taking money out of one pocket to put it into another—whereas the very objective of the [governor's proposal] was to procure money 'elsewhere'—from Europe if necessary—and to allow the banks to discount on that money as capital." [25]

The prospect of drawing on the capital resources of Europe, Cutting correctly understood, lay at the heart of the governor's plan and accounted for the part that Marcy ascribed to the Chenango loan in his plan of relief. Notwithstanding the political risks that the use of the canal issue involved in the Chenango Valley or in the Erie canal counties, canal stock, backed by the credit of the state and offered for sale in the foreign market, seemed the surest way of drawing capital into New York City from abroad in order to expand the resources of the banks and to broaden the foundation on which a program of relief for the business community could be built.

The governor's plan, approved by the Assembly, was voted down in the Senate, where legislators from the Erie canal counties were largely responsible for its defeat. One of them, Samuel Edwards of Onondaga County, indicated clearly the dangers

[24] New York *Post*, 18 Jan. 1836.
[25] New York *Journal of Commerce*, 19 Jan. 1836.

inherent in the governor's plan for the area that he represented. If this plan were implemented, Edwards maintained, its immediate effect would be to contract credit and, therefore, restrict business in the Erie and Champlain canal counties. Revenues of the Erie and Champlain Canal Fund could be used to pay for the construction in progress on the Chenango Canal only if they were "withdrawn from the county banks where they are deposited." [26] Residents of Onondaga County were scarcely likely to regard this prospect as a trifling matter; Onondaga was a capital-short county, and Edwards pointed out that his constituents would resent the diminution of banking facilities which would necessarily follow the implementation of the governor's plan.[27] Moreover, Edwards maintained, if tolls collected on the Erie Canal were to pay for construction anywhere, residents of Onondaga County would much prefer that they be used for the enlargement of the Erie Canal. Onondaga County straddled the Erie Canal; through the canal the county's inhabitants sent their salt, gypsum, lime, and agricultural products to market. By 1835, the immense increase of traffic on the canal made the crowding and congestion almost intolerable, particularly on the stretch east of Syracuse, where boats lined up and captains cursed at the delay in passing through the locks. Enlargement, therefore, of the "main line" was as important and vital to inhabitants of Onondaga County as completion of the canal from Binghamton to Utica seemed to residents of the Chenango Valley. Actually, only the previous year, the legislature had recognized the necessity for enlarging the Erie Canal and had provided for it.[28] Use

---

[26] *Daily Albany Argus,* 29 Jan. 1836.

[27] NYS, *Ass. Jour.,* 59 Sess., 190–191; Albany *Weekly Journal,* 29 Jan. 1836; Joshua V. H. Clark, *Onondaga . . . Reminiscences of Earlier and Later Times* (Syracuse, 1849), 61.

[28] NYS, *Laws,* ch. cclxxiv, 58 Sess. There was a widespread belief that prevailed in connection with railroads, projected or under construction and paralleling the canals, that these roads, even if completed, would not alleviate the problem of east-west transportation of freight. See Whitford, *History of the Canal System,* I, 148. The act authorizing the enlargement of the Erie Canal provided that "the cost of constructing,

of the Erie and Champlain canal revenues for any purpose other than the enlargement of the "main line" accounted, therefore, to a large extent for Edwards' opposition to the governor's plan in the legislature.

Onondaga, however, was not alone in objecting to Marcy's proposal; the remaining canal counties were equally concerned with the impact of the governor's plan on the progress of the enlargement of the Erie Canal, and it was generally felt in this area that the resources to pay for the enlargement—the revenue from tolls collected on the Erie and Champlain canals as provided in the act of 1835—had to be jealousy guarded. The Buffalo *Republican and Bulletin* carefully differentiated between residents of the canal counties, who valued the canal as a useful artery of transportation, and people of the rest of the state, who showed a marked tendency to consider the Erie Canal essentially as a money-making device, useful for defraying a large category of expenses in which expenditures for enlargement had no place. An editorial in this paper summed up the point of view of the canal counties about the time when the governor's plan for relieving the city of New York by manipulating the Chenango loan and the Erie canal tolls was under consideration.

The revenue of our canal seems to be regarded as an inexhaustible mine to which resort is to be had on all occasions, no matter how large or how frequent the calls made upon it by the liberality or extravagance of the legislature. If we are not mistaken, a bill passed at the last session authorized an expenditure of $12,000,000 for enlarging the Erie Canal, and which expenditures were to be met by the same revenues which are now to receive the increased burden of defraying all the expenses of the state government. To those who regard the canal as only advantageous insofar as the revenue wrung from it by the most close and miserly policy . . . this may seem wise policy; but to those who look upon it as valuable principally on

completing and maintaining the works . . . shall be paid . . . out of any moneys which may be on hand belonging to the Erie and Champlain Canal Fund" (NYS, *Laws*, ch. cclxxiv, 58 Sess.).

account of the facilities thereby afforded transportation and traffic, the disposition manifested to encumber these revenues to this inordinate extent will be regarded as highly impolitic and reprehensible.[29]

Opposition to the governor's plan in the canal counties nevertheless did not bar completely the use of the revenues of the Canal Fund for purposes of urban relief. The relief act of 1836, which authorized the bankers in the city to borrow for the purposes of expanding their accommodations to their customers, did not specifically exclude the revenues of the Canal Fund as a source of supply. The act authorized banks that borrowed stock from the city or obtained loans "elsewhere" for no less than a period of twelve months, or no longer than two years, "to discount upon the amount so borrowed as capital." [30]

Legal authorization to borrow "elsewhere," a subterfuge no doubt resorted to in order to avoid specific mention of the Canal Fund, was received by the commissioners as a signal that the revenues under their control could be used, legally, for the purpose of relief. Almost immediately the commissioners informed eight banks in the city of their rights under the act and indicated that if the banks consented to pay 5 per cent per annum on loans that the Canal Fund already had made to them the commissioners would then be able to guarantee that the loans would not be called before 1 July 1837.[31]

The Commercial Bank of New York responded immediately to the offer of the commissioners and opened negotiations for a loan that it could use within the provisions of the relief act. These negotiations revealed that at the time of the fire the Canal Fund already had a total of $812,000 distributed among banks in the city in the form of loans that yielded from 4½ per cent to 5 per cent per annum. Noting that the "said sums" were not "loaned for a specific period" and that they were subject to withdrawal "on a notice of sixty days," the commissioners observed

[29] Buffalo *Republican and Bulletin*, 25 March 1836.
[30] NYS, *Laws*, ch. xxi, 59 Sess.
[31] Flagg to John J. Palmer, 12 Feb. 1836, LRC, III, 312.

that these loans did not provide an adequate basis for the expansion of credit that the community required following the fire. It was this condition that the commissioners hoped to rectify by making their revenues available to banks for an extended period under the provisions of the relief act. By consenting to pay the higher interest rate of 5 per cent, the Commercial Bank, along with several others, received new loans or retained old ones on a new basis. Such loans, the commissioners guaranteed, would not be called before 1 July 1837, so that the banks receiving them could expand their accommodations to local citizens whose need for credit had increased as a result of the fire.[32]

In part, the commissioners imposed the higher rate of interest on the banks in order to prevent an outburst of criticism in rural areas comparable to the kind that had already arisen in Onondaga County and elsewhere. City banks that took advantage of the relief act were required to pay the higher interest rate; meanwhile the toll-receiving banks in the country would continue to pay the Canal Fund only 4½ per cent per annum for their deposits. So long as the city banks paid the higher rate to the Canal Fund, the country banks could not legitimately object to the additional privilege that the banks in the city received by way of a guarantee that the loans of the Canal Fund would remain untouched until 1 July 1837; nor could they reasonably object to being drawn on for purposes of paying costs of maintenance, operations, and repairs of the canals.

Even the revenues of the Chenango canal issue, which had figured so largely in Governor Marcy's plan, did not completely escape being pressed into service for the purpose of urban relief. When Flagg informed George Newbold, cashier of the Bank of America, that the commissioners were "willing to issue all the stock they are authorized to issue" and to deposit the proceeds of such loans in the banks, he undoubtedly had the Chenango loan particularly in mind. Flagg informed Newbold that the commissioners would have to draw on the proceeds of the

[32] Misc. Canal Papers, Pkg. 2399, NYSL.

Chenango loan, once deposited in the banks, at a monthly rate varying between $50,000 and $75,000 from March to December 1836 in order to meet the costs of construction of the Chenango Canal. Recourse to the proceeds of the loan for purposes of construction distinctly limited its usefulness as far as the banks and the business community were concerned; but the commissioners volunteered to exercise their customary powers in order to mitigate any hardships that the banks might experience as a result of these monthly withdrawals. They proposed to replace the sums withdrawn by substituting for them revenues from the tolls of the Erie and Champlain canals "as fast" as funds "might be withdrawn from the Chenango Canal." [33]

Outwardly, this arrangement resembled the rejected plan of Governor Marcy; actually, the resemblance was a remote one, since short-term loans from the Erie and Champlain Canal Fund, notably those made after July 1836, would not come within the scope of the relief act and therefore would not constitute a means for expanding bank credit.[34]

The comptroller was certain that $200,000 of the total $860,-000 of the Chenango loan would not be required before 1 July 1837. This being the case, Flagg informed George C. Strong, cashier of the Commercial Bank of New York, of the fact, urging that the sum "would be a loan on which you could bank" should the Bank of New York see fit to outbid all other institutions for the stock. The Bank of New York, apparently, was interested only in a loan of $100,000. It therefore bid "high" for that amount of stock, retained the proceeds of the loan for its own use, and, presumably, "banked" on it as capital according to the provisions of the relief act.[35]

Flagg explained to George Newbold that the commissioners' desire to speed the city's recovery was scarcely a matter of selfless benevolence. The well-being of the citizens of New York was intimately tied to the "finances of the state," and it was for this

[33] Flagg to George Newbold, 8 Feb. 1836, LRC, III, 310.
[34] *Ibid.*   [35] Flagg to Strong, 18 Feb. 1836, LRC, III, 313.

reason that the commissioners pledged themselves to do "the utmost in our power to aid in furnishing facilities for the successful commencement of the spring business, an object alike important to the city and country, and in which the finances of the state are materially concerned." [36]

Neither the commissioners nor the bankers of the city were ever interested in measuring, quantitatively, the extent to which the banks were enabled to expand their credit facilities on the basis of the revenues of the Canal Fund after the fire. Since no pertinent figures were compiled at the time, it becomes extremely difficult to estimate with any accuracy the significance of the Canal Fund as a source of disaster relief. Four banks, definitely known to have received loans from the Canal Fund under the terms of the relief law, were enabled collectively to increase their credit accommodations to the community by $725,000. In addition, the comptroller noted that banks of New York City, to which the Canal Fund had made loans at an interest rate of 5 per cent per annum, "generally acceded" to his proposition that they retain these loans until 1 July 1837.[37] Had all the banks that held Canal Fund loans and deposits at the required interest rate taken advantage of the comptroller's proposal, the total expansion of credit in the city made possible by the relief act and based on the revenues of the Canal Fund would have amounted to $1,433,750. In all probability, the figure never exceeded $1,-300,000.

Following the fire, the commissioners resorted once again to the procedure of halting redemption of stock in order to prevent the banks from being drawn on at a time when it was important for them to retain as much of their resources as possible. This procedure, first employed during the panic, was not instituted abruptly, since the commissioners had begun decreasing the rate of redemption shortly before the fire. At the time, Flagg had informed White, the transfer officer, that the commissioners' reason for doing so reflected their purpose of using more of the

[36] *Ibid.*   [37] NYS, *Ass. Docs.*, 60 Sess., I, Doc. no. 3, 2.

available revenues of the Canal Fund to pay for the enlargement
of the Erie Canal. The comptroller, therefore, instructed the
transfer officer to inform brokers who dealt in stocks and creditors of the Canal Fund that the high premiums which the commissioners had formerly paid for outstanding issues would be
discontinued. The fire, however, brought redemption to a complete standstill, a move that the commissioners deemed essential,
because by this time most of the outstanding certificates of stock
were in the hands of foreigners. To import rather than to export
capital was what the situation demanded. It was for this reason
that Flagg informed White that the "Commissioners are inclined
to discontinue purchases at this time." The reason he offered was
that

more than ¾ of the outstanding stock is held abroad, and the effect
of continuing the purchases must be to withdraw money from New
York at a time when the recent calamity to the citizens of New
York induces the Commissioners to make every arrangement in their
power to relieve the city from embarrassment.[38]

Negotiations between the Merchants Bank and the commissioners for a loan from the Canal Fund demonstrates the determination of the administration to assist the business community
following the fire and indicates how abruptly the commissioners
altered their administrative policies in order to do so. When the
Merchants Bank applied for a loan before the fire, it was supported in its request by T. W. Olcott of Albany, president of the
Mechanics and Farmers Bank of that city, a quiet but powerful
figure in the Democratic party and on intimate terms with the
dominant members of the Regency. Despite Olcott's intervention, the commissioners refused to grant the requested loan, in-
sisting that they were incapable of lending at the time because
they were still "purchasing canal stock rather freely." Apparently, Flagg and his colleagues were determined to maintain this
policy unchanged, despite the formidable political pressure that

[38] Flagg to Robert White, 22 Dec. 1835, LRC, III, 287.

had arisen in favor of altering it. But where Olcott had failed, the fire was almost immediately successful; the commissioners notified the Merchants Bank within a week following the fire that they had reversed their previous decision. "Your intimate connection with the businessmen who have suffered by the recent fire, induces the Commissioners to suppose that a loan at this time would be convenient to your bank," Flagg informed John J. Palmer, the bank's cashier. For the sake of the business community, "in which finances of the state [were] materially concerned," the commissioners now felt justified in offering the Merchants Bank a loan of $100,000 at 5 per cent per annum, which it accepted.[39]

Had the commissioners charted a new course in using the funds at their disposal for relief and reconstruction? Hardly so, since the methods that they used following the fire had been made use of before. Further, just as the methods were familiar, even more familiar were the general policies that justified state action for the purpose of advancing economic development, particularly under conditions of hardship.

[39] Flagg to John J. Palmer, 21 Dec. 1835, LRC, III, 286; NYS, *Ass. Docs.*, II, Doc. no. 78, 4.

Part Four

THE CANAL FUND AND THE

ANGLO-AMERICAN ECONOMY

XI

The Panic of 1837

THE brief enjoyment of a condition of well-being and prosperity that followed New York City's spectacular recovery from the fire ended with the Panic of 1837. The fire had been a local catastrophe, although of proportions great enough so that some of its effects were felt beyond the borders of the state; the Panic of 1837 was indisputably an economic crisis that was national and international in scope. It shook banking houses in England and in the United States; it struck down enterprises, wiped out savings, destroyed the value of produce, and deflated the hopes of thousands. New Yorkers who had an understanding of domestic and foreign trade, of banking, manufacturing, and finance, saw evidences of the approaching economic crisis almost a year in advance. By the spring of 1837, the flight of specie from the country, which was reflected in the fall in specie reserves of banks in New York City, was evidence enough for bankers that difficult times lay ahead. Their first concern was to stem the depletion of their reserves, an achievement which they realized they could not accomplish by themselves. Alarmed, the bankers turned to the state, to the sympathetic administration of William L. Marcy, which appreciated how inextricably the banks were involved with both the public and private sectors of the state's economy. The Regency did not hesitate. The state's canal stock offered a substitute for specie destined for export in the settlement of American debts abroad. This being the case, the state proposed a loan of canal stock to the city banks, a proposal that represented public support of the banks based on the credit of the state and, ultimately, on the credit of the Canal Fund. When it turned out that the state's action had come too late to prevent suspension of specie payments by the banks, the administration maintained a consistent policy by indicating that the banks could depend on it for support for the purpose of facilitating the resumption of specie payments.

Bankers and businessmen who turned to the state for aid recognized that the prosperity of the 1830's was based, in great part, on foreign credit, available largely in England. As long as Englishmen had confidence that American customers and borrowers would be able to pay, as long as American produce—cotton and cereals especially—commanded high prices in the European market, English investors were prepared to lend to Americans. They would cease lending when American imports seemed excessive, when the prices of American exports fell, or when Americans seemed to be doing too much business on too little capital of their own. Then the flow of credit to the United States would cease abruptly, and there would be a demand for the immediate settlement of foreign debts as they fell due. The cost of exchange on England would rise sharply, and, finally, there would be a steady drain on the gold reserve of the New York banks.

By 1836 it had become apparent that American businessmen had overreached themselves. Writing from London in July 1836 to his business associate in New York, Daniel James, American dealer in metals, warned his correspondent that excessive business activities, particularly by Americans, led him to believe that "hard times" were in the offing and that businessmen would be wise "to prepare for a squall." "How all the goods shipped in the last six months and still shipping are to be paid for, I cannot tell," James anxiously commented. Englishmen were alarmed at the extent of American business, he explained; "they think you are all quite wild in America . . . are half-frightened to death and think half of the Americans at least are going to fail." [1]

At home, Henry Remsen, former president of the Bank of the Manhattan Company and speculator in urban real estate, observing the domestic scene, corroborated the judgment that Americans "were apt to do too much business." Americans, Remsen declared, were impatient to accumulate large fortunes as a means of achieving their desired objective of a life of "splendor and idleness." The vast amount of "speculation in lots . . . farms . . . and the expansion of commercial business," Remsen declared, resulted from the single-minded pursuit of wealth on the part of Americans who had no time to consider the ultimate social consequences of their acts. [2]

By the middle of 1836, accommodations to American merchants were rapidly diminishing in England, so that Daniel James, writing to his partner in New York, informed him that because his English bankers had reduced credit on iron and black tin to three months their firm would have to shorten credit also to customers in the United States. [3] When the Bank of England increased its discount rate in September 1836, James warned of the inevitable panic that would follow "the rumors of the bank rejecting the paper of certain American houses." [4]

[1] James to Dodge, 7 July 1836, Phelps Dodge Papers, NYPL.

[2] Henry Remsen to Henry R. Remsen, 2 Jan. 1838, Remsen Papers, NYPL. Businessmen like Moses Taylor felt that foreign lenders anxious for profits were as culpable as American borrowers in stimulating an excess amount of business activity. Taylor singled out the London-American banker, whose "enormous credits" made possible "speculation and overtrading" (Moses Taylor to Wright Sheldon and Co., 8 April 1837, Moses Taylor Papers, V, 176, NYPL).

[3] James continued trading in tin plate, not because he wanted to or because market conditions warranted it but because he feared that if he stopped he would lose out permanently to his competitors (James to Dodge, 1 July 1836, Phelps Dodge Papers).

[4] James to Dodge, 23 Sept. 1836, Phelps Dodge Papers.

The collapse in the English market for American state stocks added to the general alarm.[5] Meanwhile, the changing conditions of Anglo-American trade agitated the financial community in New York City. Bankers feared that the urgent necessity to settle debts abroad would drain their banks of specie because of a rate of exchange that operated unfavorably for Americans. Henry Remsen remarked on this concern of the bankers early in 1837 when he noted that the banks in New York were "discounting sparingly." These institutions, he explained, feared to "lose their specie which will certainly be remitted to England and France if bills on those countries are too high in price." [6] Information concerning the low price of cotton that came from England at this time seemed to confirm the belief that the drain on the specie reserves of New York City's banks would continue.[7] The banks refused discounts even to "responsible merchants" in order to protect their specie reserves. The alternative in an increasingly stringent money market, Remsen pointed out, was for merchants and others to resort to "brokers in Wall Street" for the purpose "of having their notes cashed." [8]

But was this really an alternative? Moses Taylor's experience in applying to outstanding brokerage houses—Prime, Ward, and King, Brown Brothers, Goodhue and Company, Howland and Aspinwall, DeRham and Moore—indicated that it was not. When Taylor badgered the firm of Brown Brothers "for 60 ds. paper *satisfactory* naming at the time their own paper," the firm replied that it would not "sell at any price for even 15 ds. for the U.S. Bank with J. J. Astor to back it as security." He concluded

[5] *Ibid.;* James to Dodge, 15 Oct. 1836, Phelps Dodge Papers.

[6] Henry Remsen to Henry R. Remsen, 21 March 1837, Remsen Papers.

[7] Taylor to Drake and Coit, 5 April 1837, Moses Taylor Papers, V, 172.

[8] Henry Remsen to Henry R. Remsen, 3 April 1837, Remsen Papers. Any increase of discounts, Remsen explained, would result in an increase in the effective demand on banks for specie. This was particularly true because "bills of exchange on England were so high that it would be better for the merchant who wanted to remit, to obtain specie from the banks and remit it, than to buy bills and remit them."

that "by this you can judge the state of affairs with us & the want of confidence in the people." [9]

Remsen's prediction that there would be a demand exerted on the banks for specie for purposes of settling debts owed abroad was well founded. By mid-April, the precipitous fall since the beginning of the year in the total amount of specie that the banks held was regarded as of crisis proportions. Banks were in great danger, said Albert Gallatin, because of the prevailing efforts to settle international debts with specie. "The want of other remittances and the eagerness to export specie in lieu thereof," the banker explained, "renders the danger of a suspension of specie payments far greater than at any former period." [10]

Bankers and businessmen, including Albert Gallatin, Cornelius W. Lawrence, George Newbold, Stephen Allen, James Roosevelt, and others, assembled at the office of the mayor of New York City on 13 April, and after stating that their general objective was to provide "relief to the commercial interests and the productive industry of the community," they turned to the specific problem of protecting the specie reserves of the banks. They proposed to protect the banks' reserves by borrowing the credit of the state in the form of a "6% stock reimbursable in ten years." Actually, this plan involved a substitution of canal stock for bills of exchange, cotton, or other exportable commodities as a means of settling outstanding debts abroad. This stock, the administration could be sure, would be disposed of in a manner that would "secure the state from all hazards of loss" and would be used only for "the payment of foreign balances" or for "the immediate introduction of foreign capital" into New York City. Once the banks received the stock, the businessmen explained, it would "be sold exclusively to . . .

[9] Taylor to John Horstman, 23 March 1837; Taylor to Drake and Coit, 23 March 1837: Moses Taylor Papers, V, 150, 152–153.

[10] Memorandum Communicated to the Governor, 21 April 1837, Gallatin Papers, NYHS.

merchants, dealers, manufacturers and mechanics in actual business, who have remittances to make, or who are directly or indirectly indebted to such as have remittances to make to Europe." [11] The objectives of the plan could not be realized if the stock were bought by "capitalists and companies not indebted in Europe," who might take the stock as a speculation in the hope that it would eventually yield a 5 to 10 per cent premium as other canal issues had yielded in the past.[12]

But even if it were possible to prevent would-be speculators from acquiring some of the stock, there was still no assurance that the arrangement to lend it to the banks would save them from the necessity to suspend specie payments. Even Albert Gallatin was uncertain that the plan would work. He acknowledged that there was in Europe a "temporary want of confidence in American securities," and presumably this included New York canal stock as well.[13] But the harassed bankers saw no alternative and looked on the plan as their last resort in a desperate situation. They communicated this sense of desperation in a memorandum to the governor, in which they embodied the proposals of the meeting and asked the governor's assistance, by special message or otherwise, "to obtain the aid of the state credit."

To prevent this [suspension of specie payments] if practicable should at this moment be the main object in view. Individuals must fail and cannot be sustained. We are crippled and disabled; but we must try to save the ship. Every other consideration should yield to this. . . . People very naturally call for those palliations and that temporary relief . . . through further expansion of an exhausted credit, which if granted would necessarily produce the apprehended catastrophe. It is capital and not credit which is wanted.

The state stock would give that capital; and this is the only reason that can be alleged in justification of the interference of the state. Whether proper in every respect, or practicable is the question. But

[11] Report of a Committee to a Meeting of Citizens, 13 April 1837, Gallatin Papers.

[12] *Ibid.*   [13] *Ibid.*

however decided, that alone and applied so as to prevent the exportation of specie can be of any use. Any other temporary relief, of an internal nature, would, it is feared, only produce mischief and increase the danger.[14]

These conclusions were communicated to Governor Marcy and Comptroller Flagg at the governor's home in Albany on the evening of 21 April by a committee of bankers and merchants headed by Albert Gallatin. The committee noted that the "large foreign commerical debt" exerted a mounting "pressure" on the specie reserves of the banks, and it urged the administration to accept the recommendations for action by the state that were originally advanced at the meeting in New York City a week earlier.[15] The administration made the business community's cause its own. The next day, Flagg discussed the matter with the Commissioners of the Canal Fund, who consented to lend the banks $3,395,000 of canal stock that had been originally issued for the purpose of financing the construction or the extension of the Black River, Genesee Valley, and Chenango canals, lateral canals constituting an enlargement of the Erie canal system.[16]

[14] Memorandum Communicated to the Governor, 21 April 1837, Gallatin Papers.

[15] A. C. Flagg, *A Few Historical Facts Respecting the Establishment and Progress of Banks and the Business of Banking in the State of New York from the Adoption of the Constitution in 1777 to 1854* (New York, 1868), 27; Report of a Committee to a Meeting of Citizens, 13 April 1837.

[16] Only the Chenango Canal, extending from the city of Binghamton along the valley of the Chenango River and intersecting the Erie Canal at Utica, had been built and was in operation, although a considerable movement favoring its connection with the North Branch canal of Pennsylvania was already under way. The other two canals, for which the bulk of the borrowing was authorized, had been agitated for over the years by local supporters but after numerous surveys still remained in the planning stage. Construction of both these canals was finally authorized in 1836, and it was only after June 1837 that work on both of them began. The Genesee Valley canal, it was hoped, would ultimately link the Erie Canal with the Allegheny River at Olean; the Black River Canal was planned to extend from the high falls in the Black River to the Erie Canal at Rome. All three of these canals failed to pay for their construction

The decision to lend the credit of the Canal Fund to the banks was reached in less than twenty-four hours and reflected the sense of urgency that prevailed in the governor's conference and in the meeting of the Commissioners of the Canal Fund. Under the conditions of the loan, the banks would take the whole of the amount of stock issued at par; they would be responsible for paying the interest on the stock as long as they were indebted to the fund for it, and they would "secure the payment of the principal moneys for which said stock is issued as the same may be required . . . to carry on and complete the public works for which these several amounts are authorized to be borrowed." [17] It was proposed to divide the $3,395,000 of canal stock among eight banks in New York City, in proportion to their capital, and each bank would, in turn, sell its certificates to merchants, importers, and manufacturers who were indebted to foreigners.

The usual formalities were followed. Public notice was given that the stock would be issued and that sealed bids were to be submitted and would be opened on 10 May at 4 P.M. The bids of eight banks were received and accepted for the entire issue. Early in the morning of 10 May, however, news reached Albany that the Mechanics Bank of New York, a bank of "the largest Class" and one to which stock had been awarded, would suspend specie payments that day. [18] The news alarmed the commissioners who decided to postpone issuing the stock until they knew "the precise condition" of the banks. The same day Comptroller Flagg and Secretary of State John A. Dix started for New York, "with full authority to issue or withhold the stock as they should

---

costs, repairs, and maintenance and eventually became a heavy burden on the state (Whitford, *History of the Canal System*, 529, 535, 549–550, 693, 696, 711–713, 775).

[17] A. C. Flagg to Albert Gallatin, 22 April, 9 May 1837, Gallatin Papers.

[18] Rough Minutes of the Commissioners of the Canal Fund, 1836–1845, 3 Oct. 1837.

judge expedient, after ascertaining the condition of the banks." [19]
When they arrived on the morning of 11 May, they discovered
that every bank in the city, by mutual consent, had suspended
specie payments. "In this state of things," Flagg declared, "we
did not feel willing to issue the stocks, and the officers of the
banks generally were not disposed to have it issued except in
aid of the resumption of specie payments." The comptroller and
secretary of state intimated to some of the bankers, however,
"that when the banks were ready to resume specie payments, we
should be ready and willing to issue the stock, if it was not otherwise disposed of." [20]

The suspension of specie payments created new problems for
the state. Under the circumstances, how would the state maintain
its own credit? Could it pay the principal of the canal stocks,
due for redemption on 1 July, and the regular quarterly interest
payments, due on the same date, in irredeemable paper? Isaac
Carow, a broker in New York City, raised the question. "In
what medium," Carow asked, did the commissioners propose "to
pay the stockholders of the Erie and Champlain canal stock?" [21]

The commissioners made it clear that they intended to protect the credit of the state. They would, declared Comptroller
Flagg, "pay the stock of 1837 in a manner perfectly acceptable
to the creditors," so that "the holders of the stock could not
call into question the good faith of the state." [22] Albert Gallatin
hailed this decision. He understood that the credit of the state and
the economic welfare of the community were intimately related
to each other and that any aid that the state was prepared to

[19] *Ibid.*

[20] Flagg to J. G. Beers, 15 June 1837, LRC, IV, 126; Rough Minutes
of the Commissioners, 3 Oct. 1837.

[21] Flagg to Isaac Carow, 24 May 1837, LRC, IV, 110; Flagg to Gallatin,
15 June 1837, Gallatin Papers. A total of $1,122,000 of Erie and Champlain
canal stock was scheduled for redemption, and $78,000 in interest pay-
ments.

[22] Flagg to Gallatin, 15 June 1837, Gallatin Papers.

grant to the banks would make that relationship an even closer one. "I am happy to hear that in the general wreck, you intend to sustain the credit of the state and to fulfill its engagements with fidelity," the banker wrote to Flagg.[23] On the basis of the commissioners' decision, Gallatin was inclined to minimize the expected depression in the price of stocks in London once news of the suspension reached England. The depression in the prices of canal stock would be checked and reversed, he said, and "the stocks of New York will rise as soon as it is known that the state preserves its faith inviolate." [24]

When the commissioners realized that the suspension would "furnish a reason for the holders of the stock to decline to receive . . . drafts upon the banks," they were left with the alternative of redeeming stock in "debased currency" and with the added obligation of compensating creditors for the decline in the value of the circulating medium in which they would be paid.[25] For a while the commissioners believed that the banks could be persuaded to make up the difference between the debased currency and specie. Albert Gallatin had led the commissioners into entertaining this mistaken belief. Gallatin, an early and staunch advocate of resumption, was persuaded that, if the Canal Fund were obliged to pay its creditors in specie or its equivalent, then banks indebted to the fund were under a similar obligation to it. Gallatin informed Flagg that his own bank would willingly conform to the specie standard provided that all other banks in the city which had received loans from the Canal Fund would consent to do likewise.[26]

Acting on Gallatin's suggestions, Flagg issued a circular to the banks that held loans or deposits from the Canal Fund and requested them to assume the loss that the state would otherwise have to bear in reimbursing its creditors in the equivalent of

[23] Gallatin to Flagg, 14 June 1837, Gallatin Papers.
[24] Gallatin to Flagg, 24 June 1837, Gallatin Papers.
[25] Flagg to Carow, 24 May 1837, LRC, IV, 110.
[26] Gallatin to Flagg, 14 June 1837, Gallatin Papers.

specie. Flagg informed the banks that the commissioners, if they were to "maintain the credit of the canal stock and preserve the faith of the state," could not resort to ordinary drafts on them because of the suspension and because of "the consequent depression in bank paper." The commissioners could avoid the use of "debased currency" by offering creditors new stock for old "to be estimated at its value in specie"; if the new stock were estimated below par, the holders of the old stock would be paid the difference in specie. For those who would find such an exchange unacceptable, the commissioners would have no other recourse but to draw $110 on the banks in New York City for every $100 in stock in order to "make the payments equal to specie." The commissioners suggested that the 10 per cent loss "ought to be borne by the banks in which public moneys have long since been placed for the payment of the debt which falls due on the first of July." They referred the banks to their annual report of 1833 in order to justify this position and pointed to evidence of the "pecuniary sacrifices" that the Canal Fund had made to reduce the canal debt prior to July 1837, so that the banks would not be called on in 1837 to furnish a large sum that would be "inconvenient" for them to pay. They stressed that the report of 1833 had been made "principally" so that "their remarks [could] reach the institutions interested and prepare them for the events apprehended." [27] What the commissioners wished to emphasize was that they had given the banks adequate warning to prepare for the day when the debt of 1837 would have to be redeemed and, in addition, that the Canal Fund, at its own expense, had paid high premiums in order to ease the situation of the banks on the day when the issues became payable.

In their circular to the banks, the commissioners brought up another question discussed in the earlier report, which indicated how deeply they had considered all aspects of the redemption problem and, too, how they had become involved in the process

[27] NYS, *Ass. Docs.*, 61 Sess., I, Doc. no. 5, 47–51; Gallatin to Flagg, 14 June 1837, Gallatin Papers.

of managing the economy so far as their operations could affect it. In 1833 the commissioners had urged stockholders to redeem their holdings immediately, so that they could reinvest the principal at maximum advantage to themselves. They had pointed out how much more narrow the opportunities for investment would be if all the holders of stock payable in 1837 waited until the date of maturity before they redeemed their stock. They had conjured up a picture of a small army of stockholders trying to reinvest $3,500,000 at the same time and ruining each other's "chance of doing so on satisfactory terms." Their concern with this problem had been motivated by a consideration for the over-all economy. Individuals, they had maintained, were not likely to estimate what the effect of redemption of the entire debt of 1837 on the due date would be

upon the business of the country, so far as these moneys have been employed in furnishing facilities to that business. But with the state, which is receiving an annual revenue of more than a million and a half dollars from tolls, salt duties and auction sales, and the amount of which revenue depends essentially upon a prosperous business throughout the state, the considerations before referred to are entitled to much weight and may be properly taken into account in fixing the rate of premium to be paid for the gradual redemption of the stock.[28]

Flagg's arguments seemed sound enough to a city banker like Gallatin; to a country banker like Alexander B. Johnson, president of the Ontario Branch Bank at Utica, they were specious and downright dangerous. Johnson, in spite of his admiration of Gallatin, was a banker in an overwhelmingly debtor area; Gallatin, although debtor-conscious in relation to the English money market, was creditor-oriented toward the rest of the country. Johnson answered the comptroller's "argumentative" circular by maintaining that the policy of paying premiums by the Commissioners of the Canal Fund had not been the result of their desire to "befriend and benefit the banks"—"on the contrary," the

[28] NYS, *Ass. Docs.*, 61 Sess., I, Doc. no. 5, 50.

reasons for the "sacrifices were such as they ought to have been; they were to benefit the state at large, and not the banks in particular, they were to benefit the whole people, and not a few banks." He supported his argument by quoting the comptroller's assertion that the commissioners were responsible for maintaining prosperity throughout the state, and he noted the comptroller's concern for enlarging the opportunities for reinvestment for holders of canal stock. The comptroller had not acted out of special regard for the banks, said Johnson, and therefore had little claim on the banks for "gratitude" in the form of meeting the expense of making up the difference between paper and specie. On the contrary, Johnson insisted, if gratitude were to be expressed, then the expression should come from the commissioners to the banks:

I allude to the admission of the commissioners that they know of no other equally profitable mode of investing their funds. Nay, if I were disposed to be captious . . . I might say that the mode in which the canal tolls are collected for the banks and the high interest paid by the banks for the use of them (amounting to about $187,000 a year) and the punctuality and safety with which the banks have discharged their fiscal duties to the state, give banks more claims for gratitude on the commissioners of the canal fund than the commissioners have on the banks. And though gratitude to banks has never been awarded, yet if I remember correctly, in some one of the reports of the commissioners of the canal fund the commissioners patriotically exult . . . that the world may be challenged to produce a parallel instance in which an amount of annual revenue equal to that of the canals has for years been collected without loss or expense to the state that collects it "of a single dollar," except of course the salaries of the toll collectors.[29]

What if he insisted on payment in specie of a note or mortgage, as the commissioners did of the banks, Johnson continued to argue, would not the "community . . . be indignant at my extortion?" Yet this was essentially the precedent that the com-

[29] A. B. Johnson to Flagg, 5 July 1837, Flagg Papers.

missioners seemed anxious to set. It was, however, the underlying
assumption on which the commissioners based their argument
that really aroused Johnson's indignation: "Your claim can be
founded on nothing but a tacit understanding that the banks are
culpable in the suspension of specie payments." This was a conclusion that he rejected without qualification. "The culpability
of the banks has, I know, been assumed in all quarters"; and
although he failed to specify where the "culpability," in his
opinion, lay, he noted that "the public are constantly overlooking
their own delinquency and contemplating the delinquency of
the banks." Johnson concluded that there could be no double
standard that applied to the banks and not to other debtors. "So
long as the banks can pay their debts in as good funds as any
other debtors, I have yet to learn wherein banks are more culpable for not paying specie than other debtors." Johnson miti-
gated his assault on the commissioners, and particularly the
comptroller, by indicating an appreciation of past policies of the
state toward the banking institutions. He conceded that a general
opinion prevailed that the commissioners had always been solicitous of the welfare of the banking community, that they
"deemed the banks a branch of the public interest" worthy "in
common with other great branches of industry and capital [of]
the protecting care of the state authorities." [30]

Most of the banking community followed Johnson's lead in
rejecting the proposal that the banks pay the difference between
the price of depreciated paper in circulation and the price of
specie. As a result, there was no alternative but for the Canal
Fund to assume these costs if the credit of the state were to be
protected. Faced with the technical problem of determining
what the Canal Fund would have to pay "in New York City
paper to render the payment equivalent to specie," the commissioners turned to a committee of three bankers, consisting of
Gallatin, George Newbold, president of the Bank of America,
and Robert White, cashier of the Bank of the Manhattan Com-

[30] *Ibid.*

pany. These bankers were also asked to determine the specie value of the 5 per cents and 6 per cents of 1845 and the 5 per cents of 1850 and 1860, which the commissioners proposed to offer to stockholders who consented to accept them in exchange for their issues of 1837. Gallatin, Newbold, and White were ardent advocates of resumption and, therefore, could be expected to be scrupulously careful in their treatment of the creditors of the state.

The minute details of the evaluation of stocks and currency cluttered Gallatin's letters to the comptroller with arithmetical calculations. But more important than these details was the underlying objective that the three bankers sought to achieve. "Our intention," Gallatin informed Flagg after the bankers had reached their decision, "was that the owner of the 1837 stock should receive in London the same amount in gold which he would have received in New York had he been paid for that stock in specie." In the same way, an estimate was agreed on with respect to the evaluation of the stock of 1845, so that "the owner of the 1845 stock may [by selling in London] receive for it as much gold in England as he would have received had it [the principal of the 1845 stock] been paid to him in New York before the suspension of specie payments." Gallatin was satisfied with his own work and that of his colleagues. He observed that if the evaluations showed a slight trace of generosity in favor of the creditors of the Canal Fund, it was a generosity that served to preclude any accusation that the state failed to maintain its credit.[31]

The Commissioners of the Canal Fund were "determined to pay the interest on the canal debt in specie." By this they meant

[31] Gallatin to Flagg, 24 June 1837, Gallatin Papers. The bankers estimated that New York bank paper was exchangeable at $109 for $100 in gold, and they assigned values to the various stocks that were exchangeable for the 1837 issues as follows: 5 per cent stock, redeemable in 1845, was evaluated at 98 per cent of its face value; 5 per cents of 1850, 99 per cent; 5 per cents of 1860, 102 per cent; and 6 per cents of 1845, 104 per cent. See Rough Minutes of the Commissioners, 29 June 1837.

the entire canal debt, that is, the entire outstanding stock amounting to $6,300,000, on which quarterly interest payment was due 1 July 1837 in the amount of about $75,000. Their immediate problem was to acquire this moderate amount of specie—moderate for normal times but large for times when suspension produced hoarding and gave people an exaggerated notion of the value of gold. The banks, whose specie reserves had dwindled so considerably, had to be persuaded to part with even a small portion of their precious holdings. The commissioners, therefore, offered the banks the alternative of being drawn on to the extent of 25 per cent of their canal revenues in paper or 10 per cent in specie. By the second week in June, the comptroller informed A. M. Schermerhorn of the Bank of Monroe in Rochester that the banks in New York City and those along the canals had acceded to the proposition of substituting a payment of 10 per cent of their deposits or loans in specie in lieu of 25 per cent in paper, and he expressed confidence that "others of them will do the same." The comptroller assured Schermerhorn that, should this proposal not yield sufficient specie, the commissioners would draw on the banks with the utmost care so that the sacrifice would be divided as equitably as possible. "The amount of our drafts," the comptroller wrote, "we will endeavor to spread . . . over as large a surface as practicable and lighten the burdens of each bank as far as it can be done consistently with the public arrangements." [32]

The banks had refused to assume the cost of paying for the difference between paper and specie when the commissioners drew on their loans and deposits for the purpose of redeeming the debt of 1837; but apparently this was as far as they felt they could go. "I have issued a *specie circular* upon a small scale," Flagg wrote to Robert White on 20 June. "It ought to produce enough to pay the interest on the debt; about half enough has

[32] Flagg to Schermerhorn, 13 June 1837; Flagg to F. M. Haight *et al.*, 15 June 1837: LRC, IV, 123, 131.

already been promised . . . it is very desirable to pay the interest on the whole debt in specie." [33]

The responses of the banks to the appeal for specie varied. The Wayne County Bank, for example, was in an extremely weakened position; it frankly informed the comptroller that its specie reserve had been "much reduced by the continued payment of small sums"; the bank, therefore, chose to pay $7,600 in bills rather than $3,000 in specie.[34] Levi Beardsley of the Central Valley Bank told the same story of a loss of specie through constant demand for change that threatened to exhaust the specie reserves of his bank if the process continued unhalted. Beardsley indicated his desire to co-operate with the commissioners but hoped that if the commissioners could get the entire amount from other banks, thereby making a contribution from the Central Valley Bank unnecessary, he would be grateful.[35]

By 26 June, Flagg reported that more than $60,000 of the necessary $75,000 had been promised. The following day, Flagg informed H. W. Palmer of the Bank of Whitehall that at least temporarily the credit of the state had been preserved. "The banks of the North have responded to my 'specie circular' with-

[33] Flagg to Robert White, 20 June 1837, LRC, IV, 133. The question of what to do about the state stock lent to the Delaware and Hudson Canal Company arose, too, since the credit of the state stood behind that issue as well. Flagg wrote to President John Wurts of the coal company that he felt that the company was obliged to pay in specie or its equivalent the quarterly interest on the stock lent to the company. "As the faith of the state is pledged for that stock," wrote Flagg, "no discrimination will be made by holders between it and the stock on which the state pays the interest" (Flagg to Wurts, 16 June 1837, LRC, IV, 131). Fortunately for Flagg as well as for the credit of the state, the company proved co-operative, although had it been otherwise, a record of how both the company and the state interpreted their relationship to each other might have emerged as an instructive piece of information for those who study the nature of mixed enterprise (Flagg to White, 20 June 1837, LRC, IV, 135–136).

[34] J. S. Fenton to Flagg, 28 June 1837, GCC.

[35] Beardsley to Flagg, 24 June 1837, GCC.

out exception," wrote the exultant comptroller. "We have $75,000 in motion, which is sufficient to pay the interest on the whole debt in specie." [36]

The comptroller and the Commissioners of the Canal Fund had conducted their campaign for specie shrewdly. They had publicized their demand for specie and revealed in the press the names of the banks that had complied with it. Banks that were weak and refused to furnish specie, therefore, virtually declared their weakness publicly; hence, every effort was made to accommodate the commissioners. When, therefore, the Ogdensburg Bank was not included on a list containing the names of banks that had complied with the comptroller's "little specie circular," which had been published in the *Albany Argus,* the president of the bank, J. H. Judson, complained to the comptroller. Judson was especially annoyed because his bank had actually exceeded the 10 per cent limit requested by the commissioners.

I submit to you whether it is not a matter of justice to this institution that it should be included in the list or else the particulars of the transaction mentioned— I am the more desirous that it should be done as our first August statement showed a diminution of specie to about the amount of the payment, and if not accounted for might create the impression we had sold it— We have it is true an amount made good to this time but we have been at the expense of procuring it.[37]

Thus, the Commissioners of the Canal Fund weathered the storm of the suspension crisis of July 1837, maintaining specie payments for the state when the rest of the state and nation operated on a paper standard and doing so because of their realization that the American economy, nurtured from London, was dependent on this source of credit to maintain the rate of economic development to which it had become accustomed. Bank-

---

[36] Flagg to A. G. Story, 26 June 1837; Flagg to H. W. Palmer, 27 June 1837: LRC, IV, 141, 142.
[37] Judson to Flagg, 25 Sept. 1837, GCC.

ers of New York City, such as Albert Gallatin, Robert White, and George Newbold, stood shoulder to shoulder with the commissioners; they had a stake in the credit of the state, intimately related as it was to private credit in an economy that depended on an influx of capital from abroad.

XII

Support for the Banks

IN April, when the suspension crisis was impending, Governor Marcy had committed his administration to the support of the New York banks by use of the credit of the Canal Fund. After the banks suspended, the officials of the state affirmed that the banks could, nevertheless, depend on the state for assistance in the future. The state's willingness to support the banks is not surprising, for it shared with them a common objective in maintaining specie payments. The state was as dependent on the English money market as were bankers and importers, and the effort that the Commissioners of the Canal Fund made to maintain payments in gold on the interest of its canal stock revealed a sensitivity such as any businessman might show who saw his credit status endangered. "Our object is the same," wrote Albert Gallatin to Comptroller Flagg in October 1837, when he summed up the broad basis of agreement on policy between the state administration and a large segment of New York City's financial community.[1]

For these reasons, the administration in Albany approved and aided the movement for resumption instigated by city bankers

[1] Albert Gallatin to A. C. Flagg, 10 Oct. 1837, Gallatin Papers.

under the leadership of Albert Gallatin. Governor Marcy's administration was resumptionist to the core, and it remained ready to aid resumptionist bankers in any way that it could. Gallatin, George Newbold, and C. H. Lawrence provided the leadership in calling a meeting on 15 August in order to initiate a nation-wide movement for resumption. The bankers who attended approved the proposal that a national bankers' convention be called for the purpose of designating a suitable date for resumption, and these three men were authorized to compose the circular to be sent to bankers in all parts of the country explaining the purpose of the convention. The circular's message to the bankers of the interior noted the involvement of the city banks with bankers and businessmen throughout the country but demonstrated especially a great sensitivity to the implications of the country's subordinate and dependent position in the Anglo-American financial community. News of the fluctuations of the prices of American stocks, bonds, and produce in the London money market arrived with every packet from England and made its deepest impressions on the merchants and bankers of the eastern cities. Such news lost its force as it was communicated inland. This was to be expected, since the condition of the international balance of payments was of more immediate concern to bankers in the large port cities than to those in the interior of the country. Therefore, although the message that the New York committee sent out emphasized the connection between the international balance of payments and the possibility of resumption, it stressed as well the more familiar difficulties that bankers and businessmen experienced all over the country as a result of "a depreciated paper, differing in value in different places and subject to daily fluctuations in the same place." Moral principles, along with the most practical considerations, were advanced by the committee to justify a return to the specie standard. Resumption was a "paramount and most sacred duty," declared the committee. The bankers "had contracted the obligation of redeeming their issues at all times and under any circumstances whatever." [2]

Practical considerations, rather than concepts of morality, were responsible for the tone of exhortation that marked the message. Gallatin and his colleagues pointed out bluntly that what was involved in the suspension was nothing less than a "breach of contract," a paralyzing virus in domestic trade, and an absolutely mortal disease in an underdeveloped economy, which depended for a large portion of its sustenance on imported investment capital. The bankers of New York City were cautious and proposed to make haste slowly so as not to alarm their colleagues in the interior. They mentioned resumption in terms of the future, although they meant the not-too-distant future, since the banks of New York City were required to resume specie payments by law on or before 10 May 1838 or forfeit their charters. With complete honesty, they could say that resumption would have to wait until "a favorable alteration shall occur in the rate of foreign exchanges." [3] As far as the bankers of the interior were concerned, this was comforting news since an early resumption would be likely to spell disaster for them.

The next cotton crop might be helpful in readjusting the balance of payments, the bankers suggested, but this was purely a conjectural matter, on which they hesitated to depend. They were certain, however, that a "general cooperation" among the principal banks of the country would be necessary before specie payments could be resumed, even if a favorable reduction in the rate of exchange took place beforehand.

The meeting of bankers of New York indicated the firm intention of the city's banking community to resume specie payments as quickly as it could. Both George Newbold, president of the Bank of America in New York, and Albert Gallatin, presi-

[2] Circular sent to the Bank of Kentucky and to the Northern Bank of Kentucky by Albert Gallatin, George Newbold, and C. H. Lawrence, 18 Aug. 1837, Gallatin Papers.
[3] *Ibid.*

dent of the National Bank, sent copies of the circular to Comptroller Flagg. Gallatin noted that the circular showed "the incipient steps" that the banks of the city had taken in the direction of resumption, and he explained to the comptroller that, with the co-operation of banks of other states and the general expectation that foreign exchanges would be reduced to true specie par by the end of the year, prospects for resumption would improve. Resumption, the banker pointed out, would also depend on the extent to which the banks reduced their outstanding loans and discounts. "Curtailment," Gallatin explained, was necessary "in order to lessen and raise the value of our circulation . . . and . . . [to] prevent as far as possible a renewal of active business before our foreign debt is paid." Curtailment in itself was not a positive program, as Gallatin recognized; it "will add but little if anything to the active resources of the [city's] banks," which collectively held only about $2,000,000 in specie.[4] The banker judged that the banks would require an additional $3,000,000 in specie before they could resume with safety, and he believed that this could be acquired only by a loan of the state stock. State assistance was basic to the bankers' plan for resumption. "For that purpose and that alone are they wanted," declared the banker, as he pressed for a "positive contract" between the Commissioners of the Canal Fund and the city banks for a loan of canal stocks of the kind that had been agreed upon before the panic had swept the country.[5]

Flagg informed Gallatin that the Commissioners of the Canal Fund approved his suggestions and would "cooperate in carrying them into effect." He explained that the commissioners' initial decision to assist the bankers, and thereby the community, had been made on the assumption "that this measure would essentially aid" the banks in continuing specie payments and that only the importance of preserving a healthy currency justified issuing the canal stock before the money was actually needed for the construction of the public works. For much the same reasons,

[4] *Ibid.*   [5] Gallatin to Flagg, Aug. 1837, Gallatin Papers.

the comptroller emphasized, the commissioners were willing to enter once again into an agreement with the banks comparable to the one that had been abruptly terminated on the previous 10 May. Flagg sought to make sure that the bankers clearly understood the commissioners:

In renewing the negotiation we desire to have it distinctly understood that the restoration of a sound currency and a return of the banks to a redemption of their notes in specie is the paramount object with the commissioners in issuing the stock faster than the funds are required for the prosecution of the public works. The attainment of this great public object is necessary to justify the commissioners in loaning the credit of the people to the banks: and the commissioners are desirous of having such arrangements made as will ensure the application of the stock to the intended object.[6]

The "great public object" which the commissioners hoped to attain and which the bankers believed depended in "a great degree on their obtaining . . . state stocks" transcended traditional considerations of paternalism toward business. These considerations were, indeed, present, as was the commissioners' understanding of the relationship of the state's canal business to the business of its citizens. But an equally important question in the minds of the commissioners was the status of the credit of the Canal Fund in the money market. The Albany Regency may present at this point, the appearance of doctrinaire, hard-money Jacksonians, but in reality, their attitudes toward resumption were conditioned by their dependence on the London money market, where a borrower's status was largely determined by his past history as a debtor. The London money market imposed the specie standard on bankers in New York as well as on politicians in Albany and during the resumption crisis made them natural allies. The need to maintain this standard accounted for Flagg's "specie circular" as well as for Albert Gallatin's leadership in the resumptionist movement.

For twelve weeks, the banker, Albert Gallatin, and the comp-

[6] Flagg to Gallatin, 31 Aug. 1837, Gallatin Papers.

troller, Azariah C. Flagg, worked together on a plan to lend
canal stocks to the banks, and the result of their collaboration
was an arrangement for a loan of $2,230,526.55 of stock to seven
banks in New York City.[7] This loan involved two separate canal
issues that the legislature had authorized during the previous
year for the construction of the Genesee Valley and Black River
canals.[8] To participate in the loan, the banks had to comply with
a set of "Terms and Conditions" that largely represented the
work of Gallatin. One of the most important of these conditions
was designed to prevent speculation in the borrowed stock, a
precaution that was necessary if the objective of the entire
arrangement were not to be defeated. Participating bankers
were reminded: "This loan being made by the Commissioners of
the Canal Fund for the purpose of facilitating an early resumption of specie payments by the banks, it is understood that the
bank is pledged on its part to apply the said stock solely for the
purpose of obtaining specie." [9]

The agreement with the banks protected and satisfied fundamental needs of the Commissioners of the Canal Fund. It provided that the banks would meet the quarterly interest payments
on canal stock in specie, that the principal of the loan would be
repaid in specie, and that the revenues from the loan would be
available when needed for the construction of the Genesee and
Black River canals. The agreement represented a distinct gain
for the Canal Fund from the point of view of assuring the commissioners adequate specie for meeting the quarterly interest payments on canal stock during the period of suspension. Because
the commissioners were so concerned about maintaining interest

[7] The participating banks were the Bank of New York, the Merchants
Bank, the Bank of the Manhattan Company, Union Bank, National Bank,
Bank of the State of New York, and the Bank of America (NYS, *Ass.
Docs.*, 61 Sess., I, Doc. no. 5, 18).

[8] Rough Minutes of the Commissioners, 3 Oct. 1837; NYS, *Ass. Docs.*,
61 Sess., I, Doc. no. 5, 18. The loans provided for an annual interest
rate of 5 per cent.

[9] NYS, *Ass. Docs.*, 61 Sess., I, Doc. no. 5, 18.

payments in specie, Gallatin's draft of the agreement between the banks and the commissioners contained the requirement that the banks repay collectively $80,000 in specie at the beginning of each quarter just so long as specie payments were suspended.[10]

Negotiations for the loan of stock to the banks threatened to continue, however, beyond 1 October, and again the question of the quarterly interest payment due on that date arose. The commissioners felt compelled to enter into an arrangement with the Bank of America that almost wrecked the entire plan for lending state stocks to the banks. By this arrangement, the commissioners agreed to lend to the bank $500,000 in 5 per cent canal stock due in 1860, in return for which the bank pledged itself to furnish the commissioners with about $75,000 in specie on 1 October.[11] Only the commissioners' desire to avoid the harrowing experience of the previous June could explain this arrangement with the Bank of America. News of the agreement threw into an uproar the remaining institutions that had agreed to borrow state stocks. Officials of these banks declared that George Newbold, president of the Bank of America, had obtained a special advantage at their expense; they would receive both 1850 and 1860 stocks, whereas Newbold received the latter kind exclusively. Moreover, Newbold had not pledged to use his stock for the purpose of building up the bank's specie reserve, despite his insistence that he was making every effort to do so after the commissioners turned the stock over to the Bank of America. Campbell White maintained that the agreement with the Bank of America would "entirely defeat the negotiation"; Gallatin declared that the Bank of America was not "entitled to better conditions than the others"; and John J. Palmer of the Merchants Bank told the comptroller flatly that "we are desirous

[10] It was calculated that such payments would be necessary only on 1 Oct. 1837, 1 Jan. 1838, and 1 April 1838, because the banks were required to resume by 10 May 1838 or forfeit their charters.

[11] The sum was eventually $73,193.34, and the medium was defined as "specie or its equivalent" (Rough Minutes of the Commissioners, 3 Oct. 1837; NYS, *Ass. Docs.*, 61 Sess., I, Doc. no. 5, 18).

of being placed on as favorable a footing as any of our neighbors and have no reason to expect otherwise." [12]

Gallatin cautioned against a falling out among the bankers, despite the fact that he did not approve of the arrangement with the Bank of America. There was the larger objective of resumption at stake, he warned, and urged that "we must at all events keep our temper and not quarrel amongst ourselves." [13] Why the Bank of America received the more desirable issue of stock only and why the commissioners neglected to extract a pledge from the bank that it would be used solely to increase its specie reserve were never adequately explained. Certainly, Newbold's political affiliations and those of his directors did not help, although their co-operation with the administration in the past undoubtedly did them no harm. Flagg justified the contract by declaring that $80,000 in specie was "a strong temptation" and, looking forward to 1 October, added, "I do not know well how we can get along without it." [14]

To meet the remaining quarterly interest payments of 1 January and 1 April 1838 prior to the time when resumption became mandatory under the law, the commissioners required the banks that participated in the stock loan to furnish 5 per cent of the principal of the loan in specie on the first day of each quarter. Thus the commissioners solved their immediate problem of obtaining sufficient specie for the quarterly interest payment while the suspension persisted.

The commissioners made as certain as they possibly could that, once the Genesee Valley and Black River canals were under construction, the revenues from stocks lent to the banks would be available. They provided, too, a schedule of repayments in specie or specie funds of the principal of the loan to the banks: the loan would be repaid by 1841 in annual payments of

---

[12] Gallatin to Flagg, 25 Sept. 1837; Campbell P. White to Flagg, 18 Sept. 1837: Flagg Papers; John J. Palmer to Flagg, 6 Oct. 1837, GCC.

[13] Gallatin to Flagg, 19 Sept. 1837, Gallatin Papers.

[14] Flagg to Gallatin, 14 Sept. 1837, Gallatin Papers.

roughly $600,000 a year, unless "the progress of the canals authorized to be constructed . . . shall require a greater expenditure of money in any one of the three years." Should this prove necessary, provisions were made for the commissioners to call for and receive larger sums on the condition that the banks were given preliminary notice.[15] This last provision, Flagg explained, arose out of the fact that the commissioners were primarily responsible for the uninterrupted progress of the state's canal program. As far as the commissioners' official duties were concerned, the arrangement with the banks was a secondary consideration. Flagg explained at length to Gallatin that the commissioners had to

meet the demands growing out of the actual construction of the works. What these demands will be we cannot estimate with accuracy two, three and four years ahead: and we should be justly censurable if we issued the stock long before the money were required for the canals and then loaned it on such terms that it could not be reached when it should actually be required for the prosecution of the public works.[16]

The commissioners were careful to avoid lending the stock to banks of doubtful solvency. For this reason, they refused to include the Mechanics Bank in the stock loan, despite Gallatin's opinion that this bank "of old standing, popular and with a large capital . . . [was] a most important bank to preserve . . . provided they will help themselves and by the sale of the stocks pledged to them, extricate themselves from their difficulties and render your assistance safe to the state and efficient

[15] NYS, *Ass. Docs.*, 61 Sess., I, Doc. no. 5, 18. The draft of the stock agreement, unsigned, undated, in Gallatin's handwriting, is in the Flagg Papers, NYPL. There is ample confirmation that the agreement was drafted by Gallatin in the Gallatin Papers already cited and in Flagg, *A Few Historical Facts Respecting the Establishment and Progress of Banks*, 29.

[16] Flagg to Gallatin, 24 Oct. 1837, Flagg Papers; Flagg to Newbold, 27 Oct. 1837, LRC, IV, 236.

to its object." [17] Gallatin, at the same time, was rather cautious in his recommendation. He advised that the banking commissioners of the state examine the affairs of the Mechanics Bank and, as an afterthought, proposed, too, that all the banks that would receive state stock be examined as well. Flagg and the rest of the Commissioners of the Canal Fund were adamant in their refusal to include the Mechanics Bank in the stock loan despite the favored treatment that the national Democratic administration had accorded it, previously, as a depository of federal funds. In a letter to Charles Stebbins, one of the state's banking commissioners, he declared that

I cannot get over the fact that the Mechanics Bank, one of the original pets, with 2 or 3 millions of public moneys allowed a combination of brokers to control an amount equal to three-quarters of its capital for the purpose of shaving the life blood out of the merchants at the rate of 2, 3, and 4% a month.[18]

The question, however, was not only one of morality as far as Flagg was concerned. He granted the possibility that banks that had already received loans of canal stock might well "have lent themselves to the same practices," but if they had done so, they had neither succeeded in undermining their own credit nor inflicted as much injury on the banking community in general as the Mechanics Bank had done. The commissioners' refusal to lend stock to this bank, whose directors had expected to be included in the state loan from the time that it was first proposed in the early part of the year, brought a sharp protest from its president, J. Lorillard. Lorillard declared that the decision of the commissioners was both unjustified and illogical. He maintained that the "recent misfortunes" of the Mechanics Bank was no reason for the state to deny it the aid that it was willing to grant to others; on the contrary, he insisted that circumstances "would seem to require" that it receive "the special fostering

[17] Gallatin to Flagg, 30 Sept., 11 Oct. 1837, Gallatin Papers.
[18] Flagg to Charles Stebbins, 18 Oct. 1837, LRC, IV, 227.

care of the state." Admitting that the bank was heavily in debt and that its loans were too great, Lorillard asked whether these were not adequate reasons for a loan of stock to the bank, in order to "extract the institution from this state of things without pressing a large and respectable class of borrowers into a state of bankruptcy?" Was it right that in its "time of need" the Mechanics Bank should be "excluded from participating in the paternal favors bestowed on others not more deserving . . . ?" The banker insisted that the duty of the commissioners was to save the bank from "the discredit that appears to be cast upon it" and he assured the commissioners that any aid they granted "will be gratefully received and applied to the promotion of the public good." [19]

In response, Flagg referred to the difficulties in which the bank had become involved under Lorillard's "immediate predecessor," who had committed suicide rather than face the disgrace that the bank's shady operations had brought to his reputation. The "misfortunes" of the bank, Flagg explained, scarcely justified entrusting it with a loan of stock; if they were any "reason to question the perfect security of the bank," the comptroller declared, the commissioners were compelled to withhold the loan. The commissioners had to see to it that "the security of the public money be placed beyond question," Flagg insisted; there was risk enough, he felt, in using canal stock for purposes which the legislature had never contemplated. Pointing out that the commissioners decided to reject Gallatin's expressed desire that the Mechanics Bank be included in the loan of state stock, Flagg, speaking for the commissioners, declared that "we are taking upon ourselves a very high responsibility to loan this stock to the banks three and four years before the money is required for public use; and that if there is any question about the sufficiency of the security the loan ought not to be made in any case." [20]

To Gallatin, whom Flagg respected and admired, Flagg wrote,

[19] J. Lorillard to Flagg, 13 Oct. 1837, Flagg Papers.
[20] Flagg to Lorillard, 26 Oct. 1837, LRC, IV, 235.

nevertheless, in the firmest terms. He asked Gallatin to consider the possibilities of a legislative investigation of the Mechanics Bank and the justifiable criticism that would be directed at the commissioners for "having loaned the state credit to succour an institution which had thus been perverted from the legitimate objects of its creation." The commissioners turned down the pet bank's request on the basis of sound fiscal and public policy. They suspected that the bank would be primarily concerned with using the state loan to strengthen itself rather than to meet the needs of the community. Flagg explained that

in loaning the public stocks to institutions which are in a sound condition and strong in their own resources, we have a reasonable guarantee that the public at large will be benefitted by such an application of the public funds. But where public money is loaned to a bank in a crippled condition, the law of self-preservation controls the application of such sum . . . as is necessary to enable the corporation to bear up against the ill effects of its own managers before any additional facilities are afforded to the business community.[21]

Gallatin did not put up a struggle for the Mechanics Bank. He kept his eye focused on the main issue of resumption, and when assured that the possibility of sudden demands for repayment of the stock loan would be limited to considerations determined only by the rate of construction of the public works, he was content. "I am satisfied with the agreement," the banker wrote to the comptroller on 26 October. "Permit me only to request," he added, "that the agreements may be forwarded [to the banks] without further delay, as we may wish to send part of the stock by next packet to be sold abroad for specie." [22]

[21] Flagg to Gallatin, 6 March 1838, Gallatin Papers.
[22] Gallatin to Flagg, 26 Oct. 1837, Gallatin Papers.

XIII

Banks, Politics, and the
Struggle with Philadelphia

THE determination of the administration of the state and of
some of the leading bankers in New York City to resume specie
payments as early as possible was vigorously resisted by Nicholas
Biddle, president of the United States Bank of Pennsylvania,
successor to the second Bank of the United States. As early as
May 1837, however, Biddle had written like a true resumptionist. "Nothing can save the country but an early return to
specie payments," he had then declared. But this was before his
bank began to fall heavily in debt to state banks.[1] Its indebtedness, moreover, increased markedly just before the convention
of bankers assembled in New York in November for the purpose of setting a date for resumption of specie payments. Biddle
refused to appear at the convention, despite Gallatin's urgings
that he be present. "Your presence is essentially necessary for
the purpose of effecting any practicable arrangement," Gallatin declared. Unless New York received the co-operation of

[1] Walter B. Smith, *Economic Aspects of the Second Bank of the United
States* (Cambridge, Mass., 1953), 199, 202–203.

the banks of other cities, Gallatin pointed out, resumption on the part of New York institutions would be most difficult.

Without the cooperation of the banks of the principal cities, I might say of those of Philadelphia, or rather of the Bank of the United States we cannot otherwise return to specie payments but by our inconvenient reduction of our business and withdrawing of our circulation as would be extremely difficult, inconvenient and distressing.[2]

Biddle shunned the convention; and the convention, taking its cue from the Philadelphia banker, shunned the naming of an early date for resumption. Biddle, obviously, had moved over to an antiresumptionist position, partly because of his bank's extensive ties with the west and south, debtor areas which were opposed to early resumption, and partly because any deflationary policy might wreck the enormous cotton speculation that he was engaged in, the purpose of which was to withhold the crop from the English market until the price rose.[3]

The interests of the United States Bank of Pennsylvania were now in direct opposition to those of the banks of New York City, and it exerted great efforts to delay resumption. Such a marked clash of objectives between the business communities of Philadelphia and New York City could not be hidden for long; by the end of November, the *Times* of London called these differences to the attention of its readers who hitherto had been aware only of the more easily discernible regional differences that distinguished the American north from the south. The *Times* called its readers' attention to the "division of interest and envious distrust" that characterized the relations of the two northern states, Pennsylvania and New York, and explained that it originated in a "clash of local and state interests" that were fundamentally of economic origin. Having surveyed the American press, the *Times* guessed that the differences between the two cities ran deeper than the issue of resumption; inherent

[2] Gallatin to Biddle, 23 Nov. 1837, Gallatin Papers.
[3] Smith, *Economic Aspects*, 207.

in the antiresumptionist policy of the United States Bank of Pennsylvania was a long-standing commercial and business rivalry between the two cities. The bank's immediate objective, said the *Times*, was to control "the money and commercial business of the whole union; to constitute it the arbiter not only of the foreign but of the domestic exchanges; to make it the regulator of prices, whether of cotton or other produce."

But the objectives of the bank were tied in with an even broader master plan that had been drawn up in Philadelphia. This plan would make Philadelphia the financial capital of the nation, whose port, bank, railroad, and canal system, then under construction, was expected to carry it to economic preeminence over New York.

In furthering such a plan, the directors of the United States Bank could lend their assistance with a kind of relish. The opposition of banks in New York to rechartering the second Bank of the United States was still fresh in their memories; the *Times* quoted a Buffalo paper, noting incidentally that at one time there had been a branch of the second national bank in Buffalo, to indicate the fears that the vigorous policy of the offshoot of the old national bank threw into the hearts of some New Yorkers.

Fought out of New York—battled at every turn and corner by New York politicians—we do not wonder that Mr. Biddle should feel an interest in pushing ahead the prosperity of Pennsylvania. Why should he not indeed? He has been told plainly that New York would crush his bank. Can we expect him to consult New York interests? Surely not. He has taken the very course that that state has pointed out. It is using the instrument of a $35,000,000 bank to perfect a system of internal improvement that will set Pennsylvania on the pinnacle of prosperity. He is about driving through without delay her avenue for the western trade that can best compete with the New York avenue.[4]

[4] *Times* (London), 25 Nov. 1837.

To some New Yorkers, the link between the bank in Philadelphia and the large-scale plans for internal improvements in Pennsylvania was real enough. The bill to incorporate the bank had been introduced in the Assembly of Pennsylvania by the chairman of the Committee on Inland Navigation and Internal Improvements; the act of incorporation was entitled, in part, "An Act . . . to continue and extend the improvement of the State by railroads and canals and to charter a State Bank," and the act itself provided that the bank would be required to support specific projects of internal improvements out of its own resources, obviously in part payment for its charter.[5]

If this were not sufficient demonstration that a basic economic rivalry existed between the states of New York and Pennsylvania, in which the "monster" bank played an important part, the *Times* went on to indicate that it had detected much hard feeling among New Yorkers toward Philadelphia, which, through the activities of the bank, had "filched from them the profitable business of exchanges." In addition, the English newspaper declared that New Yorkers looked on Biddle's cotton operation as another form of competition for the buying and selling of staple commodities which normally were handled in New York.[6]

Luther Bradish, soon to be elected lieutenant governor of New York, fully appreciated the interstate rivalry that became more apparent after the onset of the panic. Bradish deplored the renewed "war against the old monster or frightening the timid by pointing to the reappearance of the old ghost." He felt that if the state of New York "roused itself," embraced a "liberal system of internal improvements," and guaranteed itself indefinitely a monopoly of the "golden harvest of the West"

[5] Smith, *Economic Aspects*, 178–179; *Laws of the General Assembly of the Commonwealth of Pennsylvania, Passed at the Session of 1835–36* (Harrisburg, 1836), no. 22.

[6] *Times* (London), 25 Nov. 1837.

New Yorkers would have nothing to fear from competition of the Pennsylvanians.[7]

Bradish's seeming contempt for the "old ghost" was designed to allay the fears that the antiresumptionist policies of the United States Bank of Pennsylvania generated in New York, even among members of the Whig party.[8] The bank and the question of resumption posed perplexing problems for politicians who appreciated their political significance but who turned in vain to the business community for guidance in these matters.

The New York *Commercial Advertiser* noted that even businessmen of New York City were divided in their opinions on the question of the early resumption of specie payments. "One class of importers," this newspaper discovered, "whose affairs" were "snug and manageable" and who had "but a small amount of what is called dry goods paper in the bank and that of unquestioned character," believed that resumption would restore confidence on the part of the business community and that such resumption could be achieved without "a much more rigid contraction by the banks than has already been made." On the other hand, there was the "Pearl Street interest," described as "dry goods merchants—together with some importers." These, the newspaper declared, maintained that "a speedy resumption will but complete the work of general destruction." Then, despairing of a solution, which defied even the business community, the paper concluded: "If then the merchants maintain doctrines and opinions so widely different, how can we, who are mere theorists in these matters, arrive at conclusions that shall always give satisfaction to all?" [9]

Whatever the confusion was that characterized the business community, politicians were faced with the necessity of taking a stand on the issue of assisting the banks to resume specie pay-

[7] Luther Bradish to Silas M. Stilwell, 16 Dec. 1837, Bradish Papers, NYHS.

[8] Thomas P. Govan, *Nicholas Biddle, Nationalist and Public Banker, 1786-1844* (Chicago, 1959), 329-330; *infra*, 241.

[9] New York *Commercial Advertiser*, 28 Nov. 1837.

ments. Once they took such a stand, they defended their positions vigorously and lashed out at their opponents with the kind of energy that they hoped would bring them favorable results at the polls.

If the affairs of the "Pearl Street interest" were not "snug and manageable," how had they got that way, asked Mr. Hunter, a Democrat in the Senate, in the presence of some "Pearl Street" merchants whom he knew were in the Senate chamber that day. Hunter declared that he "would speak out boldly and avow the opinion that too many of that class were speculators—mercantile, it is true, but speculators, nevertheless." Hunter elaborated. He referred to cases of failures where firms "with less capital than $50,000 had liabilities to the amount of $1,100,000. If this is not speculation," he asked, "what is it?" Moreover, he noted that the Pearl Street merchants were visiting Albany in order to petition the legislature to allow the banks to issue post notes payable a year from the date of issue. Speculators like Biddle, Hunter inferred, could be expected to favor "irredeemable paper." The senator "knew of no person now in favor of irredeemable paper who was not a friend of the U.S. Bank." [10]

The proposal to authorize the banks to issue post notes "to purchase on credit specie and convertible paper and public stocks," became the basis of the Whig plan to assist the banks to resume. [11] Democrats denounced this proposal as a sham—in reality, a means of prolonging the suspension—and, moreover, called attention to the fact that the United States Bank of Pennsylvania had issued $4,000,000 in post notes as recently as April 1837, in an effort to avoid a drain on its specie reserve because of its indebtedness to state banks in Pennsylvania and New York. [12] The Whigs were doubly damned for following in the footsteps of Biddle in advocating such authorization and for prolonging the suspension. "A partial suspension" Gallatin called it; go "the whole figure at once" and no "after-clap"

[10] New York *Journal of Commerce*, 21 April 1838. [11] *Ibid.*
[12] Smith, *Economic Aspects*, 192.

urged the New York *Journal of Commerce*.[13] Much of the Whig party's program in the New York Assembly seemed, indeed, as if it were the work of Biddle, who early in April, shortly before the second banking convention, in an open letter to John Quincy Adams had indicated to New Yorkers "with perfect frankness" and in considerable detail, why the Philadelphia banks "do not mean to unite with her [New York] in this forced resumption." The report of a Committee of the Assembly of the State of New York, stating its opposition to Governor Marcy's plan for aid to the banks, seemed like a short summary of this letter.[14]

The committee emphasized that the causes of the suspension were domestic and were largely the result of the fiscal policies of the Jacksonian administration and not the result of wanton curtailment of English credit, as some Democrats claimed. Its report indicated that "the government . . . repudiated the policy of a national bank" and the advantages of the "concert of action" that such an institution provided in enabling the country to resume specie payments "with as little suffering as possible" after the War of 1812. The report declared that the national government had not given any indication that it would "receive in payment the bills of all solvent and specie paying banks in order to sustain them and public confidence in their resumption." The banks in New York, the report noted, had "but too well and anxiously" prepared for resumption, reducing discounts and diminishing the circulation, with results that "have involved our commercial emporium in the deepest distress; arrested enterprise and improvement everywhere; made the wheels

[13] Albert Gallatin, *The Writings of Albert Gallatin*, ed. by Henry Adams (Philadelphia, 1879), II, 525; New York *Journal of Commerce*, 20 April 1838. Apparently Gallatin's attitude toward post notes altered somewhat in a period of less than three weeks. See Gallatin, *Writings*, II, 25.

[14] The New York *Journal of Commerce*, 10 April 1838, published Biddle's entire letter to Adams. For large excerpts of the letter, see Smith, *Economic Aspects*, 205–207.

of our manufactures to stand still . . . and ultimately reaching the farmer have caused his productions and his lands to sink in value."

Biddle had made all these points in his letter and had climaxed his argument with an appropriate plea for leniency to the debtor community which the Whigs in New York now declared had been sacrificed by the banks. Apparently the Committee of the Assembly agreed with Biddle that "the great restorer was time; time to settle; time to adjust accounts; time to send the debtors' crops to market; time to dispose of his property with the least sacrifice; time to bring out his resources to pay his debts." [15] The Whig party in New York, therefore, was officially committed to oppose the administration's drive for early resumption and to continue to block it whenever it could do so with political impunity.

Even as the banking convention met in New York in November 1837 and decided to postpone naming the date for resumption, New York bankers noted that "exchange had fallen below specie par" and the exportation of specie had ceased.[16] The resumptionists exulted, and suspensionists were thrown on the defensive. Partly for this reason, Biddle published his letter warning against "premature resumption" based on a misinterpretation of the low rate of exchange on England. Was this not the result of the "unnatural condition" that the New York banks' measures of curtailment had produced, Biddle asked. By 16 December, the *Times* of London commented on the changed conditions and declared that American stocks, public and private, were coming "into circulation" once again. Exchange now so clearly favored the United States that at the end of February 1838 the Committee on the Resumption of Specie Payments in New York indicated that it was "absolutely cer-

[15] New York *Journal of Commerce*, 10 April 1838.

[16] Gallatin, *Writings*, III, 475; *Report of the Delegates of the Banks of the City of New York to the Bank Convention Held at New York on the 27th of November to 1st of December 1837* (New York, 1837), 3–14.

tain that no exportation of specie can take place, and more than a considerable influx may be expected." Here was the answer, declared the committee, to those who had regarded their "efforts" for an "early resumption premature." [17] The New York *Journal of Commerce* summed up the situation in a sentence: "If the banks but stand still," this newspaper suggested, "resumption will come of itself." [18]

Then why did the resumptionists once again request government aid? Why not "stand still" as the editor of the *Journal of Commerce* proposed?

The "protracted reluctance" of the banks of Pennsylvania to resume and the failure of the Senate of that state to vote affirmatively on a bill requiring the banks to return to the specie standard by mid-May indicated to the bankers of New York City that they would be resuming alone. This seemed true because so many of the nation's financial institutions looked to the great bank in Philadelphia for leadership. Thus isolated, any attempt of the New York banks to resume, bankers thought, more than ever would require substantial assistance from the state. Otherwise they feared that the people would lose confidence in the banks because, in resuming alone, they would be "exposed to specie drafts from states in which banks may still refuse to pay their debts in specie." This danger would limit the extent of the accommodations that the bankers could provide to the community and would necessarily restrict their discounts "to a sum not much exceeding the amount of their capital and surplus." Commercial and business activities would be stifled, and resumption would merely constitute "a payment of former engagements and not a resumption of banking business on its ordinary scale." The bankers declared that their

[17] Report of the Committee on the Resumption of Specie Payments to the Meeting of Officers of the Banks of the City of New York, 28 Feb. 1838, Flagg Papers.
[18] 11 April 1838.

request for further state aid was based more on their concern
for maintaining adequate accommodations for their customers
than for the "safety of the banks." They asked the state once
more to "interpose its credit by the issue of canal stock to be
loaned" to the banks so that they could "continue to accommodate the commercial community and . . . prevent the great
distress" that would result from unilateral resumption.[19]

The bankers believed that the stock, when sold or pledged,
would "shield the banks against the apprehended foreign demand" and would have a great "moral effect" in counteracting
suspensionist pressures that the Philadelphia banks were expected
to exert in the approaching convention of bankers, scheduled
for 11 April. As the time for the convention drew near, both
sides engaged in some plain talk. Biddle issued his letter about
a week before the convention met. Gallatin abandoned cir-
cumlocutions and declared that the United States Bank of
Pennsylvania was at the heart of the antiresumptionist movement. He informed Willis Hall, chairman of the Committee on
Banks in the State Senate, that the question of early resumption
depended on whether the "Philadelphia (and particularly the
U. States Bank) may be induced to agree." [20]

By the first week in April, Gallatin declared that the need
for a loan to the banks depended entirely on the policy of the
United States Bank. "If deemed necessary to specify the con-
tingency on which the stock should be issued," Gallatin wrote,
"I say without hesitation, that it is wanted only in case the
Banks of Philadelphia, or to speak with more precision, the

[19] Gallatin to Gov. William L. Marcy, 20 March 1838, in Gallatin,
Writings, II, 526–529. Henry Adams, editor of Gallatin's *Writings*,
omitted the signatories to the message to the governor. They included
Albert Gallatin, Peter Stagg, George Newbold, Cornelius Heyer, John
J. Palmer, C. W. Lawrence, and F. W. Edmonds. See MS version in
Gallatin Papers.

[20] Gallatin, *Writings*, II, 531–532; Gallatin to Willis Hall, 28 March
1838, Gallatin Papers.

United States Bank of Pennsylvania, should not resume simultaneously or shortly after those of New York." [21]

The resumptionist New York press attacked Biddle in language of unbridled sarcasm. The *Evening Post* declared that "he who is able to pay his debts and will not, is a rogue; he who cannot, is an insolvent." [22] The New York *Journal of Commerce*, seldom in agreement with the *Evening Post*, took the same position. The *Journal* saw that "our mercantile honor abroad" was on the way to being sacrificed. The paper commented that the banks were either able or unable to resume and noted that "but few of them will dare to say that they are unable." Or, it suggested further, could the banks insist that they "were able to pay and yet refuse to pay?" Would this not "serve as a high example to universal dishonesty?" The *Journal* expressed confidence that the state would extend its aid to the banks. "The whole power of the Empire State will be put forth to sustain our banks," it declared, "and through them to sustain the whole line of resumption." [23]

Almost to the very day that the convention met, Gallatin, as the leader of the New York resumptionists, continued to urge key officials in the legislature and in the administration to commit the state to a policy of supporting the banks. He informed Samuel B. Ruggles, Whig chairman of the Ways and Means Committee of the Assembly, that if his committee had decided to act favorably on aid to the banks it would do well to act "at once, in order to produce the desired effect on the convention." "There will be found in that body many timid and undecided men," said Gallatin, "and the knowledge that the great state of New York will sustain and aid the resumption cannot fail to have a powerful influence." [24] Gallatin scrupulously refrained from any reference to Philadelphia and its banks

[21] Gallatin to Jonathan Goodhue, 5 April 1838, Gallatin Papers; Gallatin, *Writings*, II, 535–537.

[22] 11 April 1838.   [23] 11 April 1838.

[24] Gallatin, *Writings*, II, 538–539.

in his communication with the Whig chairman of the Assembly's Banking Committee. In his letter to Governor Marcy, however, this was a point that Gallatin stressed: "The want of cooperation on the part of Philadelphia alone" was the basis of the bankers' request for aid, and the governor's immediate pronouncement that it would be forthcoming was needed to influence the banking convention and to "encourage the timid and decide the wavering." [25]

When delegates from seventeen states and the District of Columbia assembled at the City Hall in New York, there was no delegation from Philadelphia, but there was a message from the president of the United States Bank of Pennsylvania to spearhead the antiresumptionist movement. There was a message, too, from Governor Marcy, the same one that he sent to the legislature, indicating that he approved lending the credit of the state to the banks for the purpose of facilitating the resumption of specie payments. In it, Marcy urged the legislature to support the banks of New York with a second loan of canal stock based on issues that would eventually be required for the enlargement of the Erie Canal and for the completion of the Genesee and Black River canals. The stock would have to be issued in any case, the governor declared, adding that many citizens doubted whether the banks would ever have to rely on this aid at all. Marcy thought, however, that it would be wise to have the stock on hand "if . . . apprehended emergencies arise demanding its use."

The governor did not hesitate to say that the United States Bank of Pennsylvania was the chief source of the difficulties that the New York banks were encountering in their efforts to resume specie payments. He made specific reference to the Philadelphia bank when he urged that the state "sustain [its] institutions against hostile attacks from whatever quarter they may come." Marcy alluded to the fact that the capital of the Philadelphia bank exceeded that of all the banks in New York

[25] *Ibid.*, II, 538.

combined and declared that, when the state of New York resumed, bankers might be reluctant to grant their customers the usual accommodations out of fear of the "monster." To avoid a contraction of loans and discounts upon resumption, the governor advocated the additional loan of state stock to the banks. Such assistance, Marcy held, would "invigorate all branches of industry, call forth the energies of the state, and give an onward movement to its business concerns." Failure to grant such assistance, the governor warned, would result in a situation where

the public will not be essentially relieved; the laboring class will look in vain for their accustomed employment; most kinds of agricultural products will decline in price; our manufacturing establishments cannot be put in successful operation; various branches of mechanical business will be deprived of a wholesome degree of encouragement; trade will continue in its depressed condition; the disorders of the currency will be but partially removed, and the immoral practices which spring from such disorders, will be but partially remedied.

New Yorkers, Marcy declared, looked to the state to "stand forth in its strength, and by the use of its credit, and the sanction of its name . . . shield its institutions and its citizens from harm." [26]

The governor's message was no match for the pressure exerted on the banking convention from Philadelphia. The convention rejected an early resumption as advocated by the New Yorkers and, in effect, endorsed Biddle's thesis that "the great restorer was time." It recommended the relatively distant date of January 1839 for resumption by the banks and thereby administered a major defeat to the banking community and the state administration of New York.[27]

[26] Lincoln, ed., *Messages*, III, 694–705.

[27] *The Financial Register of the United States: Devoted Chiefly to Finance and Currency and to Banking and Commercial Statistics* (Philadelphia, 1838), II, 337–344.

To regard the struggle on the floor of the convention as a clash between "Chestnut Street" and "Wall Street" tends to oversimplify its total meaning and obscures, to some extent, the stake of local politicians and businessmen of the state in it. Clearly, businessmen of New York were divided on the issue of resumption, with not a few Whigs fearful of Biddle's policy and intent on denying the banker their support. Francis Granger, eminent in the higher echelons of the Whig party in New York, was one of these. Granger confided to Thurlow Weed that Biddle was rapidly developing into a political liability as far as Whigs of New York were concerned and described Biddle's letter to the banking convention as a "manifesto of dictation." He accused the Philadelphia banker of "trying to raise the devil" and advised the party faithful to proceed with caution in relation to him and his bank lest Biddle "use up the Whig cause" and make all the party's "victories" account for "nothing." [28] The history of the opposition of businessmen in the Whig party to Biddle and to his great bank reached back to an earlier time when the Bank of the United States had not yet been transformed into the United States Bank of Pennsylvania; Whig politicians, apparently, reflected some of the doubts of these businessmen, at least, behind the scenes.[29]

With regard to their public performance, Whigs in the Assembly had no choice but to join in universal condemnation of Biddle's letter if only to prove that their loyalty to their state was beyond question. Having done so, they felt free to turn their attention to the administration and to assail Governor Marcy for his policies and practices. They denounced Marcy's attack on the bank as being shrewdly designed to divert "the attention of the people from the errors of the national administration to a supposed issue between the banks of this

[28] Granger to Weed, 9 April 1838, Weed Collection, Rush Rhees Library, University of Rochester (photostatic copy, original in Library of Congress).

[29] *Supra*, 162, 168, 210–211.

state and that of the Pennsylvania Bank of the United States."
The proper attitude for New Yorkers toward the Pennsylvania
bank was one of cool indifference, which the governor of the
state had failed to assume:

This legislature knows that institution [the United States Bank of
Pennsylvania] as one created by the state in which it is located, for
the advantage of its own citizens. With it, the people of this state
have no common interest, and they certainly look to it for no favor,
as it would be unworthy of them to regard it with any fear. While
the committee regard as presumptuous and indefensible the suggestion made in a recent publication by the President of that bank
that this Legislature shall depart from its settled policy in regard to
the period fixed for the resumption of specie payments by our own
state banks, and giving notice to the world of the course that he
shall persue [*sic*], if it shall not comply with his suggestion they
cannot view with greater favor the language of jealousy and suspi-
cion contained in the special message of his Excellency [Governor
Marcy] in regard to that publication. They see in both the publication and the message only cause to regret the errors of policy which
have thus fearfully provoked conflicting interests and excited re-
criminations.[30]

The Whigs in the Assembly were opposed to the governor's
plan on another count. They maintained that the six to eight million dollars' worth of stock, along with the stock that had been
issued earlier that year to the banks, would scarcely suffice if
the banks of New York resumed alone and if they had to "redeem not only their own bills, but those of 700 banks of the
whole union." Moreover, they held that the governor's plan
involved a dangerous expansion of the functions of the Commissioners of the Canal Fund, which constituted a danger to the
welfare of the state. The committee regarded Marcy's proposal as "inconsistent with the interests of the state," and they
felt that their approval of the plan would be an improper exercise of "their legislative functions." For did not the plan "de-

[30] NYS, *Ass. Docs.*, 61 Sess., VI, Doc. no. 352, 12–13.

volve upon the Canal Board," consisting of "subordinates and merely administrative officers, so vast and dangerous a delegation of sovereign power, as that of issuing stocks, or pledging the credit of the state at their pleasure, and according to their sense of the importance of any public contingency," that it posed a danger to the state? [31]

Although the Whigs upbraided the governor for not displaying an appropriate remoteness toward the Philadelphia bank, it is not too certain that they were as unconcerned as they pretended to be. They did express the hope that the hostile attitudes, which New York and Pennsylvania had assumed toward each other, would soon be relaxed and took the opportunity to ascribe the conflict that had arisen between the business communities of the two states to the failure of the national government to act in the emergency. It became apparent, however, that the Whigs, too, were uncertain how far the unpredictable Biddle might go, when after rejecting Marcy's plan for aid to the banks they declared that if New York had to resume specie payments alone "without concert with those [banks] of other states and exposed to their hostility" they would then advise the governor to reconvene the legislature for purposes of considering what further steps ought to be taken.[32]

The separate bills that the Senate and the Assembly fashioned for the relief of the banks had little to do with the immediate problem and much to do with the impending election. There was no possibility that a Whig Assembly and a Democratic Senate could agree on a financial issue that found even the business community divided. Hence the Senate sought to embody the spirit of the long war on the second national bank in the sixth clause of the bill that it wrote. This bill, which contained the governor's basic proposal for a loan of stock to the banks, required that any bank seeking to borrow such stock would have to prove in writing, to the satisfaction of the commissioners, that the loan was necessary to sustain the bank

[31] *Ibid.*   [32] *Ibid.*

"against hostile operations of any non-specie paying bank . . . of any other state or country." [33]

The Whigs of the Assembly, who had made their "detached" view of the United States Bank of Pennsylvania well known, felt that this was an intolerable suggestion. They proposed a bill, instead, that bore the appearance, but lacked the substance, of resumption. The bill authorized specie-paying banks to issue post notes up to a stated maximum, for a period of two years, in denominations of not less than $100, with each note payable within twelve months of issue. In addition, the bill provided that the banks of the state could subscribe to canal stock as issued for the construction of internal improvements "and to dispose of and sell such stocks." The Assembly's bill made no provision to lend canal stock to the banks.[34]

The expected stalemate ensued in the legislature and doomed the governor's program for aiding the banks of the state on the basis of its credit. "With shame, mortification and regret," the New York *Journal of Commerce* reported to its readers that the administration's bill had been lost and ascribed the defeat of the bill to politics.[35] Other papers were more searching in their analysis, not so much because they were anxious to ferret out the truth but because they hoped to ferret out some votes in the next election. A great debate ensued between the Albany *Argus*, mouthpiece of the Regency, and the Albany *Evening Journal*, edited by Thurlow Weed, who by this time was well on his way toward manufacturing a Whig governor for the state of New York. The *Argus* cited the claim of the New York *American*, a Whig paper, which declared that Samuel B. Ruggles and John A. King had committed their party to support a measure that would have authorized the banks to subscribe to state stocks. According to the *Argus*, the *American* had described this measure as one that would have aided the banks

[33] Quoted in the Albany *Evening Journal*, 28 April 1838.
[34] NYS, *Ass. Docs.*, 61 Sess., VI, Doc. no. 354, 1–3.
[35] 20 April 1838.

in a manner comparable to the arrangement for aid that had been worked out in October 1837. The governor then turned his back on this agreement, the Whig newspaper claimed, and instead approved the Senate bill that contained the "infamous" sixth clause. Governor Marcy and Comptroller Flagg had violated the bipartisan agreement, claimed the *American*, not Ruggles and King.

The *Argus* set about clarifying certain alleged distortions in the story that the Whig paper had published. It explained that when the "most respectable merchants and businessmen in New York" requested "the interposition of the state to sustain the institutions of the trade and commerce of the state . . . in the crisis of the resumption of specie payments by the banks" they asked for a loan of the state's stocks, not the right of the banks to subscribe to such stock. Essentially, what the bankers sought to "procure" was the "credit of the state" in aid of the banks, and for the purpose of achieving this end, Ruggles and King had reached an agreement with the governor and the comptroller which Ruggles forthwith had published in the columns of the New York *American*. The *Argus* quoted Ruggles' message to the *American*, which summarized Marcy's recommendation to the legislature and which indicated that there would be bipartisan support of this recommendation as soon as it was ascertained "that the Pennsylvania banks will not resume specie payments." Ruggles had declared that

THE GOVERNOR WILL BE FULLY SUSTAINED BY BOTH PARTIES IN BOTH HOUSES . . . the stock is to be loaned to the banks until the avails shall be wanted from time to time to prosecute the public works.

The friends of an honest resumption may rest assured that the Governor and his party are fully determined to do their duty—of course, the Whigs will do theirs.

What had altered this forthright commitment of the two leading Whigs? The *Argus* maintained that Ruggles' bipartisanship was enunciated when Biddle's "influence had not extensively pervaded the Assembly," despite the fact that the banker's position on resumption had been known. Soon after, Marcy's program had "alarmed the money autocrat"; Biddle issued his "manifesto," and gone was the "patriotism . . . of the Whig members of the Assembly," who "ranged themselves under the banner of the Irredeemable paper party." The *Argus* embellished its account by describing the anguish of Ruggles and King as they repudiated their earlier agreement for the sake of party harmony; they "yielded with reluctance, and after a painful struggle," and abandoned the measures of relief that "the merchants and businessmen of New York had requested of the legislature." [36]

The *Argus* marshaled journalistic opinion from various parts of the state to indicate the widespread support that could be found among newspapers for the administration's policy on resumption. It published the most pertinent extracts of a dozen papers in one issue, which together constituted the Democratic attack on the Whig policy in connection with state aid to the banks. The *Orange County Independent Republican* reflected on the "astonishment" that "capitalists of England" would show when they learned that the small banks of New York had resumed and "the regulator of the currency," the United States Bank of Pennsylvania, remained "the great head of irredeemable paper issues." The *Westchester Spy* condemned post notes as an extension of suspension and advocated the loan of canal stock "required for the completion of the public works of the state" to the banks to enable them to resume despite the position of Biddle. The *Ulster Republican* challenged the Whigs to "tear off their veil of duplicity," declare their "yearnings for a national bank . . . and confess" their willingness to "prostrate commerce, annihilate trade and sink the country in misery in order to achieve their objective." By contrast, the Plattsburg *Republican* saluted the governor for "throwing" the "shield of public credit" in front of the banking institutions of the state

[36] *Daily Albany Argus*, 25 April 1838.

in order to protect "our altars and our firesides against the threatened attack of foreign institutions." [37]

The Albany *Evening Journal* employed the same technique as the *Argus* and culled excerpts from Whig papers that presented most vigorously the Whig point of view. The *Journal* cited the Poughkeepsie *Eagle's* call for a "political revolution"; it echoed the *Eagle's* exhortations for preparations for the "November election" which "would permit New Yorkers to seek redress through the ballot boxes." The *Journal* reprinted the *Eagle's* article in which the Poughkeepsie paper upheld its party's post-note policy, approved authorization of the banks to subscribe to state stocks, and condemned "the demon spirit of loco-focoism" responsible for the Senate's bill that required would-be borrowing banks to testify to their own unstable conditions. After a bank "has established its insolvency," the Poughkeepsie *Eagle* declared, "it may receive a *little aid* provided the Commissioners of the Canal Fund, alias the Albany Regency see fit to grant it." Would any bank, "not rotten and worthless . . . take a dollar of state stocks upon the degrading conditions here offered . . . ?" Obviously, the proposal to aid the banks that the Senate advanced was, according to the Whigs, pure sham.[38] The *Long Island Star*, apologizing for the obvious pun, declared that the governor and the Senate wanted to "put our state *in the stocks*—in humiliation and in tribulation when the people were looking for relief."

The *Journal* presented its own version of the story of how the plan for bipartisan action on resumption had broken down. Ruggles and King had conferred with Governor Marcy and Comptroller Flagg, it conceded, and the Whigs had acted in their customary spirit of "frankness and magnanimity"; the Democrats, on the other hand, had resorted to their usual "craft and selfishness." Apparently, the *Journal* sought to have its readers conclude that it was impossible to reach a working

[37] *Ibid.*, 15 May 1838.
[38] Albany *Evening Journal*, 25 April 1838.

agreement with Democrats because they operated on such a low ethical level.

Like the Whigs in the Assembly, the *Journal* concentrated on the vast amount of power that the Senate bill proposed to vest in the Commissioners of the Canal Fund and the requirement that banks present evidence of hostile activities by an out-of-state bank, before they would be eligible for aid. The Senate bill, "so corrupting in design," was clearly what was to be expected of a "Van Buren Bank Committee in the Senate." Could Governor Marcy have expected Ruggles and King to support such a bill? "Could any man other than the collared minions of Van Buren, thus prostitute his vote?" Moreover, a close examination of the Senate bill revealed that the distribution of stock would be vested in the commissioners who would be free to place their own value on them. "Were all the banks . . . to receive a portion of . . . stocks? By no means," declared the *Journal*, and for perfectly good reason.

The party would have made nothing out of such an operation. That would have been too fair and equitable. The Commissioners were authorized to "distribute" the stocks among the applicant banks "*in such manner and at such prices*" as they deemed proper! The people of this state are familiar with the Regency mode of distributing stock.[39]

The newspaper war, essentially a war for votes, tended to obscure the economic facts that would hurry the New York banks back to the specie standard. Even before the second banking convention assembled on 11 April, the New York *Journal of Commerce* declared that the conditions of international exchange had altered to such an extent that the country was already beginning to receive specie from abroad. Quoting the Albany *Evening Journal*, the *Journal of Commerce* pointed out that "specie is flowing into the country so profusely that all sound banks have it in their power to redeem their promises

[39] *Ibid.*

to the people"; needless to say, this paper declared that such banks "should be required to do so." [40] The same paper, while commending the governor for his "honorable" message that urged assistance to the banks, reassessed its significance by 13 April and declared that the message's importance was based on its usefulness in lifting public morale. The banks, the *Journal of Commerce* declared, would never need the assistance that the governor asked for, but the message was useful "in quieting the misgivings of the timid." "Resumption," however, the paper declared, "will come of itself and under the guidance of laws of higher authority and more resistless force than any acts of the legislature." [41]

Less than a week later, the brokerage house of Prime, Ward, and King corroborated the judgment of the newspaper. "For the information of the banking convention," the firm informed Gallatin that the Bank of England had decided to send a large amount of " £'s in specie" to the United States and that £100,-000 had already reached New York. [42] The following day, the *Journal of Commerce* reported the arrival of almost $1,500,000 in specie from England and France, entitling the article with the eye-catching phrase, "Specie by Wholesale." But the million and a half represented "a mere pittance compared with what is yet to come," declared the *Journal*. The Bank of England, through the agency of Baring Brothers, had decided to send £1,000,000 in specie, the paper went on to say. [43]

The laws of higher authority that the *Journal* had referred to involved, in part, the stake that English manufacturers, bankers, and exporters had in Anglo-American trade, a stake which was, of course, considerable. The United States was England's best customer, and it was to this country that many Englishmen had looked, and would continue to look for many more years, as an

---

[40] New York *Journal of Commerce*, 11 April 1838.
[41] *Ibid.*, 13 April 1838.
[42] Prime, Ward, and King to Gallatin, 16 April 1838, Gallatin Papers.
[43] New York *Journal of Commerce*, 17 April 1838.

area of potential investment. The catastrophe of 1837 made the outlook seem dismal for Englishmen involved directly or indirectly in Anglo-American trade. The *Times* of London pointed out that Americans would be required, for several years, to diminish the debts that they owed to foreigners. This would mean that they would have to export their produce, mostly cotton, and to realize good prices for the crops during 1838 and 1839. Meanwhile, they would be required to practice a kind of austerity and avoid importation of English manufactures "beyond the actual wants of the country." This, indeed, posed gloomy prospects for the English manufacturer and exporter. Although such austerity might well solve the problems of the United States as a debtor nation, the *Times* commented, if the plan succeeded it would be "a very bad omen for the manufacturing interest of England." [44]

Export of specie from England to the United States was expected to solve the immediate problem of resumption as a preliminary to restoring Anglo-American trade to a more normal condition. The house of Baring that shipped the gold declared that the influx of specie would enable the banks of New York "to resume specie payments and to maintain them." It would provide the incentive for banks of other seaport towns to follow the example of the New Yorkers, so that the immediate effect would be to "place the trade upon a securer footing . . . restore confidence . . . and diminish the pressure which the fears of the banks and their consequent reductions of issues must produce." James Gore King, of Prime, Ward, and King, judged that the gold could not have arrived at a more propitious time, in view of the violence of Biddle's assault on the resumptionist movement as embodied in his letter to Adams. According to King, the purpose of Biddle's letter was to undermine the movement for resumption for which "the labors of the Best Heads in New York and Boston had been exerted." [45]

[44] *Times* (London), 12 April 1838.
[45] Ralph W. Hidy, *The House of Baring in American Trade and Fi-*

William S. Cruft, a businessman from Boston, who was in England in 1838, assessed the English interest in American resumption and related it to Anglo-American trade. The "deranged trade" in the United States had contributed to the depressed condition of the "manufacturing districts" in England, which he described as being "in a state of paralysis." Cruft believed that this condition would continue until the American banks resumed specie payments.[46] Cruft's analysis was supported two years later by two directors of the Bank of England, John Horsley Palmer and George Warde Norman. At that time, Palmer and Norman testified before an investigatory committee of Parliament on the specific question of the export of bullion to the United States in 1838. Palmer held that this export was a profitable undertaking, coming at a time when exchange had fallen in England and American imports had almost ceased. But aside from the matter of profit, he stressed the desirable effect that the move had in hastening the resumption of specie payments in America. Resumption, the witness held, was an antecedent step to recovery in the American import trade, which, he avowed, was a matter of great interest to English manufacturers. When Palmer was specifically asked if the purpose of exporting specie to America was to revive Anglo-American trade, he categorically affirmed that it was so.

Further testimony offered by George Warde Norman confirmed much that Palmer had asserted. In addition, however, Norman indicated that the decision to send gold to America had been reached as a result of representations made to the Bank of England which emphasized the great benefits likely to accrue to English commercial interests from a restoration of credit in America. Norman explained that Americans had incurred a

---

nance (Cambridge, Mass., 1949), 244. Purchasers of this specie included the Mechanics Bank of New York, the Merchants Bank of Boston, and the United States Bank of Pennsylvania; some of it was invested in Ohio 6 per cent bonds. With regard to the remainder, see *ibid.*, 245.

[46] William S. Cruft to George Newbold, 16 May 1838, Newbold Papers; *Times* (London), 14 March 1838.

large indebtedness to the Bank of England as a result of advances made by that institution to American houses in England. The restoration of American credit was expected to revive the languishing Anglo-American trade and also to hasten the repayment of "large sums" owed by Americans to English creditors, among whom the Bank of England was, admittedly, one of considerable importance.[47] Norman pointed out that many American houses had frozen assets that could be thawed by means of English assistance. Fortunately, the Bank of England was particularly well situated to act at this time. It had an "abundant stock of gold available," as Norman indicated, and this was undoubtedly the most important single factor that led it to invest in a project the purpose of which was to stimulate American economic recovery.[48]

The testimony of Palmer and Norman suggests that the Bank of England played a major part in enabling the New York state banks to resume specie payments. This is an exaggeration.[49] The state's loan of stocks to the banks had, indeed, augmented their specie reserves.[50] Most important, however, is the fact that the economic picture had brightened considerably by late November and early December before the Bank of England acted.[51]

The motives of the Whigs in opposing a second loan of canal stock to the banks were mixed. The political factor was clearly present. Any positive action that the administration took, particularly at a time when conditions were improving, represented a potential claim on the vote of the electorate which the Whigs as a party sought to avoid. Whig opposition to a second loan no doubt reflected some of the sentiment of

---

[47] New York *Journal of Commerce*, 25 Oct. 1837. "A large amount of the protested bills on the Anglo-American houses came into the possession of the bank so that the institution is to a very great extent, the creditor of our merchants."

[48] Great Britain, Parliament, *Sessional Papers*, vol. IV for 1840: *Report from Select Committee on Banks of Issue*, 1325–1333, 1855–1865.

[49] Redlich, *Molding of American Banking*, pt. II, 67.

[50] Gallatin, *Writings*, III, 400.   [51] *Supra*, 248–249.

the debtor element in the state, particularly that of the debtor businessman of the "Pearl Street" type. Unquestionably, some of the Whigs believed, too, that the improvement in economic conditions already apparent in the spring of 1838 would take place soon enough without further interference of the state, whereas any attempt that the administration made to hasten the process would only cause greater hardship. Such Whigs, naturally, would favor a "gradualist" policy as did Biddle in the matter of resumption.

Whatever the explanation of the Whig opposition to a second loan of canal stock, it scarcely involved a rejection of the state as a force in the economy. Victory for the Whigs in the election of 1838 brought to office far more ardent advocates of state enterprise and intervention than the Democrats ever produced—men who had great plans for accelerating economic development through the agency of the state. These men minimized the difficulties attached to financing or subsidizing further construction of canals and railroads and emphasized the importance of the state's assuming leadership in and responsibility for this basic form of economic development on which so much else depended.

Foremost among these men was the new governor, William H. Seward, who viewed the state as a useful and insufficiently employed instrument of economic development. Time dealt harshly with Seward and with his plans. By the time his administration ended, he had earned the sobriquet of "$40,000,000 debt Seward" and had unwittingly furnished a variety of reasons for reducing the role of the state in the economy to a large group of citizens who were becoming increasingly receptive to this line of thought.

Part Five

CONCLUSION

XIV

The Enterprise of a Free People

OPTIMISM, ambition, and the expectation of economic growth characterized New Yorkers at the beginning of the nineteenth century. The endowments of nature suggested a variety of opportunities that awaited men with sufficient enterprise and imagination to take advantage of them. There was no shortage of men of this kind in New York, where human resources were impressive and where enterprise meant a host of skills and occupations available for productive use.

Worldly bankers, brokers, and real-estate operators exemplified the business spirit that pervaded the "great emporium" at the mouth of the Hudson River. Wall Street, after the War of 1812, was already a famous urban artery and a recognized symbol of business. It was a place where informed men bought and sold stocks, discussed the condition of the money market, exchanged information regarding the price of cotton at Liverpool, argued the merits of insurance, and indicated a keen analytical grasp of problems of borrowing, lending, and investment. Here could be found businessmen who showed rigorous self-discipline, who preached saving as a virtue, and who urged this virtue on others by stressing the necessity of thrift and by encouraging the savings bank movement.

The spirit and standards of the marketplace penetrated the hinterlands, along the rivers, roads, and lanes of rural New York. The frontier of commercial agriculture advanced so steadily that Peter B. Porter, land speculator and future investor in turnpikes and railroads, as early as 1810 regarded subsistence farming on the Niagara frontier as a thing of the past. The greatest need of western farmers, Porter urged, was "a vent for their productions," a need that explained Porter's early enthusiasm for a canal between the Hudson River and Lake Erie and his service as a canal commissioner in New York.

Economic traditions inherited from the colonial period that were mercantilistic in character served the requirements of a developing economy. Enterprising men were accustomed to function within the framework of these traditions and to pursue their objectives under the protection and regulation, and often with the assistance, of the state. The public works program that the state inaugurated in 1817 represented, therefore, an enlargement rather than a departure from its customary activities. Improved transportation facilities, so essential to further economic growth, so expensive, and in such demand by citizens seemed far beyond the capacities of individuals and corporations, as the experience of the Western Inland Lock Navigation Company proved. State action in connection with internal improvements, therefore, was justified by necessity and sanctioned by the mercantilistic tradition. Those who shied away from the bold approach to economic development that the canal enthusiasts employed had many reasons for doing so, but seldom were their objections matters of principle or motivated by fundamental ideological convictions. Even such *avant-garde* advocates of laissez-faire economics as the Reverend John McVickar and Samuel Young temporarily set aside principles in favor of canals.

The Erie and Champlain canals produced varied and widespread reactions in New York and throughout the nation. Their completion and efficient operation seemed incontestable vindication of the form of state enterprise that produced them. Within the state, in regions that suffered from inferior transportation facilities, the benefits that accrued to the areas through which the canals passed were especially impressive. Inhabitants of "sequestered" regions noted the sharply accelerated pace of economic development in the canal counties and concluded that logic and a code of equal justice demanded that what had been done for other sections of the state should be done for theirs also. The state responded to the clamor. It extended its canal system by constructing a number of costly and unprofitable feeders and by granting aid to canal and railroad corporations.

The Western, Northern, and Seneca Lock Navigation companies constituted several well-known precedents for state aid to corporations engaged in improving transportation facilities. In 1827, the Delaware and Hudson Canal Company, whose canal between the anthracite region of Pennsylvania and the Hudson River was under construction, received the first of two grants of aid from the state.[1] The arguments that were advanced in favor of aid to this company contrasted the benefits that the Erie and Champlain canals produced locally and those that the company was expected to render in the more southern counties of the state by providing them with better transportation to New York City and the Hudson River Valley, especially for the shipment of coal.[2] Thereafter, petitions to the legislature for aid to railroad corporations, which originated either with the inhabitants of the affected region or with the corporations themselves, invariably mentioned the canals, the company, or both, as precedents and justification for the aid sought.

[1] NYS, *Laws*, ch. lxii, 50 Sess.; ch. cccxlvi, 52 Sess.

[2] "That the state of New York is justly bound to give reasonable facilities to those counties laying along the southern line of the state as a fair offset to the advantage already given to the northern counties, no one will deny. . . . With the connection formed by the Hudson and Delaware Canal to tidewater, it will open a channel of communication with the commercial emporium which will be of immense importance to the state" (Benjamin Wright to DeWitt Clinton, 21 July, 1826, DWC Papers).

Beyond the borders of New York, citizens of other states observed with trepidation how successfully the Empire State was keeping pace with the growing requirements for transportation connections with the expanding west. Other coastal states, with more enthusiasm than discretion, rushed headlong into internal improvement projects of all sorts, seemingly blind to the costs, the technological problems involved, and the amount of likely traffic that could be expected once the projects were completed. Some of these projects were public and some combined the use of private and public resources, but most were in some measure inspired by the achievements of New York or motivated by the fear that in the race for western markets states that failed to emulate New York were doomed to economic stagnation.

Recent studies indicate, to a greater or lesser degree, how the forces responsible for the varied functions that the state assumed in New York were operating in other states.[3] If the most dramatic examples of state interventionism occurred in building and financing canals and railroads, this was because the large costs, the dearth of capital, and the difficult technical problems made such intervention necessary. Legislatures of the different states independently reached the same conclusion that the risk, effort, and expense of providing improved transportation facilities required participation by their respective governments. States differed in the kind and extent of their aid, and these differences were significant in terms of local needs, resources, and politics; but of greater pertinence here is the fact that ascribing economic functions to state governments was widely acceptable.

[3] Hartz, *Economic Policy, passim;* Handlin, *Commonwealth, passim;* Milton S. Heath, *Constructive Liberalism: The Role of the State in Economic Development in Georgia to 1860* (Cambridge, Mass., 1954), *passim;* Carter Goodrich, *Government Promotion of American Canals and Railroads, 1800–1890* (New York, 1960), 51–120; James N. Primm, *Economic Policy in the Development of a Western State: Missouri, 1820–1860* (Cambridge, Mass., 1954), *passim.*

The legislature of New York rejected numerous bills providing for aid to private enterprise or for new public projects during the period under consideration. Such bills were usually voted down for political, sectional, or other reasons, but never for reasons that suggested an abandonment of the state's long practice of economic interventionism despite the greater evidence of laissez-faire thought and advocacy toward the end of the period.

It is notable that government intervention in the economy continued without interruption or alteration even as the structure and organization of the state government was drastically revised in accordance with the provisions of the Constitution of 1821. That constitution was drafted while the Erie and Champlain canals were under construction and represented a smashing defeat for the old Federalist-aristocratic element in the state—a defeat made more impressive by the vigor and eloquence that opponents of constitutional revision employed to fight for a lost cause. Almost precisely when the state committed itself to an enlarged responsibility for economic development, its political institutions were being refashioned along more democratic lines, with the result that universal suffrage was almost, if not totally, achieved and the Councils of Revision and Appointment, notorious as instruments designed to frustrate the popular will, were abolished.[4] Obviously, New Yorkers saw no contradiction between the state's assumption of large economic functions and the institutions and practices of democracy; current conceptions of progress were broad enough to embrace an acceptance of expanded activity of the state government in the economy along with its increased subjection to the popular will.

Officials of the state understood the importance of foreign capital for local development as fully then as do public officials of countries today who are anxious to make the long, quick leap from a primitive agrarian economy into a condition of

[4] Fox, *Decline of Aristocracy*, 230–267.

advanced twentieth-century industrialism. Along with businessmen familiar with the money market, such officials regarded
the bridge of credit that linked the more advanced economies
of western Europe, particularly England, with that of the
United States as a delicate structure at best. They trembled
when it trembled, and state officials and businessmen joined
forces to support it when it showed signs of collapsing. Indeed, the essential unity of the two aspects of the problem of
the movement of capital into New York from abroad considered above should not be overlooked. The pattern of investment and the way that it developed in connection with
financing the Erie and Champlain canals between 1817 and
1825 and the effort to sustain the banks and to maintain the
credit of the state in 1837 are inseparable details of a single
story. When the state borrowed to build the canals, it had to
furnish evidence that it and its citizens were self-reliant, well
disciplined, and responsible—qualities that were measurable in
their willingness to allocate revenues from taxation and to
demonstrate by their own exertions a desire and a capacity to
further economic development in the state. Acceptance of the
financial plan for the construction of the canals satisfied the
first requirement, and completion of the middle section satisfied the second; together, they were instrumental in earning
the confidence of potential investors at home and abroad. The
conclusion that in New York State the English investor found
an advanced outpost of enterprise familiar to him, where profits
were possible and the risk was reasonable but not excessive,
was absolutely clear by 1822. It was this image of the state and
its citizens that the Commissioners of the Canal Fund sought
to preserve when they came to the aid of the banks in 1837
and assured creditors of the Canal Fund that whatever others
might do they would cling to the specie standard. The motives
behind their determination to do so were rooted in the history
of the state and the province; imported capital had been an essential ingredient of economic development and remained a

continuing necessity. Long-standing ties of New Yorkers with foreign business houses and the export of canal stock abroad along with other American securities proved the point.

Suspension of specie payments by the banks in 1837 blurred once again the line that separated private interest from public responsibility. The state administration was as anxious to facilitate a return to the specie standards by the banks as it was to maintain its own credit. In actuality, officials of the state scarcely differentiated one from the other. The commissioners lent canal stock to eight banks in New York City in a move to bolster the private sector of the economy through the use of public credit. The immediate objective was to sustain the banks and to assist them along the road to resumption; it was also an attempt to strengthen the position of businessmen who were immediately involved in the Anglo-American trade. Even more important, however, was the fact that the loan of stock was expected to pave the way toward the re-establishment of normal financial relations with London, which, translated into realistic terms, meant the re-creation of trust in New York State and its citizens in the largest money market of the world.

The Canal Fund became a development bank less by design than by dint of circumstances. The commissioners were as reluctant a group of bankers as the world had ever seen; to begin with, they were racked with fears when their loans and deposits moved into the channels of business via the banks, which, inspected or not, always seemed to them likely to be less secure than was apparent on the surface. The concatenation of circumstances that made the Canal Fund more than a sinking fund and the commissioners more than commissioners of a canal fund required these officials to remain alert to economic changes and trends. Increasingly, the commissioners, who were first and foremost politicians, became burdened with large economic responsibilities. They were forced to subject established policies to review and to examine those under consideration for clues that might reveal their effect on the private sector of the economy. As they proceeded in their tasks from day to day, their familiarity with the financial and economic problems that beset the state and its citizens deepened, their perspectives broadened, and they became increasingly sensitive to sudden changes in economic conditions to which they frequently responded sharply and decisively. In 1834, the commissioners abruptly altered their banking policies and abandoned their carefully conceived program for redeeming canal stock in response to pressures that the panic of that year imposed on the business community. The lessons learned in this crisis guided them in 1835 when the great fire reduced a large section of the city of New York to ashes. The commissioners proposed to use the resources at their command to finance relief and recovery by maintaining, or better still by raising, the level of banking resources in the city. They stopped redemption of stock and sought to siphon deposits from upstate banks to banks in New York City in order to achieve their purpose.

The determination to direct the flow of funds to an area that needed them badly proved to be the commissioners' boldest effort in connection with the fire. It involved a problem of choice that bedevils all administrators of capital-short economies, whether in the latter half of the twentieth century or at the beginning of the nineteenth. How to allocate scarce resources was a decision that the commissioners then resolved in favor of the city. Articulate spokesmen for the inhabitants of the Chenango Valley and for those who lived along the lines of the Erie Canal protested the commissioners' plan. They opposed it not because of a want of sympathy for the plight of the stricken city or because they failed to realize the importance of the city in the total picture of business and agriculture in the state. Their opposition was based on the belief that, large as the revenues of the Canal Fund were, the demands of a growing economy were larger and any diversion of the revenues from their sections would retard local development. This consideration was sufficiently meaningful to them so that despite their evident sympathy they preferred that aid to the city be drawn from another source.

The factor of the shortage of capital hovers in the background of every example of state intervention. It was a crucial factor in converting the Canal Fund into a development bank and in the 1830's raised that fund to a level of importance never reached again. During this period, the fund's importance was great precisely because it had relatively large revenues at its disposal at a time when the resources of banking institutions and individuals were meager. Not for a long time would the commissioners again have such surpluses on hand; indeed, the sums that they made available to banks in the thirties for loans and deposits were not exceeded in amount on an annual basis until the Civil War.[5]

By the 1850's, the resources of the banks in New York State expanded considerably so that proportionately loans and deposits of the Canal Fund were not as important as they had been for some banks in the 1830's.[6] These loans and deposits were still large enough in 1857, however, to cause the commissioners the same concern that their predecessors in the middle thirties experienced when they anxiously contemplated the effect that large withdrawals of canal revenues from the banks would have on the private sector of the economy.[7]

The record of the Commissioners of the Canal Fund is indispensable if the role of the state in the economy of New York for the period under consideration is to be understood. This record reveals more than the decisions bearing on the financial management of the canals and more than the processes by which revenues of the Canal Fund were "diffused through all the departments of the economy." It is a record of the depend-

[5] A comparison was made of the figures in the anual reports of the Commissioners of the Canal Fund. For the high figures during the Civil War, see NYS, *Ass. Docs.*, 86 Sess., I, Doc. no. 4, 89–91; 87 Sess., I, Doc. no. 5, 96–98.

[6] NYS, *Ass. Docs.*, 74 Sess., III, Doc. no. 87, 1–39.

[7] NYS, *Sen. Docs.*, 80 Sess., I, Doc. no. 10, 51.

ence of young economies on matured ones and of how a community with abundant resources, varied skills, a tradition of self-discipline, savings, and investment could, in DeWitt Clinton's oft-repeated biblical quotation, succeed in making the desert "blossom as the rose." It is a record, too, of the forces that give rise to the assumption of responsibility of government for the course and progress of economic development under certain conditions. In addition, the record indicates that the large part that the state played in the economy was compatible with a concurrent development involving the extension and strengthening of institutions of democracy.

The ultimate objective for making use of the state in order to advance economic development was to create a more favorable economic environment for inhabitants of the state. The concept of "the enterprise of a free people" was based on the proposition that New Yorkers, alone or in association with others, engaged in agriculture, commerce, or manufacturing for their own profit and satisfaction. If, however, the state could mitigate some of the larger and more persistent difficulties of economic development, citizens of New York saw no reason why their government should not assist them in the effort.

APPENDIXES

BIBLIOGRAPHY

INDEX

APPENDIX I

Loans from the Canal Fund to Banks as Designated at the End of the Fiscal Year

Bank	Year inc.	Capital	1st canal loan	1832	1833	1834	1835	1836	1837
Bk. of Albany	1792	$ 240,000	1833		$ 50,000	$ 78,500	$ 78,500	$ 78,500	$ 53,050
Albany City Bk.	1834	100,000	1835				108,000	123,000	100,700
Bk. of America, N.Y.C.	1812	2,001,200	1832	$150,000	112,500	112,500			
Bk. of Auburn	1817	200,000							
Broome Co. Bk., Binghamton	1831	100,000	1834			20,000	10,000		
Bk. of Buffalo	1831	200,000	1837						33,800
Canal Bk., Albany	1829	300,000	1832	130,000	105,000	105,000	105,000	125,000	111,750
Cayuga Co. Bk., Auburn	1833	250,000	1837						49,150
Central Bk., Cherry Valley	1818	120,000	1834			25,000	25,000	25,000	20,000
Chautauqua Co. Bk., Jamestown	1831	100,000	1834			10,000	20,000	20,000	18,000
Chemung Canal Bk., Elmira	1833	200,000	1837						8,800
Clinton Co. Bk., Plattsburg	1836	200,000	1837						10,006
Commercial Bk., Albany	1825	225,000	1832	100,000	75,000	102,500	102,500	161,636	69,250
Commercial Bk., Buffalo	1834	400,000	1835				50,000	50,000	40,000
Commercial Bk., N.Y.C.	1834	500,000	1835				100,000	100,000	80,000
Dry Dock Bk., N.Y.C.	1825	200,000	1835				100,000	100,000	90,000
Essex Co. Bk., Keeseville	1832	100,000	1834			20,000	20,000	20,000	16,000
Farmers Bk., Troy	1801	278,000	1832	32,000	50,000	50,000	50,000	50,000	33,800
Bk. of Genesee, Batavia	1829	100,000	1832	36,000	27,000	27,000	27,000	27,000	
Bk. of Geneva	1817	400,000	1832	20,000	20,000	20,000	20,000	20,000	16,100
Greenwich Bk., N.Y.C.	1830	200,000	1832	50,000	37,500	37,500	37,500	50,000	40,000

APPENDIX I (*continued*)

Bank	Year inc.	Capital	1st canal loan	1832	1833	1834	1835	1836	1837
Herkimer Co. Bk., Little Falls	1833	200,000	1837						8,800
Bk. of Ithaca	1829	200,000	1832	38,000	28,500	25,000	25,000	25,000	16,900
LaFayette Bk., N.Y.C.	1834	500,000	1835				100,000	100,000	73,750
Leather Mfgrs. Bk., N.Y.C.	1832	600,000	1833		50,000	50,000	100,000	100,000	80,000
Lewis Co. Bk., Martinsburg	1833	100,000	1836					20,000	16,200
Livingston Co. Bk., Geneseo	1830	100,000	1835				25,000	25,000	20,500
Lockport Bk.	1829	100,000	1837						29,700
Bk. of Lyons	1836	200,000							
Madison Co. Bk., Cazenovia	1831	100,000	1832	36,000	27,000	27,000	27,000	27,000	13,000
Bk. of the Manhattan Co., N.Y.C.	1799	2,050,000							
Mechanics & Farmers Bk., Albany	1811	442,000							
Merchants & Mechanics Bk., Troy	1829	300,000	1832	88,254	146,569	155,784	155,784	155,784	135,400
Merchants Bk., N.Y.C.		1,490,000	1836					150,000	95,000
Merchants Exchange Bk., N.Y.C.	1829	750,000	1832	50,000	37,500	12,500		50,000	40,000
Mohawk Bk., Schenectady	1807	165,000	1837						54,000
Bk. of Monroe, Rochester	1829	300,000	1833		100,000	100,000	100,000	150,000	149,500
Montgomery Co. Bk., Johnstown	1831	100,000							
National Bk., N.Y.C.	1829	750,000	1832	150,000	112,500	62,500	162,500	100,000	60,000
Bk. of New York, N.Y.C.	1784	1,000,000						100,000	

Bank	Year inc.	Capital	1st canal loan	1832	1833	1834	1835	1836	1837
N.Y. State Bk., Albany	1803	369,600	1836					50,000	48,500
Ogdensburg Bk.	1829	100,000	1833		30,000	30,000	30,000	30,000	24,601
Onondaga Co. Bk., Syracuse	1830	150,000							
Ontario Branch Bk., Utica	1815	250,000	1832	20,000	70,000	70,000	80,000	80,000	54,000
Bk. of Orleans, Albion	1834	200,000	1835				25,000	25,000	21,000
Bk. of Oswego	1831	150,000	1837						33,313
Otsego Co. Bk., Cooperstown	1830	100,000	1834			25,000			
Phoenix Bk., N.Y.C.	1812	500,000	1832	150,000	112,500	50,000	112,500	112,500	36,500
Bk. of Rochester	1824	250,000	1833		100,000	100,000	100,000	100,000	78,300
Rochester City Bk.	1836								21,800
Bk. of Rome	1832	100,000	1837						16,200
Sackets Harbor Bk.	1834	200,000	1836					20,000	18,000
Bk. of Salina, Syracuse	1832	150,000	1837						20,300
Saratoga Co. Bk., Waterford	1830	100,000							
Schenectady Bk.	1832	150,000	1834			20,000	20,000	20,000	16,200
Seneca Co. Bk., Waterloo	1833	200,000	1834			10,000	20,000	20,000	13,500
Steuben Co. Bk., Bath	1833	150,000	1834			30,000	20,000	20,000	13,500
Tradesmens Bk., N.Y.C.	1823	400,000	1834			50,000			
Bk. of Troy	1811	440,000	1832	50,000	150,000	150,000	150,000	170,000	160,000
Troy City Bk.	1833	300,000	1834			70,000	100,000	100,000	85,000
Union Bk., N.Y.C.	1811	1,000,000	1833		50,000	50,000	100,000	100,000	60,000
Bk. of Utica	1812	450,000	1832	100,000	100,000	70,000			31,100
Wayne Co. Bk., Palmyra	1829	100,000	1833		30,000	30,000	30,000	30,000	23,000
Bk. of Whitehall	1829	100,000	1837						24,300
Yates Co. Bk., Penn Yan	1831	100,000	1833		20,000	20,000	20,000	20,000	13,500

Source: Annual reports of the Commissioners of the Canal Fund, 1832–1837.

APPENDIX II

Deposits from the Canal Fund in Banks as Designated at the End of Each Fiscal Year

Bank	Year inc.	Capital	1831	1832	1833	1834	1835	1836	1837
Bk. of Albany	1792	$ 240,000							
Albany City Bk.	1834	100,000							
Bk. of America, N.Y.C.	1812	2,001,200							
Bk. of Auburn	1817	200,000		$ 5,685					
Broome Co. Bk., Binghamton	1831	100,000							$ 586
Bk. of Buffalo	1831	200,000		33,515	$ 71,839	$109,057	$65,504	$70,396	34,080
Canal Bk., Albany	1829	300,000							
Cayuga Co. Bk., Auburn	1833	250,000				45,873	53,518	67,481	9,152
Central Bk., Cherry Valley	1818	120,000							
Chatauqua Co. Bk., Jamestown	1831	100,000							
Chemung Canal Bk., Elmira	1833	200,000				3,521	14,768	13,387	1,031
Clinton Co. Bk., Plattsburg	1836	200,000							
Commercial Bk., Albany	1825	225,000							
Commercial Bk., Buffalo	1834	400,000							
Commercial Bk., N.Y.C.	1834	500,000							
Dry Dock Bk., N.Y.C.	1825	200,000							
Essex Co. Bk., Keeseville	1832	100,000							
Farmers Bk., Troy	1801	278,000							
Bk. of Genesee, Batavia	1829	100,000							
Bk. of Geneva	1817	400,000	$32,913	80,000	59,369	45,001	32,761	26,302	
Greenwich Bk., N.Y.C.	1830	200,000							379

Bank	Year inc.	Capital	1831	1832	1833	1834	1835	1836	1837
Herkimer Co. Bk., Little Falls	1833	200,000				10,053	21,473	13,115	1,269
Bk. of Ithaca	1829	200,000							
LaFayette Bk., N.Y.C.	1834	500,000							
Leather Mfgrs. Bk., N.Y.C.	1832	600,000							
Lewis Co. Bk., Martinsburg	1833	100,000							
Livingston Co. Bk., Geneseo	1830	100,000							
Lockport Bk.	1829	100,000	32,626	46,266	62,147	60,396	54,979	33,396	715
Bk. of Lyons	1836	200,000							1,107
Madison Co. Bk., Cazenovia	1831	100,000							
Bk. of the Manhattan Co., N.Y.C.	1799	2,050,000	19,615						
Mechanics & Farmers Bk., Albany	1811	442,000	749,567	184,139	57,439	11,490	23,777	53,359	199,307
Merchants & Mechanics Bk., Troy	1829	300,000			6,279	22,098	1,430	4,581	12,283
Merchants Bk., N.Y.C.		1,490,000							
Merchants Exchange Bk., N.Y.C.	1829	750,000							
Mohawk Bk., Schenectady	1807	165,000	12,062	6,674	34,400	43,416	35,908	30,861	4,335
Bk. of Monroe, Rochester	1829	300,000		104,338	36,154	58,349	35,471	27,926	708
Montgomery Co. Bk., Johnstown	1831	100,000						7,777	
National Bk., N.Y.C.	1829	750,000							
Bk. of New York, N.Y.C.	1784	1,000,000	748,971	184,187	66,289				
N.Y. State Bk., Albany	1803	369,000				19,686	32,177	48,144	1,435

APPENDIX II (*continued*)

Bank	Year inc.	Capital	1831	1832	1833	1834	1835	1836	1837
Ogdensburg Bk.	1829	100,000							
Onondaga Co. Bk., Syracuse	1829	100,000	13,036	153,733	184,821	172,322	98,741	72,489	59,381
Ontario Branch Bk., Utica	1815	250,000	28,382	72,665	30,644	10,000			
Bk. of Orleans, Albion	1834	200,000					3,108	6,411	1,617
Bk. of Oswego	1831	150,000		3,128	10,728	27,964	42,458	41,397	6,465
Otsego Co. Bk., Cooperstown	1830	100,000							
Phoenix Bk., N.Y.C.	1812	500,000							
Bk. of Rochester	1824	250,000	94,452	176,617	32,297	68,583	48,602	51,019	16,446
Bk. of Rome	1832	100,000			14,880	33,826	11,498	18,054	5,714
Sackets Harbor Bk.	1834	200,000							
Bk. of Salina, Syracuse	1832	150,000			24,455	79,067	53,646	33,024	7,754
Saratoga Co. Bk., Waterford	1830	100,000	8,329	44,741	46,519	21,602	24,722	13,551	8,611
Schenectady Bk.	1832	150,000							1,954
Seneca Co. Bk., Waterloo	1833	200,000				11,058	22,667	14,933	5,056
Steuben Co. Bk., Bath	1833	150,000				1,304	7,057	7,133	3,715
Tradesmens Bk., N.Y.C.	1823	400,000							
Bk. of Troy	1811	440,000	76,972	184,450	33,943	30,158	1,531	4,581	207
Troy City Bk.	1833	300,000							
Union Bk., N.Y.C.	1811	1,000,000							
Bk. of Utica	1812	450,000		21,735	21,757	26,968	55,472	46,235	5,787
Wayne Co. Bk., Palmyra	1829	100,000	16,300	57,604	19,942	22,927	4,683	4,258	25,750
Bk. of Whitehall	1829	100,000		30,510	55,459	72,000	39,259	32,740	8,038
Yates Co. Bk., Penn Yan	1831	100,000				1,309	6,368	6,481	3,183

Source: Annual reports of the Commissioners of the Canal Fund, 1831–1837.

Two "Loan-Contractor" Banks

The New York State Bank and the Mechanics and Farmers Bank frequently acted as loan contractors between 1817 and 1823, along with individual brokers and "brokerage houses" that performed the same function during the same period and thereafter. These banks, however, were especially conspicuous as "loan contractors" during the period 1817–1821 (NYS, *Ass. Docs.*, 60 Sess., I, Doc. no. 4, 53). They bought canal stock in order to make quick sales, which were frequently consummated within a matter of days after the certificates came into their possession, as a sampling of the transferred certificates indicates (Misc. Canal Papers, NYSL). Evidence dating from 1821 indicates that the distinct advantage that these banks derived from such transactions was to extend the circulation of their bills. They offered considerably higher premiums than did rival bidders for stock on the condition that their bills would be used to pay contractors, and, hence, laborers employed in building the canals (*NY Canal Laws*, II, 554). These banks were closely connected with the state. The state owned 40 per cent of the stock of the New York State Bank and 10 per cent of the stock of the Mechanics and Farmers Bank. State directors sat on the boards of both banks (Letterbooks of the Comptroller, 1821–1822, *passim*). The part that these two banks played in floating the very early canal loans was probably for them a "shoestring operation" of the kind that characterized so many of the operations of banks at this time (B. Hammond, *Banking and Politics*, 274–276, 282), and it is regrettable that the details involved in these activities are lacking. A clearer picture of the risks they ran would emerge if their actual resources and obligations at the time were accurately known. Azariah Flagg, who touched on the subject of the "aid" that the New York State Bank and the Mechanics and Farmers Bank provided in connection with marketing the early loans, gives none of the missing data. See A. C. Flagg, *A Few Historical Facts Respecting the Establishment and Progress of Banks and the Business of Banking in the State of New York from the Adoption of the Constitu-*

tion in 1777 to 1864 (New York, 1868), 2–3. To understand the money market and the availability of investment capital, it is important to determine what happened to canal stock after it passed through the brief possession of banks and brokers. As Albert Gallatin pointed out many years later, after studying the relationship of canal stock to the credit of the state, "the value of a new stock is not settled until it has fallen into the hands of those who intend to make it a permanent investment" (Albert Gallatin, *The Writings of Albert Gallatin*, ed. by Henry Adams [Philadelphia, 1879], II, 540–544). For a general discussion of the role of banks and individuals as "loan contractors" see Redlich, *Molding of American Banking*, pt. II, 327–337.

Bibliography

MANUSCRIPT COLLECTIONS

Columbia University Library
DeWitt Clinton Papers (cited as DWC Papers)

New-York Historical Society
Bradish Papers
Gallatin Papers
Diary of Philip Hone (MS)
Rufus King Papers
Newbold Papers

New York Public Library
Bronson Papers
Bronson Papers, Martin Collection
Constable Papers
Flagg Papers
Phelps Dodge Papers
Remsen Papers
Schuyler Papers
Moses Taylor Papers
Townsend Papers

New York State Department of Audit and Control

Letterbooks of the Comptroller, 1817–1826
Letterbooks of the Comptroller Relating to Canals, 1817–1846 (cited as LRC)
Rough Minutes of the Commissioners of the Canal Fund, 1836–1845

New York State Library, Albany

General Correspondence of the Comptroller (cited as GCC)
Miscellaneous Assembly Papers
Miscellaneous Canal Papers

GOVERNMENT PUBLICATIONS

Great Britain

Parliament Sessional Papers. Vol. IV for 1840: *Report from Select Committee on Banks of Issue.*

United States

Congress. *American State Papers: Documents, Legislative and Executive.* 38 vols. Washington, 1832–1861.
———. *Congressional Globe, Containing the Debates and Proceedings, 1833–1873.* 109 vols. Washington, 1834–1873.
———. *The Debates and Proceedings in the Congress of the United States, 1789–1824.* 42 vols. Washington, 1834–1856. (Cited as *Annals of Cong.*)
———. *Register of Debates in Congress, 1825–1837.* 29 vols. Washington, 1825–1837. (Cited as *Cong. Debates.*)
Richardson, James D., ed. *Compilation of the Messages and Papers of the Presidents, 1789–1897.* 10 vols. Washington, 1907.
Statutes at Large of the United States of America. Boston, 1850–1873.

New York State

Assembly. *Documents of the Assembly of the State of New York.* Albany, 1830–1846.
———. *Journal of the Assembly of the State of New York.* Albany, 1792–1838.

Board of Agriculture. *Memoirs of the Board of Agriculture of the State of New York.* 3 vols. Albany, 1821–1826.

Census of the State of New York for 1855. Albany, 1857.

Laws of the State of New York. Albany, 1792–1838.

Laws of the State of New York in Relation to the Erie and Champlain Canals, Together with the Annual Reports of the Canal Commissioners and Other Documents. 2 vols. Albany, 1825.

Lincoln, C. Z., ed. *Messages from the Governors.* 11 vols. Albany, 1909.

Senate. *Documents of the Senate of the State of New York.* Albany, 1830–1846.

———. *Journal of the Senate of the State of New York.* Albany, 1792–1838.

ALBANY

Report of the Chamberlain of the Corporation of the City of Albany. Albany, 1822.

NEW YORK CITY

Board of Assistants. *Documents.* New York, 1838–1868.

Common Council. *Minutes of the Common Council of the City of New York, 1784–1831.* 21 vols. New York, 1917–1930.

Pennsylvania

Laws of the General Assembly of the Commonwealth of Pennsylvania, Passed at the Session of 1835–1836. Harrisburg, 1836.

MAGAZINES

Analectic Magazine (Philadelphia)
The Gentleman's Magazine and Historical Chronicle (London)
The Monthly Magazine; or, British Register (London)

NEWSPAPERS

Albany
Daily Advertiser
Daily Albany Argus

Evening Journal
Gazette and Daily Advertiser
Weekly Journal

Baltimore
Niles' Weekly Register

Buffalo
Republican and Bulletin

London
The Times

Newburgh, New York
Political Index

New York City
Commercial Advertiser
Evening Post
General Shipping and Commercial List
Herald
Journal and Patriotic Register
Journal of Commerce
Post

BOOKS

Adams, Herbert B. *Maryland's Influence upon Land Cessions in the United States.* (Johns Hopkins University Studies in History and Political Science, III, no. 1.) Baltimore, 1885.

Albion, Robert G. *The Rise of New York Port (1815–1860).* New York, 1939.

American Almanac: New York Register and City Directory. New York, 1816.

Axon, William E. *The Annals of Manchester.* London, 1886.

Barnard, Daniel D. *A Discourse on the Life and Character of Stephen Van Rensselaer.* Albany, 1839.

Bidwell, Percy W., and John I. Falconer. *History of Agriculture in the Northern United States, 1620–1860.* Washington, 1925.

Bingham, Robert W., ed. *Holland Land Company Papers: Reports of Joseph Ellicott.* (Buffalo Historical Society Publications, XXXIII.) Buffalo, 1941.

Brant, Irving. *James Madison.* 4 vols. New York, 1941–1953.

Burt, A. L. *The United States, Great Britain, and British North America from the Revolution to the Establishment of Peace after the War of 1812.* New Haven, 1940.

Calhoun, Daniel H. *The American Civil Engineer: Origins and Conflict.* Cambridge, Mass., 1960.

Campbell, William W., ed. *The Life and Writings of DeWitt Clinton.* New York, 1849.

Carey, Mathew. *Essays on Political Economy.* Philadelphia, 1822.

Catterall, Ralph C. H. *The Second Bank of the United States.* Chicago, 1903.

Clark, Joshua V. H. *Onondaga . . . Reminiscences of Earlier and Later Times.* Syracuse, 1849.

Clark, Victor S. *History of Manufactures in the United States, 1607–1860.* 3 vols. Washington, 1929.

Clay, Henry. *Works of Henry Clay, Comprising His Life, Correspondence, and Speeches.* Ed. by Calvin Colton. 7 vols. New York, 1897.

Clinton, DeWitt (Tacitus, pseud.). *The Canal Policy of the State of New York, Delineated in a Letter to Robert Troup.* Albany, 1821.

The Coalition. Undated.

Cochran, Thomas C. *New York and the Confederation.* Philadelphia, 1932.

Cole, Arthur H. *Wholesale Commodity Prices in the United States, 1700–1861.* Cambridge, Mass., 1938.

Darusmont, Francis Wright. *Views of Society and Manners in America . . . by an Englishwoman.* London, 1821.

Davis, Joseph S. *Essays in the Earlier History of American Corporations.* 2 vols. Cambridge, Mass., 1917.

Donovan, H. D. A. *The Barnburners.* New York, 1925.

Dorfman, Joseph. *The Economic Mind in American Civilization, 1606–1865.* 2 vols. New York, 1946.

Dunaway, Wayland F. *History of the James River and Kanawha Company.* New York, 1922.

Durrenberger, Joseph A. *Turnpikes: A Study of the Toll Road Movement in the Middle Atlantic States and Maryland.* Valdosta, 1931.

Dwight, Timothy. *Travels in New England and New York.* New Haven, 1822.

Edson, Obed. *History of Chautauqua County, New York.* Boston, 1894.

Ellis, David M. *Landlords and Farmers in the Hudson-Mohawk Region, 1790–1850.* Ithaca, 1946.

Evans, Paul D. *The Holland Land Company.* Buffalo, 1924.

The Financial Register of the United States, Devoted Chiefly to Finance and Currency and to Banking and Commercial Statistics. Philadelphia, 1838.

Flagg, A. C. *A Few Historical Facts Respecting the Establishment and Progress of Banks and the Business of Banking in the State of New York from the Adoption of the Constitution in 1777 to 1854.* New York, 1868.

Flick, Alexander, ed. *History of the State of New York.* 10 vols. New York, 1934.

Fox, Dixon R. *The Decline of Aristocracy in the Politics of New York.* New York, 1919.

Gallatin, Albert. *The Writings of Albert Gallatin.* Ed. by Henry Adams. 3 vols. Philadelphia, 1879.

Gray, Thomas. *Observations on a General Iron Railway; or, Land Steam Conveyance.* London, 1825.

Haines, Charles G. *Considerations on the Western Canal from the Hudson to Lake Erie.* Brooklyn, 1818.

Hammond, Bray. *Banking and Politics in America.* Princeton, 1957.

Hammond, Jabez D. *History of Political Parties in the State of New York.* 3 vols. Syracuse, 1848–1852.

Handlin, Oscar and Mary F. *Commonwealth: A Study of the Role of Government in the American Economy: Massachusetts, 1774–1861.* New York, 1947.

Hartz, Louis. *Economic Policy and Democratic Thought: Pennsylvania, 1776–1860.* Cambridge, Mass., 1948.

Heath, Milton S. *Constructive Liberalism: The Role of the State* in *Economic Development in Georgia to 1860*. Cambridge, Mass., 1954.

Hidy, Ralph W. *The House of Baring in American Trade and Finance*. Cambridge, Mass., 1949.

Holdsworth, John T., and Davis R. Dewey. *The First and Second National Banks of the United States*. Washington, 1910.

Holland, Edgar S. *A History of the Family of Holland of Mobberley and Knutsford*. Ed. by William Fergusson Irvine. Edinburgh, 1902.

Holt, L. C. T. *The Inland Waterways of England*. London, 1950.

Hone, Philip. *The Diary of Philip Hone*. Ed. by Allan Nevins. 2 vols. New York, 1927.

Hosack, David. *Memoir of DeWitt Clinton*. New York, 1829.

Hurlburt, Archer B. *The Cumberland Road*. Cleveland, 1904.

Jackman, W. T. *The Development of Transportation in Modern England*. 2 vols. Cambridge, Eng., 1916.

Jefferson, Thomas. *Notes on the State of Virginia*. London, 1787.

Jensen, Merrill. *The New Nation: A History of the United States during the Confederation, 1781–1789*. New York, 1950.

Jones, Clement. *Pioneer Shipowners*. Liverpool, 1935.

King, Peter Lord. *Thoughts on the Effects of the Bank Restrictions*. London, 1804.

Knapp, Samuel L. *The Life of Thomas Eddy*. New York, 1834.

Koch, Adrienne. *Jefferson and Madison: The Great Collaboration*. New York, 1950.

Lincoln, C. Z. *The Constitutional History of New York*. 5 vols. Rochester, 1906.

Longworth's New York Almanac for 1816–1817. New York, 1817.

Lowe, Joseph. *The Present State of England in Regard to Agriculture, Trade, and Finance*. London, 1823.

Loyd, Samuel Jones (the Rt. Hon. Lord Overstone). *Tracts and Other Publications on Metallic and Paper Currency*. London, 1857.

MacBean, William N. *Biographical Register of Saint Andrews' Society of the State of New York*. New York, 1922.

McCulloch, James R., ed. *Outlines of Political Economy . . . by Rev. John McVickar*. New York, 1825.

McGrane, Reginald. *The Correspondence of Nicholas Biddle*. Boston, 1919.

———. *Foreign Bondholders and American State Debts.* New York, 1935.

McKelvey, Blake. *Rochester, the Water-Power City, 1812–1854.* Cambridge, Mass. 1945.

Mackenzie, Alexander S. *The Life of Commodore Oliver Hazard Perry.* 2 vols. New York, 1843.

McNall, Neil A. *An Agricultural History of the Genesee Valley, 1790–1860.* Philadelphia, 1952.

Meyer, B. H., ed. *History of Transportation in the United States before 1860, by Caroline Gill & a Staff of Collaborators.* New York, 1948.

Morris, Ann Cary. *The Diary and Letters of Gouverneur Morris.* 2 vols. New York, 1888.

Morris, Richard B. *Government and Labor in Early America.* New York, 1946.

Morse, Jedidiah. *The American Geography; or, A View of the Present Situation of the United States of America.* Elizabethtown, 1789.

Myers, Margaret G. *The New York Money Market.* New York, 1931.

New York Corresponding Association for the Promotion of Internal Improvements. *Public Documents Relating to New York Canals.* New York, 1821.

North, C. Douglass. *The Economic Growth of the United States, 1790–1860,* Englewood Cliffs, N.J., 1961.

O'Neall, John Belton. *Biographical Sketches of the Bench and Bar of South Carolina.* Charleston, 1859.

Pitkin, Timothy. *A Statistical View of the Commerce of the United States of America.* New York, 1817.

Pomerantz, Sidney I. *New York, an American City, 1783–1803: A Study in Urban Life.* New York, 1938.

The Post-Office: London Directory for 1821. London, 1821.

Pratt, Julius W. *Expansionists of 1812.* New York, 1925.

Primm, James N. *Economic Policy in the Development of a Western State: Missouri, 1820–1860.* Cambridge, Mass., 1954.

Ratchford, B. U. *American State Debts.* Durham, 1941.

Redlich, Fritz. *The Molding of American Banking: Men and Ideas.* 2 parts. New York, 1947–1951.

Report of the Delegates of the Banks of the City of New York to the Bank Convention Held at New York on the 27th of November to 1st of December, 1837. New York, 1837.

Sakolski, Aaron M. *The Great American Land Bubble.* New York, 1932.

Sanderlin, Walter S. *The Great National Project: A History of the Chesapeake and Ohio Canal.* (Johns Hopkins University Studies in History and Political Science, LXIV, no. 1.) Baltimore, 1946.

Scoville, Joseph A. (Walter Barrett, pseud.). *The Old Merchants of New York City.* 4 vols. New York, 1863–1866.

Severance, Frank H., ed. *The Holland Land Company and the Erie Canal: Journals and Documents.* (Buffalo Historical Society Publications, XIV.) Buffalo, 1910.

Smith, Walter B. *Economic Aspects of the Second Bank of the United States.* Cambridge, Mass., 1953.

Society for the Prevention of Pauperism in the City of New York. *Second Annual Report of the Managers.* New York, 1820.

Society for the Promotion of the Useful Arts in the State of New York. *Transactions.* Albany, 1807.

Sowers, Don C. *The Financial History of New York State from 1789–1912.* (Studies in History, Economics, and Public Law, Columbia University, LVII, no. 2.) New York, 1914.

Sparks, Jared. *The Life of Gouverneur Morris.* 3 vols. Boston, 1832.

Spencer, Ivor D. *The Victor and the Spoils: A Life of William L. Marcy.* Providence, 1959.

Sutcliffe, John. *A Treatise on Canals and Reservoirs.* Rochdale, 1816.

Van Buren, Martin. *The Autobiography of Martin Van Buren.* Ed. by J. C. Fitzpatrick. (Annual Report of the American Historical Association for the Year 1918, II.) Washington, 1920.

Washington, George. *The Writings of George Washington.* Ed. by J. C. Fitzpatrick. 39 vols. Washington, 1931–1944.

——. *The Writings of George Washington.* Ed. by W. C. Ford. 14 vols. New York, 1889–1893.

Watson, Elkanah. *History of the Rise, Progress, and Existing Condition of the Western Canals in the State of New York . . . Together with the Rise of Modern Agricultural Societies on the Berkshire System.* Albany, 1820.

Whitford, Noble E. *History of the Canal System of the State of New York.* 2 vols. Albany, 1906.

Wilson, Thomas L. V. *The Aristocracy of Boston: Who They Are and What They Were.* Boston, 1846.

Young, Samuel. *A Discourse Delivered at Schenectady, July 25, A.D. 1826, before the New York Alpha of the Phi Beta Kappa.* Ballston Spa, 1826.

ARTICLES

Bird, William A. "New York State: Early Transportation," *Buffalo Historical Society Publications,* II (1880), 17–32.

Galpin, W. Freeman. "The Genesis of Syracuse," *New York History,* XXX, no. 1 (1949), 19–32.

Goodrich, Carter. "National Planning of Internal Improvements," *Political Science Quarterly,* LXIII, no. 1 (1948), 16–44.

——. "Public Spirit and Internal Improvements," *Proceedings of the American Philosophical Society,* XCII, no. 4 (1948), 305–309.

Horsman, Reginald. "British Indian Policy in the Northwest, 1807–1812," *Mississippi Valley Historical Review,* XLV, No. 1 (1958), 51–66.

Jacobsen, Edna L., ed. "Aaron Hamton's Diary (II)," *New York History,* XXI, no. 3 (1940), 324–334, 431–442.

Lord, Clifford. "Elkanah Watson and New York's First County Fair," *New York History,* XXIII, no. 4 (1942), 437–448.

Mayer, Josephine, and Robert A. East. "The Settlement of Alexander Hamilton's Debts," *New York History,* XVIII, no. 4 (1937), 378–385.

Miller, Nathan. "Private Enterprise in Inland Navigation: The Mohawk Route Prior to the Erie Canal," *New York History,* XXXI, no. 4 (1950), 398–413.

Murphy, Joseph Hawley. "The Salt Industry of Syracuse—A Brief Review," *New York History,* XXX, no. 3 (1949), 304–315.

Robinson, Charles M. "The Life of Judge Augustus Porter," *Buffalo Historical Society Publications,* VII (1904), 229–275.

Van Deusen, John G. "Robert Troup, Agent of the Pulteney Estate," *New York History,* XXIII, no. 1 (1942), 166–180.

Wall, Alexander J., Jr. "The Great Fire of 1835," *New-York Historical Society Quarterly Bulletin,* XX, no. 1 (1936), 3–22.

Index

*Recent books published for the American Historical Association
from the income of the Albert J. Beveridge Memorial Fund*

An Agricultural History of the Genesee Valley, 1790–1860.
By Neil A. McNall.

Steam Power on the American Farm. *By Reynold M. Wik.*

Horace Greeley: Nineteenth-Century Crusader.
By Glyndon G. Van Deusen.

Era of the Oath: Northern Loyalty Tests during the
Civil War and Reconstruction. *By Harold M. Hyman.*

History of Marshall Field & Co. *By Robert W. Twyman.*

Robert Morris: Revolutionary Financier.
By Clarence L. Ver Steeg.

A History of the Freedmen's Bureau. *By George R. Bentley.*

The First Rapprochement: England and the
United States, 1795–1805. *By Bradford Perkins.*

Middle-Class Democracy and the Revolution in Massachusetts,
1691–1780. *By Robert E. Brown.*

The Development of American Petroleum Pipelines:
A Study in Private Enterprise and Public Policy, 1862–1906.
By Arthur Menzies Johnson.

Colonists from Scotland: Emigration to North America,
1707–1783. *By Ian Charles Cargill Graham.*

Professors and Public Ethics: Studies of Northern Moral
Philosophers before the Civil War. *By Wilson Smith.*

The Axis Alliance and Japanese-American Relations, 1941.
By Paul W. Schroeder.

A Frontier State at War: Kansas, 1861–1865.
By Albert Castel.

British Investments and the American Mining Frontier,
1860–1901. *By Clark C. Spence.*
Rails, Mines, and Progress: Seven American Promoters
in Mexico, 1867–1911. *By David M. Pletcher.*

LaGuardia in Congress. *By Howard Zinn.*

Tomorrow a New World: The New Deal Community Program. *By Paul K. Conkin.*

Conservative Crisis and the Rule of Law: Attitudes of Bar and Bench, 1887-1895. *By Arnold M. Paul.*

The United States and Pancho Villa: A Study in Unconventional Diplomacy. *By Clarence C. Clendenen.*

The Enterprise of a Free People: Aspects of Economic Development in New York State during the Canal Period, 1792-1838. *By Nathan Miller.*